S.

11/23.

THE LIFE OF JAMES CARDINAL GIBBONS

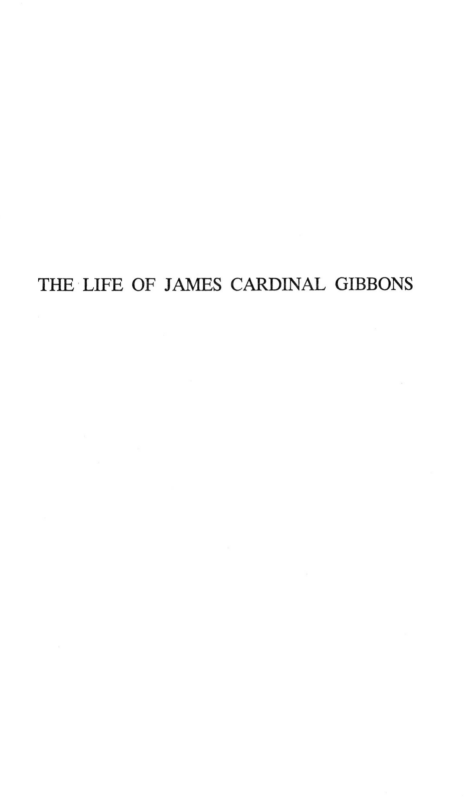

THE LIFE OF
James Cardinal Gibbons

...Popular Edition...

By

JOHN TRACY ELLIS

Edited by

FRANCIS L. BRODERICK

THE BRUCE PUBLISHING COMPANY
MILWAUKEE

NIHIL OBSTAT:

JOHN F. MURPHY, S.T.D.
Censor librorum

IMPRIMATUR:

✠ WILLIAM E. COUSINS
Archbishop of Milwaukee
May 15, 1963

Library of Congress Catalog Card Number: 63–21344
© 1963 THE BRUCE PUBLISHING COMPANY
MADE IN THE UNITED STATES OF AMERICA

Contents

THE LIFE OF JAMES CARDINAL GIBBONS

Chapter 1

The Education of a Bishop

On July 23, 1834, James Gibbons was born in a simple dwelling on the west side of Gay Street in the city of Baltimore. Twelve days later this fourth child of Thomas and Bridget Gibbons was baptized at the Cathedral of the Assumption. Thus began the association between the future cardinal and this venerable building that went on for nearly eighty-seven years before his burial in the crypt beneath the sanctuary.

James was the first boy in the Gibbons family. His parents were both natives of Ireland, and his two eldest sisters, Mary and Bridget, had been born there in the mid-1820's, before the family had emigrated to the United States. Catherine, the youngest girl, had been born in Baltimore exactly three years before James; John, the second son, nearly three years after James. The youngest child, Thomas, was born about 1842.

Thomas Gibbons had emigrated from his unhappy homeland about 1829. In Baltimore the Gibbons' fortunes picked up considerably as the father found employment as a clerk with a prosperous importing business. After six or seven years, however, Thomas Gibbons' health deteriorated, and his physician advised a sea voyage. The family undertook a trip to Ireland, intending to return to Baltimore soon. With that in mind they left their furnishings in the care of some cousins.

The three-year-old lad who left the United States in 1837 retained one recollection of the period. Over eighty years later he wrote to a correspondent:

> I was always interested in Andrew Jackson for personal reasons. When I was an infant in the year 1837, General Jackson received an ovation in Baltimore. The procession escorting him through the city happened to pass our residence and my mother held me up in her arms to contemplate the hero of New Orleans, the President of the United States,

After arriving in Ireland in 1837, the Gibbons family went back to County Mayo, and the extended holiday lengthened into sixteen years. Thomas bought some land near Ballinrobe, a small town in the southern part of the county, ten miles from his native Cortnacullin, and began anew the task of providing for his family. Gibbons carried on a grocery business on Bridge Street; he also had a publican's license for the sale of liquor.

At about the age of seven years James Gibbons started to school. In the company of Francis J. MacCormack, a future bishop of Galway, he learned his first lessons from a Mr. Jennings. Later James was sent to a private classical school conducted by John J. Rooney in the Cornmarket at Ballinrobe.

The early 1840's, when James Gibbons started to school, were a period of great tension in Irish education. In 1831 the British government had devised a system of national schools for Ireland. The provision for religious instruction in these schools satisfied no one, and the Catholics, Presbyterians, and Church of Ireland people all objected to it from various angles. The Irish hierarchy was divided: Archbishop Daniel Murray of Dublin sided with the government on the national schools, while Archbishop John MacHale of Tuam, to which Ballinrobe belonged, forbade the children of his archdiocese to attend them. Schools like Rooney's were, therefore, private in character.

With his quick mind young James took in the rudiments of English, Greek, and Latin; in Ballinrobe he first met the classics of English literature and of history. No one disputed Rooney's ability to instruct, but because the fellow was somewhat slovenly and uncouth, some townspeople decided to employ another teacher. According to an old story, Gibbons refused to transfer his allegiance. When challenged to give a reason, he replied that he would learn as much from Rooney in one week as he would from the new teacher in a month. In these early years James Gibbons first showed the love of study that characterized his entire life. He was so eager to learn that he disliked missing a single day at school. Yet Gibbons was, nonetheless, a real boy for all his love of books. In later years one of his companions in Ballinrobe recalled him as "a most gentle, amiable boy, very studious and clever, and a great favorite." He liked to swim in Lough Carra, to hike, and to play cricket, handball, and marbles. In fact, he bore through life a scar on one of his fingers from an injury in a cricket game. He was the envy of the neighborhood in playing marbles. His brother related that on one occasion he saw James "sell as many as a shilling's worth and still his pockets were full." He took many long hikes with his closest friend, Charles Clark, the only Protestant lad in town. A quarter of a century later, Gibbons, looking forward to a renewed acquaintance, reminisced about their childhood:

> How gratifying it will be to both of us to retrace our steps and revisit once more together those familiar spots where we unbosomed ourselves and where our hearts were knit like those of Jonathan and David. Our friendship has proved lasting, resisting time and all counter affections, because it was based on virtue. When I look back on that early period of my life, like you I attribute much of my subsequent strength against temptations to our pure and healthy conversations, serious and mature beyond our age. Surely our guardian angels must have been with us.

Young Gibbons, reared in the home of deeply religious people, early manifested a love for the Church and its ceremonies that showed itself in his serving Mass at St. Mary's Church in Ballinrobe from his earliest years.

When James was only eight years old, the spring and summer of 1842 brought famine to County Mayo. This severe distress was mild, however, compared to the scourge in 1845 — the failure of the potato crop. Through the succeeding two years hunger stalked the countryside, the very region in which James lived being one of the hardest hit. Although there is no record that the family experienced actual hunger, the cholera, or "famine fever" as it was called, did strike, and on April 20, 1847, Thomas Gibbons died at the early age of forty-seven. Just two years later, his youngest daughter Catherine was buried beside him. Not yet thirteen years of age, James, this eldest boy in a family of six children, felt the altered circumstances in their home keenly. The death of Catherine caused him so much grief that for a time he lost his appetite.

For six years following her husband's death, Bridget Gibbons continued to live at Ballinrobe, caring as best she could for her growing children. Yet, not surprisingly, Mrs. Gibbons again turned her eyes hopefully back across the Atlantic. Emigration to the New World had by now become an old practice among the Irish. The numbers leaving Ireland for America had shown a fairly steady increase since

1815; now the famine of the 1840's accelerated the pace. The year 1846 created a new record with 109,000 emigrants departing for North America; the succeeding year, the number doubled. Along with many of their neighbors seeking a fresh start in the United States, Mrs. Gibbons and her children prepared to leave Ireland forever.

Bridget Gibbons could not bear to return to Baltimore without the partner with whom she had shared the happiest days of her life. She chose New Orleans as the site of the family's future home. Like many large Irish families, the Gibbons family split up to make the trip to America, James, John, and their sister Bridget apparently coming first, sailing from Liverpool in January, 1853, on a ship bound for New Orleans. After about two months at sea, the ship struck a sand bar off the Bahamas near midnight of March 17. Fortunately there was not a high wind, and at daybreak the passengers were taken in small boats to the island and eventually were sent to Nassau. After a short delay they sailed again and landed at New Orleans. Soon the rest of the family followed. All now reunited in the metropolis of the South, they began a new chapter in the life of each of them.

The city where Bridget Gibbons and her five children cast their lot in the spring of 1853 had long since become the leading port of the South. A good deal of Old World atmosphere still hung about New Orleans: narrow streets, quaint shops, and dwellings that projected interesting balconies over the sidewalks. Enough of the inhabitants had retained the Latin features of their forebears who had built New Orleans to draw the comment of strangers. The year the Gibbons family arrived proved to be one of the most turbulent in the city's long history. In May, 1853, a virulent form of yellow fever, brought in from Jamaica or Brazil, swept through the city, causing thousands of deaths. Added to this havoc was the spirit of political violence, for in this year a group of Whigs introduced the Know-Nothing Party into Louisiana. When the campaign for mayor finally ended in March, 1854, election day left several killed and a considerable number seriously wounded. These disorders continued for the next four years. So bad did conditions become that Governor Robert C. Wickliffe informed the legislature in 1857 that "organized ruffians" were keeping nearly one third of the New Orleans electorate from the polls.

On his arrival in New Orleans, James Gibbons was nearing his nineteenth birthday, old enough to help support his mother, sisters, and younger brothers. Fortunately he secured employment as a clerk in the grocery store of William C. Raymond on Camp Street. Not long after entering Raymond's employ, James fell a victim to yellow fever. His oldest sister, Mary, nursed him at a great risk to herself. Following the current practice, he remained in bed under heavy coverings to induce perspiration, took hot baths, and went on a near-starvation diet. For a time his weakness became so extreme that his life was despaired of. At length he recovered and returned to work. So satisfied was Raymond with the services of his young clerk that he raised James's salary each year, and — an unusual practice, to be sure — the advances in salary were made for the previous year as well as for the coming year. While James Gibbons found both pleasure and profit in serving the families in the neighborhood, the wealthy sugar and cotton planters who purchased stock that would last them and their slaves for months ahead, and the hardy rivermen who sought provisions for trips up the Mississippi, he had other plans.

From the time when he had served Mass in the chapel back in Ballinrobe, his religion had meant more to him than it did to most boys. He thought nothing of going a distance from his family's parish church to attend a ten-day mission at St. Joseph's Church, opposite Charity Hospital, the second week in February, 1854. A band of famous missionaries was on hand: Alexander Czvitovicz, Francis X. Masson, Isaac T. Hecker, Clarence Walworth, and Augustine Hewit, all members of the Congregation of the Most Holy Redeemer, the last three, converts to the Catholic Church. Gibbons attended faithfully the exercises of the mission and found inspiration in the sermons of the distinguished preachers. For some time the young man had been considering the priesthood as a vocation. But like every serious-minded youth contemplating a step of this kind, he hesitated, not knowing whether he "should serve God in the Church as a priest, or as a layman in the world." A close reading of Orestes Brownson's apologetic essays in his famous *Review* stimulated greatly Gibbons' thoughts of how much he might accomplish for the Church in the priesthood. Now, during the mission at St. Joseph's, Father Walworth's spirited talk on the priesthood settled James's doubts and solidified his decision to devote his talents to this high calling.

Once his final decision had been made, Gibbons turned to another Redemptorist, John B. Duffy, for help. Father Duffy, a priest at St. Alphonsus Church in New Orleans, had distinguished himself during the yellow-fever epidemic of 1853 by his zeal in behalf of the sick. Along with his other duties, Father Duffy also found time to give Latin lessons to a number of boys who had manifested a desire to become priests. The earlier lessons of Jennings and Rooney in Ireland again came alive in the mind of young Gibbons. From this priest-mentor, too, came James's decision to pursue his priestly studies under the Sulpician Fathers in Baltimore. Father Duffy not only suggested the place for study, but wrote to Archbishop Francis P. Kenrick of Baltimore asking him to accept Gibbons as a student at St. Charles College. The Archbishop promptly assented. From the outset Gibbons was enrolled as a clerical student for the Archdiocese of Baltimore; that meant that he had elected to lead his life permanently in that part of the country.

While the determination of her eldest son to study in far-off Baltimore created a certain sorrow for Mrs. Gibbons, the devout widow's happiness at the thought of James's becoming a priest outweighed her loneliness at his impending departure.

In the late summer of 1855, at the age of twenty-one James Gibbons set out from New Orleans for Baltimore. The 1000-mile journey could not be made entirely by rail. Gibbons, therefore, took the easier and cheaper transportation afforded by the steamboat up the Mississippi and then over the Ohio River to Cincinnati. There he took the Baltimore and Ohio to a point west of the Allegheny Mountains, detrained, and continued over the mountains by stage. He was exactly sixteen days en route from New Orleans to Baltimore.

By 1855, Baltimore had grown to a metropolis of 188,251 persons, nearly 25 percent foreign-born. Recent immigration had added hundreds of Germans and Irish to the native population, and with both groups highly organized, "either or both could swing a close election." The presence of so many foreign-born, of course, fanned the flames of hatred among the Know-Nothings who had appeared in Baltimore politics three years before. Election day in November, 1855, was marked by rioting, and "the success of the Know-Nothings was complete. Baltimore City and thirteen out of twenty-one counties were ranged in the Know-Nothing column." Through most of Gibbons' student days in Baltimore the Know-Nothings reigned supreme;

they were dislodged from the city government only in October, 1860, after a period of violence.

Despite unpleasant incidents caused by the tactics of the Know-Nothings, the Archdiocese of Baltimore with its nearly 120,000 Catholics and 127 priests continued its quiet advance. Out in the countryside near the village of Ellicott City, St. Charles College was just past its embryonic stage. It had opened its doors seven years before, with Father Oliver L. Jenkins, S.S., as president, one other priest, a deacon, a housekeeper, and four boys as students. Before long other students were attracted to this preparatory seminary conducted by the Sulpician Fathers, and by 1855 forty-two students were crowding the accommodations sufficiently to warrant making a dormitory on the third floor of the single building that served the community for all purposes. This change created room for about seventy. A large room on the east end of the second floor was fitted up as a community chapel. The charges were $100 for board and tuition for a school year, payable half-yearly in advance. Living conditions were rather primitive. With the dormitory heated by only one central stove, the young man from New Orleans suffered from the cold that first winter, the coldest on record in Maryland since 1817.

James Gibbons was, of course, quite unfamiliar with the discipline in an institution for the training of future priests. He observed with some misgiving the silence maintained when the boys walked to their meals and when they filed into the hall for morning prayers. The friendly spirit of the new arrival from New Orleans overflowed with questions and greetings, but when he experienced nothing but silent gestures and an icy stare from the superior, Gibbons resigned himself to the rule.

Two other phases of the life at St. Charles James Gibbons found thoroughly to his liking, namely, study and recreation. Father J. B. Randanne was a hard taskmaster in the Latin classes, but Gibbons, well trained in Ballinrobe and New Orleans, experienced no difficulty. This same Father Randanne also exercised some supervision over the students' recreation. On his arrival at St. Charles Gibbons had two suits of clothes. But in the course of baseball and football games, the breeches gave way. Randanne came to the rescue with a suit of his own design. The vest came up to the seminarian's chin, the coat went down to his heels, and, as Gibbons later stated, "John L. Sullivan could have gotten into the legs of the trousers." Randanne's sole reaction to the ridiculous garment was: "I will cure you of your vanities."

In the college at Ellicott City, Gibbons again played with vigor at outdoor sports and once more took long hikes with his friends. Across the Frederick turnpike from the college campus Doughoregan Manor, the vast ancestral estate of Charles Carroll of Carrollton, was a special attraction for the students. Some of his associates at recreation later attained prominence in the American Church: Thomas M. A. Burke, who in 1894 became the fourth Bishop of Albany, and John S. Foley, the son of a well-known Baltimore Catholic family, who in 1888 had the pleasure of having his old friend, by then a cardinal, consecrate him as fourth Bishop of Detroit.

At the end of the first year young Gibbons received a first premium in Greek and in second-year French and a second premium in Church history, Latin, English, and elocution. He improved on this performance a year later when, as a member of a graduating class of five, he carried off a first premium in Greek, French, rhetoric, and elocution and a second premium in Church history and Latin.

Selected to make the student's address at the commencement on July 12, 1857, Gibbons framed a graceful tribute to Charles Carroll of Carrollton, who had given the college its property, and to Carroll's descendant, present as the guest of honor, who allowed the students to roam freely on his estate. In its final form Gibbons' speech was sufficiently good that Father Jenkins "showed his appreciation of the oration by making a copy of it to be preserved."

After a four-week vacation in New Orleans, James set out again on September 1, for the mother seminary of the United States, old St. Mary's on North Paca Street, Baltimore. A warm recommendation preceded him: "Bon ésprit; talent," Father Jenkins had written to Father François Lhomme, the superior at St. Mary's. The student body into which Gibbons entered on September 10, 1857, consisted of thirty-two young men; the faculty included five priests besides Father Lhomme. The following year, François P. Dissez joined the faculty to teach philosophy; Gibbons became especially attached to him. The friendship formed in 1858 endured through half a century until the night in 1908 when the Cardinal Archbishop of Baltimore stood sadly by the deathbed of his old professor.

Gibbons made an outstanding record at the seminary. At the end of his first year, he ranked first in his class and won a coveted appointment as "master of conference," the seminarian in charge of review for public examinations. At the end of four years, the faculty recorded its high esteem:

1. Talents & capacity more than ordinary, especially facility.
2. Success 9.
3. Disposition & temper: amiable, equanimity; cheerfulness; zeal for duty, great ardor for study, & almost too great eagerness for knowledge; for some time inspired some fears lest he might not take the right direction.
4. Regularity 9; virtue 9.
5. Preaching very successful; judgment, exposed to be carried by his imagination.
6. Manners.
7. Observations: gained the esteem & affection of all.

One of his professors gave this summary of his career at St. Mary's Seminary:

> James Gibbons manifested the *bon esprit* at St. Mary's as at St. Charles' by his affability, politeness and kindness towards all, superiors and fellow-students. He was a regular and edifying seminarian. He profited by all opportunities to increase his knowledge. Even in recreation he liked to ask his Professors about the subject-matter of his studies or readings. He had a special zeal for the study of Holy Scripture; in his private rule he set apart one hour to read it every day.

Through all these four years at St. Mary's the Sulpicians themselves bore the expenses of this candidate for the Archdiocese of Baltimore. It is small wonder, then, that Gibbons should have felt a lifelong gratitude to the Sulpicians. In the years to come he more than repaid these good priests by establishing three burses at St. Charles College, giving $15,000 for the chapel fund of St. Mary's, and bestowing on the two institutions combined a gift of $50,000.

Having received minor orders in 1859, Gibbons moved on in the summer of 1861 to the subdiaconate on June 28, and to the diaconate on June 29. Finally, with five of his classmates, he was raised to the priesthood on Sunday, June 30, 1861, by Archbishop Kenrick, whom Gibbons later recalled as "the first really great man whom I can remember to have known intimately. . . ."

By the time of James Gibbons' ordination, the long bitter controversy over slavery had culminated in civil war. Nowhere did the bitterness of the conflict divide the population more than in Baltimore. Maryland, linked for long years by close commercial, social, and historical ties to the South, was generally southern in sympathy, but Baltimore's large manufacturing interests bound the city to the North. When the Sixth Massachusetts Regiment approached Baltimore on its way to Washington in April, 1861, angry Baltimoreans of southern views set upon the troops, killing four and wounding thirty-six. In these circumstances there was strong sentiment for secession of Maryland from the Union. The government at Washington took no chances: on the night of May 13 Union troops under General Benjamin F. Butler occupied Federal Hill near Baltimore. The general election in November decided once and for all the status of Maryland within the Union. All practical hopes of the secessionists disappeared, many southern sympathizers fled, and "Maryland became in fact as well as in name a loyal state," though the diehards continued all through the war to cause incidents. A severe censorship of the press was enforced by the federal authorities. During the war nine Baltimore newspapers were suppressed at least temporarily, two of the nine were forced to suspend publication because of the arrest of their editors. The Catholic press was no exception. The *Catholic Mirror* was suspended during the week of May 23–30, 1864; in October, 1864, J. and C. Kreuzer, proprietors of the *Katholische Volkzeitung* of Baltimore, were warned by General Lew Wallace against publishing any antigovernment tracts, threatened with suspension of their newspaper should the order be disobeyed, and commanded to submit each issue to the provost marshal for examination.

Such were the general conditions in which Father James Gibbons inaugurated his priesthood in Baltimore. While the young priest, twenty-seven that summer, had lived all his life in the United States south of the Mason and Dixon Line, he did not favor the South during the Civil War.

> I had been born a Southerner and brought up a Southerner, and my heart was, of course, with the Southern States. Indeed, my brother was actually fighting in the Army of the Confederacy; but I could never believe that secession would succeed, and even if it should succeed I could not help but see that it would be the destruction of what was already a growing, and what might become a very great nation. Therefore my head was always with the Union.

It was not easy for a priest with such opinions to carry out his religious ministrations in the Baltimore of these years. So intensely did many of the Baltimore Catholic clergy feel about the righteousness of the Confederate cause that in the first year of the war the priests of the cathedral parish refused to read Archbishop Carroll's prayer for the civil authorities because it contained a petition for the preservation of the union of the American people. Archbishop Kenrick finally decided that he would read it himself, and as Gibbons related:

> I suppose during the reading of that prayer he suffered more than one could well imagine; for when he mentioned the Union of the States, many people got up and publicly left the Cathedral, and those who remained expressed their dissent from the Archbishop's petition by a great rustling of papers and silks.

Gibbons' first parochial experience came as an assistant at St. Patrick's Church in Fell's Point, a rough section of Baltimore stretching along the waterfront where the Patapsco River reached out to meet the Chesapeake Bay. The rough elements of society found in all large port cities filled some of the streets, but back a few blocks from the water, modest, respectable dwellings housed many fine families of both native and immigrant stock. Here he stayed a mere six weeks. Then, in accordance with the common practice of appointing newly ordained priests to country pastorates, he was transferred to St. Bridget's in Mount Savage, Maryland.

A pastor only six weeks after ordination, the eager priest went promptly to work. While the simple church was adequate for the religious services of his congregation, he had to make his home in a few small rooms built against the wall of the church with no provision for light or ventilation and with the floorboards resting on the ground. The neighborhood had not yet been built up; the only house close at hand was that of Mrs. Bridget Smyth, one of his parishioners, who served as a housekeeper for the priest's rooms and sent one of her sons to sleep there each night because the lonely location was thought to be dangerous.

While Father Gibbons' parishioners were not numerous, they were widely scattered; reaching them required long and sometimes exhausting trips in all kinds of weather. Most of his people were quite poor, industrial employees who worked in the copper works and rolling mills of Canton or agricultural workers who tilled their small farms and market gardens. Naturally these people could not contribute much to the support of their pastor, and Gibbons had to tax his ingenuity to meet expenses and to improve the parish. At length he held a fair in Carroll Hall in the city, and from the proceeds of this and succeeding entertainments he raised enough money to erect a neat brick rectory alongside the church.

Early the next year Archbishop Kenrick asked Father Gibbons to assume charge of St. Lawrence O'Toole Church, a mile away at Locust Point across the Patapsco River. In this new parish, he gained new insight into the hardships of the working class, for his parishioners were mainly the families of dock workers and shipbuilders. The dual assignment put a strain on the pastor's frail constitution. Each Sunday morning he had to leave Canton at six o'clock and to row in a skiff across to Locust Point where he would hear confessions, say Mass, preach, baptize, and attend sick calls. He then rowed back across the river to Canton in time for the high Mass at St. Bridget's at ten-thirty where he likewise delivered a sermon. He fasted throughout this early morning travel, of course; the ordeal left him with a lifelong ailment in the form of bad digestion.

Beyond his two parishes, the young pastor found time to act as a volunteer chaplain at the two principal military posts in Maryland: Fort Marshall, not far from St. Bridget's, and Fort McHenry, within the boundaries of the parish of St. Lawrence. On one occasion at Fort McHenry in July, 1864, Gibbons, after hearing the confession of a Confederate prisoner, sought to get some nourishment for the man, who had not been properly provided for by the hospital doctor. For this act of kindness, he was told that his services would no longer be accepted at the fortress, and that he need not return. Gibbons explained the sequel: "However, I did return, since I threatened to make known to the higher authorities what had taken place; and men who exercise martial law with little regard for the feelings of those below them are often very sensitive as to the feelings of those above them."

The young chaplain had a variety of experiences during the war. On one occasion in 1864, a Confederate soldier, visiting his family in eastern Maryland, was arrested as a spy and condemned to death. Partly through Father Gibbons' efforts, a reprieve from President Abraham Lincoln saved the soldier's life. Having escaped from the hangman's noose, the soldier reappeared after the war to ask Gibbons "to tie a more pleasing knot," and Gibbons happily officiated at the wedding. Another time he was called to Fort Marshall to attend a soldier in a delirium from fever. In an effort to bring the soldier back to his senses, Gibbons began to ask him questions. To the query as to where he was born, the soldier answered, "Ireland." To the question of what part of Ireland, the sick man replied the western section. Finally the priest learned it was Ballinrobe. He then inquired if he knew the pastor of Ballinrobe and the soldier replied yes, he was his brother. At once Gibbons exclaimed: "You are Hal Conway!" In such strange circumstances did the chaplain discover an old schoolmate from Ballinrobe.

The war years brought a major change to the Archdiocese of Baltimore. When Archbishop Kenrick died in July, 1863, the appointment of a new archbishop was delayed by the exigencies of war and by the delicate task that faced the Holy See in filling the premier see of the United States — a city southern in sympathy although lying within the Union lines — with a candidate who would offer satisfaction to various groups. Happily, the selection finally fell upon Martin John Spalding, Bishop of Louisville. He was of old Maryland stock; this factor helped to make his appointment a highly popular one. Baltimore's seventh archbishop took possession of his see on July 31, 1864.

Despite the hazards of war Father Gibbons undertook a visit to his family in New Orleans. The young priest had been greatly weakened by his strenuous work in the two parishes and military forts, and his obvious illness alarmed his family lest he be lapsing into tuberculosis. For this reason his sister Bridget, Mrs. George Swarbrick, persuaded him to go to Lewisburg, Louisiana, for a rest. There the resilient spirit and basically healthy constitution of Father Gibbons revived.

From the outset of his priestly career Gibbons had a very high ideal of the preaching office. About him there was nothing of the fiery orator, nor anything distinguished in his style of composition. But he did have to a marked degree the gift of putting religious truths in a simple and attractive dress that won the conviction of his audiences. He spoke to the people on simple yet basic subjects like pride, mortal sin, the love of God, the resurrection of the body. All his sermons showed the same unadorned recitation of dogmatic truths clarified by homely illustrations. The thought of using the pulpit for any purpose other than the inculcation of moral values and the instruction in religious truths was abhorrent to him. At St. Bridget's Church on the first Sunday of the new year 1863, he reviewed for his people the suffering that had come upon the nation by reason of the Civil War. Amid the conflict, he said, they had heard nothing from the Catholic pulpit to excite their passions or to give them a thirst for blood; rather the American Catholics had heard in their churches only of God's glory and of man's need for peace, of Christ and Him crucified. Referring to preachers who invoked the God of battle instead of the God of peace, he said: "A fearful responsibility awaits those who have sounded the new blast from their church desks, & fanned the flame of civil hatred and dissension. These will have their judgment, let us attend to ourselves."

One sermon proved to be terrifyingly apt. It was Good Friday night, April 14, 1865, and Gibbons was preaching at St. Joseph's Church in Baltimore. In commenting on the base treachery of Judas toward Jesus, Gibbons said:

> Imagine a great and good ruler, who had done everything to deserve the confidence and affection of his subjects, and who had lived only for his country and had no desire but for his country's good, imagine such a ruler struck down by the hand of an assassin! Would you not feel, my brethren, a deep indignation at his murder?

Only an hour or two after Gibbons' sermon that same evening, President Lincoln fell at Ford's Theater from the bullet of John Wilkes Booth.

As normal times returned after the war, Father Gibbons gave up his volunteer chaplaincies and devoted himself to his two parishes. He seemed perfectly content, and his mind was filled with plans for the improvement of his parishes. The new archbishop had other plans, however. Archbishop Spalding developed a strong liking for this wiry little priest whose gracious manner complemented so well his piety and his administrative ability. Before long Spalding got the idea of appointing Gibbons to the busy cathedral household as his secretary. Alternately pleased by the possibility and troubled by a departure from his parishioners, Gibbons debated sleeplessly about his answer. Did he not have a duty to remain with his parishioners? Or was he stubbornly persisting in his own will against that of his archbishop? Finally he reached the decision: he stood ready to accept the archbishop's will. When word of the appointment spread, a committee of parishioners from St. Bridget's pleaded with the archbishop to leave their pastor with them. But Spalding held to his original decision, and in mid-December, 1865, Father Gibbons joined the cathedral staff.

As secretary, Gibbons accompanied the archbishop on his visitation tours throughout the archdiocese, an experience that stood him in good stead in later years. Though secretarial duties were his primary responsibility, he also found time for the priestly ministrations that he loved so well and performed with so much profit to souls: hearing confessions regularly in the cathedral, taking his turn at the parish Masses, preaching, giving instructions in the successful Sunday school that he began conducting soon after his arrival.

Baltimore was, in a sense, the Catholic capital of the United States. Here were held the councils of the American Church and here, too, was directed much of the important business of the Holy See with the American bishops. Archbishop Spalding was in Baltimore only a few months when he began laying plans for a plenary council. By February, 1866, Pope Pius IX gave the council his approval and designated Spalding as apostolic delegate. The archbishop, in turn, sent out the letter of convocation to the American hierarchy. This activity, of course, greatly increased the archbishop's correspondence, and through the spring and summer the arrangements for the council kept Gibbons very busy.

The solemn opening of the Second Plenary Council took place in the cathedral in October. As assistant chancellor of the council, Gibbons came into direct contact with the six archbishops besides Spalding, the thirty-seven bishops, and the large number of distinguished priests who were in attendance as theologians and superiors of religious orders. It was James Gibbons' first formal introduction to the leaders of the American Church, and they, in turn, had an opportunity to observe the young priest who in a few years would be of their number.

To keep the Church apace with the expanding nation, the hierarchy had a continuing duty to suggest new dioceses to the Holy See. In a session held on October 13 the name of Gibbons was placed first on the *terna* (list of three names) chosen to fill the Vicariate Apostolic of North Carolina that the bishops were proposing to the Holy See. The council submitted to the Congregation of the Propaganda a very favorable opinion of Gibbons' qualifications for this episcopal office, the delegate speaking of him as "the most worthy of all for the Episcopacy." "He is," said Spalding, "a priest in every respect perfect."

In the spring of 1867 Archbishop Spalding decided upon a trip to

Europe to attend the celebration in Rome marking the eighteenth centennial of the martyrdom of St. Peter. During his absence the archbishop kept in touch by mail with Baltimore, and one letter referred again to the bishopric for his secretary. In his reply, Gibbons' mixed feelings were apparent:

> As your Grace seems determined to inflict a mitre on me, I think it would be a good idea to send me on from France some of the Episcopal paraphernalia. I have the blues since I read your letter. To leave Baltimore is hard enough, but to lose the genial company of the archiepiscopal house costs me a good deal, — more than I can say in words. You see I take it seriously, because your letter appears serious.

The city of Baltimore was throughout his long life the place above all where James Gibbons loved to be, and the thought of leaving it brought readily to his mind a sense of exile.

In 1868, after Archbishop Spalding's return to the United States, the Maryland legislature passed a law levying a state tax of ten cents on each $100 of taxable property to support the public schools. No provision was made for any aid to schools under denominational control, nor was any account taken of the need for religious instruction of children attending the public schools. Naturally the Archbishop of Baltimore felt that the state should be willing to give some form of financial assistance to the private schools conducted under Catholic auspices. With this in mind he asked Gibbons to prepare a report that would demonstrate the saving to the state of Maryland from the Catholic schools. Gibbons' detailed account showed that the Catholics of Baltimore alone saved the state $37,945. The report, referred to the Senate Committee on Education, died there.

Meanwhile, the threat of the miter of North Carolina finally became a reality. Once the decision had been made, plans could mature for the consecration of the young priest as a bishop. The date was set for Sunday, August 16, 1868, and the invitations went out some weeks in advance. Gibbons, the first alumnus of St. Charles to become a bishop, must have been especially pleased by the reply of an old friend of his days in the seminary, Thomas Burke: "I feel that the hand of God has been in your appointment and that in it, neither ambition nor human influence had any share."

Then he added a series of questions that now seem almost prophetic:

How many churches will there not spring up under your fostering care? How many young levites by your encouragement will consecrate themselves to God in the sacred priesthood? How many converts will be added to the fold of Christ? With what tender care will the poor despised children of Africa be instructed in the saving truths of our holy religion? In a word what charitable and religious institutions will spring up as monuments to your zeal?

One letter must have touched him deeply, a brief note from Father James Dolan at St. Patrick's in Baltimore under whom he had first served as a priest. Dolan enclosed a check for $100 for Gibbons' new mission, with the promise as well of a missal and two chasubles. Other friends in Baltimore were also generous, and a few days before Gibbons' consecration he was able to send off a check for $6,000 to purchase a lot adjoining St. Thomas Church, his little procathedral in Wilmington, North Carolina.

At length the great day arrived when James Gibbons was to be made a bishop. Thomas A. Becker, a priest of the Diocese of Richmond, was consecrated first Bishop of Wilmington, Delaware, at the same ceremony. Archbishop Spalding was the consecrator of these two priests, and the coconsecrators for Gibbons were Patrick N. Lynch, Bishop of Charleston, and Michael Domenec, C.M., Bishop of Pittsburgh. The preacher for the occasion was Father Thomas Foley of the cathedral staff.

At the time of his consecration James Gibbons had just passed his thirty-fourth birthday. He was the youngest among the more than 1000 bishops scattered throughout the Catholic world and, of course, the youngest in the United States. His ecclesiastical jurisdiction in North Carolina being only a vicariate apostolic and not a diocese, he was given the title of Bishop of Adramyttum, one of the many dioceses that had long ago passed out of existence but the titles of which were reserved for titular bishops of missionary territories. Any priest ordained only seven years and relatively uninformed about the exacting duties of episcopal administration might well have entertained misgivings at the prospect that confronted Gibbons. Never adventuresome, nor particularly endowed with initiative and originality, he was nevertheless determined in pursuing a course that he had decided was right. If the thought of his impending departure from the Baltimore that he loved so well to the North Carolina that he knew so little caused him to grow faint, his deep trust in the designs of Providence buoyed him up.

Chapter 2

North Carolina and Richmond

Although Bishop Gibbons was consecrated on August 16, he was not installed in his procathedral in North Carolina until November 1. His health was not too good that summer, and he was advised to wait for cooler weather before going South. Meanwhile he was not idle. During the late summer and autumn he kept busy performing various episcopal functions in and around Baltimore. A week after his consecration he returned to his old parish of St. Bridget in Canton where he confirmed ninety-four persons. The new bishop preached in different city churches on succeeding Sundays, and in September he paid a visit to his former parish of St. Lawrence at Locust Point. On September 18 Gibbons ordained two Jesuits, the first of 2471 priests to receive holy orders at his hands.

In early September the bishop received his first authentic word on the state of Catholicism in North Carolina. Father Henry P. Northrop reported that only three towns had churches — Raleigh, Edenton, and New Bern — although fifteen other towns and villages were named as stations where the priest visited occasionally. "Besides these," said Northrop, "there are other small points where one or two Catholics reside." Three priests served this vast area.

Before leaving for North Carolina, Bishop Gibbons visited St. Charles College and solicited candidates for the vicariate. Among the students whom he met was one named Denis J. O'Connell to whom the bishop apparently took an immediate liking. Two years later he was greatly cheered by the news that his five students at St. Charles all gave promise of making the type of priest who would serve the missions in North Carolina with credit.

By autumn the new bishop's health improved, and he could make plans for his installation on the feast of All Saints, Sunday, November 1. The little party, consisting of Archbishop Spalding, Gibbons, and Bernard J. McManus, pastor of St. John's Church in Baltimore, left the city on October 29 and arrived in Wilmington on Friday evening, October 30. On Sunday morning St. Thomas Church was crowded to capacity despite a heavy rain. After Archbishop Spalding led Bishop Gibbons to his throne and formally installed him, the latter celebrated the pontifical high Mass.

The Vicariate Apostolic of North Carolina covered the entire state, an area of almost 50,000 square miles. According to the census of 1870, over 96 percent of the 1,071,361 inhabitants were living in rural areas. Of these, only about 700, less than one in a thousand, were Catholic. Moreover, the Church's problem was aggravated by widespread illiteracy, for the school system all over the state had largely broken down during the war. Wages were low and money extremely scarce. At the outset Bishop Gibbons worked closely with his three priests — Mark S. Gross, who was with him in Wilmington, Northrop, who covered the many stations in the northeastern part of the state, and Lawrence P. O'Connell, who had charge of the missions in the southwestern area. There were no Catholic schools, hospitals, or other diocesan institutions. The modest little brick and stucco Church of St. Thomas the Apostle in Wilmington had been dedicated in July, 1847. Since there was no residence for the clergy, the bishop and Father Gross had to accommodate themselves in the four small rooms attached to the rear of the church.

From every human viewpoint it was a discouraging prospect. Archbishop Spalding sensed Gibbons' loneliness. "I was truly affected when I left you on Monday morning; I thought you looked like an orphan & desolate," he wrote back from Baltimore. Nonetheless, "I have not a doubt of your ultimate success. You will reap in joy after sowing in tears. Courage!" Spalding went on to say that he had sent to the Prefect of the Congregation of the Propaganda, a report about Gibbons which "your modesty could scarcely recognize, but which I look to you to make true in the future as I believe it has been in the past."

Meanwhile there was much work to be done; no good could come of spending time lamenting Baltimore. Five days after his installation Gibbons entered his first item in the parish register: "I baptized conditionally Abraham Franklin, aged 53 years, after having received his profession of faith. Bernard Gorman, spr." This was the first in a lengthy series of adult converts received into the Church at James Gibbons' hands in North Carolina.

On November 10 the bishop left Wilmington on a four-week visitation of his jurisdiction. He traveled 925 miles by rail, stage, and steamboat, visited sixteen towns and stations in central and eastern North Carolina, confirmed sixty-four persons of whom sixteen were converts, and baptized sixteen of whom ten were converts. In Raleigh, the state capital, he received every mark of respect. He could report happily to Spalding: "Yesterday I preached twice in the Catholic Church to crowded houses. The Legislature now in session, turned out en masse. It is here particularly that the Church gains in public estimation by the conservative cause she pursued during the war." When Edward Conigland, one of the most outstanding lawyers in North Carolina at the time, learned that Gibbons was coming to Halifax, he wrote to offer the hospitality of his home. The lawyer had just lost his wife, and he wondered if her influence in eternity had not turned him back to religion. Conigland was to be the instrument through which the bishop was to accomplish much good for the Church in the succeeding years. December 17 found Gibbons once more in Wilmington with his first visitation tour completed. He himself attested to the cordial reception he had received everywhere, telling Archbishop Spalding that he had been welcomed "both by Protestants & Catholics."

Near the end of 1868, Bishop Gibbons received his first benefaction from the Society for the Propagation of the Faith in France — 8,000 francs, or about $420. These donations from the Society, which continued for the next nine years of Gibbons' time in North Carolina, finally amounted in all to 57,280 francs, a little over $3,000. Gibbons later said of this help: "I can scarcely see how the work could have gone without such aid. The certainty of the annuity was a relief to my mind, whilst it gave a stimulus to fresh undertakings."

Early in 1869, the bishop spent a few days in New Orleans with his family. By this time his brother John's grain business was doing so well that John was able to give him "a handsome present in money & horse" for the work in North Carolina.

Gibbons lamented the lack of books of instruction for his flock, and he told Archbishop Spalding after his return from New Orleans that while the danger of losing the faith was not great for the Catholics of Wilmington, he did fear for those in the rural areas. "My one remedy," he said, "is the circulation of books. I have exhausted my supply. . . . I wish I had about a dozen copies of the 'Evidences

[Spalding's book, *General Evidences of Catholicity,* published in 1847].' " From his experiences with prospective converts and his strong feeling of the need of books on instruction there gradually took shape in Gibbons' mind the idea of writing a book that would give the essentials of Catholic doctrine in a simple way. Thus was slowly adumbrated *The Faith of Our Fathers,* destined to have such remarkable success.

Bishop Gibbons at first encountered disappointment in recruiting religious women. His appeal to Ireland for Sisters of Mercy, sent a few days after his arrival at Wilmington, met with a refusal. At last he decided to seek the assistance of Sisters nearer home. He wrote to the Sisters of Our Lady of Mercy in Charleston in August, 1869, and having received a favorable reply and won the permission of Bishop Lynch, Gibbons secured the services of three Sisters. On October 11, 1869, these Sisters opened the Academy of the Incarnation for girls, and on January 3, 1871, they began a parochial school under the title of St. Peter. The help that they gave the young bishop and his few priests in the task of instructing the children in the faith was, indeed, very great.

Gibbons' friend, the Archbishop of Baltimore, was a churchman whose wide experience in Church councils had brought a deep conviction of their usefulness. Spalding, therefore, decided to convoke the Tenth Provincial Council of Baltimore in April, 1869, and he turned to his youngest suffragan to prepare the pastoral letter that would be issued at the close of the council. He wanted the document to be fresh, terse, and practical; he said: "I therefore commit it to a fresh hand guided by a fresh heart."

Thomas Foley, chancellor of Baltimore, had the task of making the arrangements for the council, and it must have amused Gibbons to be requested to send the chancellor "the names of your Theologians & also the names of superiors of Seminaries and Heads of Religious Orders in your Vicariate, who will accompany you." Foley ended by saying the archbishop had appointed Gibbons to preach the closing sermon of the council. The vicar apostolic replied that he was glad of an opportunity of returning to his native city: "I feel in going back to Baltimore, like a boy returning home to spend the holidays."

The council in Baltimore opened on Sunday, April 25, with Archbishop Spalding, his twelve suffragan bishops, and Abbot Boniface

Wimmer, O.S.B., of St. Vincent's Abbey, Latrobe, Pennsylvania, in attendance. The main business was to decide upon the best means to carry out the decrees of the Second Plenary Council of 1866, and to consult about the council that would convene at Rome in December. The bishops were in session one week, and on the closing day, Sunday, May 2, Gibbons preached in the cathedral on "The Divine Mission and Unerring Authority of the Catholic Church." The pastoral letter, written by Gibbons and published at the end of the meeting, urged the cause of Catholic education upon parents and pointed out the dangers of a purely secular education. While the number of converts to the Catholic Church in the United States had been gratifying, the pastoral did not fail to mention that Catholics were obliged "to confess with sorrow, that a great number are lost to the Church." The bishops renewed their approval of the Catholic Publication Society of New York and warmly recommended protectories and orphan asylums to the generosity of the people. The concern of the Church for the Negroes was expressed. The bishops condemned birth control as well as obscene theatrical performances, indecent literature, and the "modern fashionable dances, commonly called German or Round dances."

The day after the council closed Gibbons had a special joy. On one of his visits to St. Charles College as a priest, he had met T. Herbert Shriver, a student there. Their friendship had ripened into a deep and abiding affection between Gibbons and the whole Shriver family, one that was to last until the very end of Gibbons' life. Now as Gibbons celebrated Mass in the cathedral, he gave first Communion to old William Shriver for whose conversion Mrs. Shriver and their children had been praying for many years.

Upon Bishop Gibbons' return to Wilmington in the spring of 1869, he made ready for his second major visitation tour, this time through the missions served by Father O'Connell in and around Charlotte. He and O'Connell left home in July and traveled through the small towns and settlements for some weeks. Finally, on August 16, he arrived home again, having gone 985 miles by rail and stage, visited eleven towns, counted 376 Catholics in O'Connell's missions, confirmed 106 of whom thirty-three were converts, and baptized six of whom four were converts. Gibbons' friend, the Archbishop of Baltimore, wrote to say that he had heard that the vicar apostolic had returned to Wilmington "like a conquering hero."

That fall the time had arrived for the bishop to leave his vicariate for over a year. Before sailing for Rome, he fulfilled a number of engagements in Baltimore that enabled him to visit his friends as well as make collections for his mission. On October 20 the archbishop and his party, including Gibbons, sailed for Europe on the *Baltimore* to attend the Vatican Council. In Paris, where they were the guests of the general motherhouse of the Sulpician Fathers, the Vicar Apostolic of North Carolina called at the headquarters of the Society for the Propagation of the Faith. He thanked the directors in person for their financial aid and explained in detail the pressing needs under which his vicariate still labored. From Paris the prelates made their way southward through France, and from Marseilles they crossed the Mediterranean. Of the sixty-some bishops in the United States at the time, forty-eight attended the council, eighteen of them, including Gibbons, resident at the American College, others scattered in various religious houses throughout Rome. During all his time away from home Bishop Gibbons remained close to his episcopal patron, Archbishop Spalding: "For ten months we sat at the same table and slept under the same roof."

It would be difficult to imagine any event in history better calculated to give a young missionary bishop a true concept of the majesty and universality of the Catholic Church than the Vatican Council. The spirit in which the discussions in the Council were conducted, the wealth of erudition unfolding finely delineated theories, impressed Gibbons. He maintained that as he listened attentively to the debates on the issue of papal infallibility, he heard "far more subtle, more plausible, and more searching objections against this prerogative of the Pope than I have ever read or heard from the pen or tongue of the most learned and formidable Protestant assailant."

On the subject of the definition of papal infallibility, the American hierarchy was divided. When in January, 1870, a petition was circulated asking that the doctrine be defined, 380 bishops, including nine Americans, signed it. But contrary petitions appeared at once. One, suggesting that the question not be brought before the council at all, carried the names of twenty American bishops. When a resolution that the debates on papal infallibilty be closed was passed on June 3, this action gave rise to a protest to which nine Americans affixed their signatures.

To all this theological controversy James Gibbons was an interested witness; but he took no active part. When the time came to pass on the question of papal infallibility in the final public session July 18, he voted with the majority as did most of the Americans. A number of bishops from the United States had gone home rather than vote in favor of the decree, and one, Edward Fitzgerald of Little Rock, at the last moment decided to attend and vote against it. Fitzgerald and Bishop Luigi Riccio of Cajazzo in the former kingdom of Naples were the only two among 535 bishops voting who returned a *non placet*.

During the nearly eight months that Bishop Gibbons spent in Rome he had had many an unforgettable experience. Through his close association with Archbishop Spalding, the vicar apostolic from North Carolina, thirty-five years old, had met personally many of the greatest men in the Church. He was present on January 29, 1870, when Pius IX paid a special compliment to the Americans by coming to the chapel of the American College to pronounce the decree declaring Giovanni Ancina as venerable. Listening week after week to the finest minds in the Church debate doctrinal and moral problems not only refreshed Gibbons' own knowledge but gave to it an enrichment that he never lost. Some of the richness of this experience shone through the series of eight unsigned articles that he and Bishop Lynch wrote in Europe and published in the *Catholic World* from February to September.

One lesson Gibbons learned on this trip pertained to the relations of Church and State. His observation of the practical working of union of Church and State in some European countries solidified his preference for the American system. At Annecy in Savoy he and Archbishop Spalding were the guests of Bishop Claude M. Magnin who received them in his splendid palace "before which guards marched up and down." The vicar apostolic from North Carolina, contrasting the magnificence of the building with his four small rooms back in Wilmington, congratulated his host, to which the latter replied: "Monsignor Gibbons! All is not gold that glitters. I cannot even build a sacristy without government approval." The incident made a profound impression on James Gibbons' mind, and it reconciled him more than ever to the independent poverty in which he administered his vicariate. With each new view of the Old World system he became a stronger defender of the free and mutually amicable relationships between Church and State in the United States. By October 4, the bishop was again in Wilmington after an absence of over a year. St. Thomas Church had been enlarged and its equipment improved. The enlargement of 24 by 40 feet was in the main intended as living quarters for the clergy, and Gibbons was pleased with the improvement which, as he wrote, "forms my present commodious dwelling." By this time the efforts of the bishop and his four priests on the missions had succeeded in increasing the number of Catholics, either by searching out lapsed ones or by conversions, to a total of 1200, about 500 above the number when Gibbons came in 1868. Yet resources were still so meager that the bishop had to depend on outside aid. With this thought in mind he wrote to the Bishop of Albany and to other friends in that diocese asking if he might go there to beg. He received a hearty welcome from Bishop John Conroy, and his friend, James Mc-Dermott, said he thought there was scarcely a priest in the Diocese of Albany "who will not give you a passibly [*sic*] decent Collection."

Before setting off for the North the bishop completed work on his first pastoral letter, a commentary on the temporal power of the Pope. Gibbons sought to prove the Pope's title to sovereignty on the basis of legitimate acquisition, long possession, and just use of the original grant to the Papacy. The tone of the pastoral was firm and clear, although the language was sufficiently restrained as to offer no opportunity for criticism to fair-minded Americans outside the Church. The document pleased John Murphy, the publisher in Baltimore, so much that he volunteered to make Gibbons no charge for printing it. Before Gibbons left Wilmington he also delivered a public lecture at the invitation of the local temperance society, "the members of which," said Gibbons, "with one exception, are non-Catholics." The lecture was a sufficient success to prompt the president of the state council of the Friends of Temperance at Raleigh to write Gibbons two days later asking that he repeat it there.

On his way to Albany in late March, 1871, Gibbons stopped off at Baltimore to visit his friends. On March 19 he delivered a lecture on the Papacy and the temporal power in the hall of the Maryland Institute. Gibbons gave the lecture, so he thought, for the benefit of a parochial school fund of one of the Baltimore parishes, but the pastor decided, without Gibbons' prior knowledge, to give over the receipts to the bishop himself for the benefit of his diocese.

His reception by the clergy of the Diocese of Albany was very cordial, and Gibbons was able to collect a considerable sum of money from the priests and people to take back to his vicariate. The first week of June found him stopping with Bishop Conroy in Albany with his tour of the diocese about ended. He confessed to his friend, Father Joseph P. Dubreul, S.S., that his labors had veen "very arduous."

During June and part of July Bishop Gibbons filled engagements to confirm in a number of parishes in the Archdiocese of Baltimore. While on his tour he confirmed and preached at Barnesville, a little village in Montgomery County. Not long afterward a woman wrote him that she was present on that occasion and she was now seeking further information. "Believe me I shall never forget your sermon nor you. I am a Protestant and have been an earnest searcher after truth. Whether I have found it or not remains yet to be tested." This inquiry was one of the first among dozens sent to Gibbons by Protestants after hearing him preach or after reading one of his books.

In the fall of 1871 there occurred one of the most remarkable incidents of James Gibbons' North Carolina career. A country doctor by the name of John C. Monk was living with his family at a rural settlement called Newton Grove between Raleigh and Wilmington. The doctor had for some time been giving serious thought to the subject of religion. He chanced on an old issue of the New York *Herald* that contained a sermon by Archbishop John McCloskey on the true Church. He was so impressed by what he had read that he sent off a letter addressed to "Any Catholic Priest in Wilmington, N. C." in which he asked for further enlightenment. Mark Gross answered the call by a visit to Newton Grove where he began a series of instructions for the doctor and preached in the open to the people from the neighboring countryside. Dr. Monk's position of influence in the community proved to be a powerful attraction and soon a lively interest in Catholicism sprang up in a region where before it had been the subject of ridicule and reprobation. At length the doctor finished his instructions and came to Wilmington where, on October 27, 1871, Bishop Gibbons baptized him after receiving his profession of faith. He proved to be so ardent a Catholic and set so splendid an example that soon his wife and children, his brother and his family, and a number of their neighbors followed him into the Church.

In March, 1872, Gibbons visited Newton Grove. He had to rise at four o'clock in the morning to catch a very early train out of Wilmington and, there being no carriages about, he was compelled — with the aid of a small boy — to carry his heavy traveling bag filled with mission articles a mile to the station. Upon arrival at Newton Grove in a very severe storm he was met by a local resident with a carriage. Gibbons later wrote that his host carried an ax "to cut our way through the forests, for the sleet and snow had covered the country, and bowed to the earth, and in many places across our course, the pine saplings that grew in dense bodies up to the margin of the road." For twenty-one miles they crossed the country in the teeth of wind, rain, sleet, and snow. "After a short exposure I was all but frozen by the violence of the storm and intense cold." Gibbons recovered quickly after reaching his destination, however, and the next day he celebrated Mass in a private home and preached to a large gathering of people. In a short time many entered the Church, and ultimately a crude little wooden church was constructed to accommodate them when the priest came on his occasional visits. Experiences such as these — and he had several others that were not so striking — gave heart and courage to Gibbons to continue his efforts in spite of all difficulties.

The new year 1872 brought alarming reports from Baltimore concerning the health of Archbishop Spalding. Father Dubreul told Gibbons the archbishop had been anointed. "He may recover yet," said Dubreul, "but is continually in danger of being strangled. . . . His sufferings are great. We are all praying for him." Even before the ordeal of the archbishop ended, death struck in another part of the Province of Baltimore when John McGill, Bishop of Richmond, died on January 14. On his return from the funeral in Richmond Gibbons found awaiting him a telegram appointing him administrator of the vacant diocese; Archbishop Spalding wished Gibbons to make his residence in Richmond. By his nature, James Gibbons disliked radical changes in his customary way of living. When he was appointed to the cathedral in Baltimore, he was reluctant to leave St. Bridget's Parish; now that he had become used to his home in Wilmington, he was again loath to leave it. He did not feel he could refuse the appointment of the archbishop, however, so he wrote off his assent.

Just three weeks later, Martin John Spalding died on February 7. Gibbons confided to his diary: "Archbishop Spalding died. A great light is extinguished in Israel. I attended his funeral, having before his death, given him the H. Viaticum & read for him the Profession of Faith." In the death of Spalding, Gibbons lost a powerful friend. On March 20 the month's mind Mass was celebrated for the late archbishop in the cathedral of Baltimore. Gibbons, selected to preach the sermon, traced his relationship to Archbishop Spalding since 1865; he said that their friendship was of a most intimate and affectionate nature. "I reverenced him as a father, and he deigned to honor me as a son."

The responsibility for administering the vacant see of Richmond along with the vicariate was, of course, a heavy one. It necessitated repeated trips between Richmond and Wilmington and a good deal of added travel in visiting the scattered missions in Virginia and North Carolina. But any hope that Gibbons might have entertained of being relieved of one of the two jurisdictions was dashed on August 29, 1872, when Alessandro Cardinal Barnabò, Prefect of the Congregation of the Propaganda, notified Gibbons by letter that he had been named Bishop of Richmond by Pius IX. Barnabò also stated that Gibbons was to administer the Vicariate of North Carolina until the Holy See appointed a successor. The bulls for his promotion to Richmond were dated July 30; on the same day James Roosevelt Bayley, Bishop of Newark, had been named Archbishop of Baltimore to succeed Spalding.

Gibbons soon prepared to leave North Carolina. On September 5, a week after receiving the bulls, he wrote to Pius IX and Cardinal Barnabò accepting the appointment as Bishop of Richmond. On October 6 he preached his farewell sermon in St. Thomas Church. He told his Wilmington Catholics: "Like an absent father who reads with nervous hands the letters of his devoted children far away, I will watch you my spiritual children, for such you still remain." He never lost his high regard for those North Carolinians, and in after years he stated that he found the audiences in North Carolina more receptive to the teachings of the Church than those in Virginia.

In the interval since Gibbons' arrival in 1868 the number of priests in the vicariate had increased to eight; two parochial schools and a number of new churches and mission stations had appeared; and the total number of Catholics in North Carolina had doubled to 1400. One of the missionary priests wrote some years later that "The transfer of Bishop Gibbons was universally regretted," for the bishop's ability to speak and to write attractively, as well as his personal amiability and unaffected manners, had won him friends and admirers. He remarked that Gibbons was capable of accomplishing an incredible amount of work, that his visitation tours, by all modes of conveyance, "new and obsolete," brought an acquaintance with his people so intimate that "He knew all the adult Catholics in North Carolina personally and called them by name." Gibbons' method of apologetics for the Church likewise drew admiration, for he could always refute error "without wounding charity or interrupting the amenities of social intercourse."

At thirty-eight years of age, then, with four years of experience as a bishop, James Gibbons set out from Wilmington for Richmond, where the Catholics of the Old Dominion were prepared to welcome in his person the fourth bishop of their episcopal see.

The installation of James Gibbons as Bishop of Richmond took place in St. Peter's Cathedral on October 20, 1872. So great a crowd lined the sidewalks for nearly a block that "the utmost efforts of a squad of police . . . were necessary to prevent accidents." When the doors of the cathedral opened, Archbishop Bayley installed Gibbons and Bishop Thomas A. Becker of Wilmington celebrated the pontifical Mass. At the end of the ceremony Gibbons himself gave the principal address. Commending the faithful, he linked their loyalty to the Church with their loyalty to the nation:

> And we have unbounded confidence in your enlightened obedience, beloved children of the laity. It has been tauntingly said by the enemies of the Church that the submission of the Catholic laity to their pastors was forced and servile, and that their loyalty to their Church would melt away amid the free air of America. The Catholics of the United States have triumphantly repelled, by their acts, the insulting insinuation. As there are none more loyal than they to their country, so there are none more devoted to their Church.

The Diocese of Richmond comprised eight counties in West Virginia together with all the state of Virginia except twenty counties. The combined area that now became the spiritual responsibility of Bishop Gibbons covered 34,808 square miles. In the year of Gibbons' arrival in Richmond the diocese had fifteen churches, an equal number of chapels and stations, five schools for girls with about 800 students, eight schools for boys with 600 students, one hospital, two orphan asylums caring for 119 orphans, and an estimated

Catholic population of around 17,000. To care for the spiritual needs of the diocese there were seventeen priests; nine students were preparing for the ministry in various seminaries.

While the situation of the Church in Virginia was, indeed, better than in North Carolina, the overwhelmingly non-Catholic character of the population made Virginia missionary territory for Catholicism. In 1870 only a fraction over one in seventy-two of the total population were Catholics. As in North Carolina, the population was largely scattered, more than 88 percent of the inhabitants living in rural areas. Richmond, the largest city, was showing signs of development as an industrial center with iron works, flour mills, and a large cotton mill doing a fairly thriving business. Railroad communication, opened between Richmond and the West in 1873, contributed to the city's prosperity.

The new year 1873 brought a donation of about $150 for the Diocese of Richmond from the Paris headquarters of the Society for the Propagation of the Faith, the first of a series of benefactions that would ultimately total over 34,000 francs or $1,700 for Gibbons' years in the diocese. Needless to say, these sums were speedily put to work, for it was not easy to find money to help support priests on the mission and to pay for the expenses of students for the diocesan priesthood. The diocese needed priests, but Gibbons, short of money, asked the rector of All Hallows College in Ireland to cancel any adoption of students for Richmond.

A few weeks after the arrival of James Gibbons in Richmond, a Catholic temperance society was organized in the cathedral parish with his approval. All through his life the bishop gave his hearty blessing to the temperance movement, although at no time was he a teetotaler. In the fall of 1873, the cathedral school for boys at Ninth and Marshall Streets was dedicated. A few weeks later the bishop was visited by the assistant Mother of the Little Sisters of the Poor who came to inspect a building on Brooke Avenue that Gibbons had proposed as a home for the aged poor in his diocese. This became one of his favorite projects; through the generosity of William Shakespeare Caldwell, a wealthy layman of New York, he was able to make his dream a reality. In 1874 Caldwell deeded a house on Marshall Street to the bishop for an old people's home and provided an endowment to help support it.

On his repeated missionary journeys through Virginia and North

Carolina Gibbons encountered some strange experiences. Early in 1874 he had gone south to Halifax, Virginia, where on a dark, rainy night he had preached to about twenty persons in the courthouse. About four-thirty the next morning he was awakened by the barking of dogs. He soon discovered that there was a thief in his room. The bishop called out several times but received no answer; whereupon he jumped out of bed, and the robber ran, leaving behind Gibbons' vest which contained about $150.

One of the severest trials of his life as a bishop was just ahead of him. Father J. V. McNamara, the pastor at Raleigh, North Carolina, forbade his people to hold a ball on St. Patrick's night because he felt that scandal would arise from it. The bishop disagreed with him, and the incident brought on a crisis in their relations. The priest had been gravely disobedient for years, had given scandal, and had abused his people through his ungovernable temper. Finally Gibbons' patience was worn out, and he suspended McNamara. When the bishop went to Raleigh in the spring of 1874 to try to bring order to the parish, McNamara, as the bishop described it, "had the hardihood to sit in the sanctuary on last Sunday during late Mass, & attempted to speak after I had preached, but I forbade him." McNamara appealed to the Holy See, and the bishop was compelled to defend his own course of action to the Prefect of the Congregation of the Propaganda. Ultimately, McNamara was replaced as pastor at Raleigh, but the incident had been a sore trial that the young bishop did not soon forget.

North Carolina gave rise to another disturbing incident of a different character. In May, 1874, Thomas Atkinson, Protestant Episcopal Bishop of North Carolina, delivered an attack on the Catholic teaching on the sacrament of penance and on the moral influence of the confessional. Gibbons regarded the attack as serious enough to warrant an answer. He, therefore, prepared a fairly elaborate reply, had it printed in the form of a brochure entitled *The Sacrament of Penance and the Moral Influence of Sacramental Confession*. In it Gibbons endeavored to answer the two main charges of Atkinson, namely, the alleged human origin and immoral tendency of confession, and the religious superiority of Protestant over Catholic countries.

James Gibbons was again in North Carolina in June, 1875; he spent most of the month on a tour of the missions. On this trip he was offered a tract of 500 acres of good land by Father Jeremiah O'Connell. O'Connell felt that the farm would afford an opportunity for the bishop to engage the services of a group of religious who might live off the land and at the same time take care of the Catholics in the surrounding settlements. Gibbons acted promptly, and after about six months of negotiation finally induced Abbot Wimmer of St. Vincent's Abbey to send a colony of monks to cultivate the farm. On March 25, 1876, Gibbons transferred the deed to the Benedictines.

One of the last recorded visits to North Carolina that Gibbons made before his promotion to Baltimore was in the late winter of 1876. He traveled to Greensboro by boat on the Tar River and preached that night in the Methodist church. As he wrote, "The Methodist bell summoned the people to church, & some Protestant ladies sang & played on the occasion. The attendance was large." On Easter Tuesday he reached Raleigh, where he confirmed and preached; as he told Archbishop Bayley, "preaching is almost the alpha & omega of Episcopal life in N. Carolina." It was now over seven years since Gibbons had assumed charge of the Church in North Carolina. While its progress still left much to be desired, his repeated visitation tours and his sermons and ministrations had done much to give spirit to the priests and laity scattered over the vast stretches of the Old North State.

Bishop Gibbons kept in frequent touch with his metropolitan in Baltimore, and it was evident from their correspondence that their ties of friendship were growing closer as time passed. Soon — certainly by 1874 — Bayley gave intimation that he had Gibbons in mind as coadjutor of Baltimore with the right of succession. Through the next three years the steps taken by the archbishop made it a virtual certainty that James Gibbons' residence in Richmond would soon be ended.

Toward the end of 1874 the interest of the English-speaking world was enlivened notably by the public controversy between Henry Edward Cardinal Manning and William Ewart Gladstone over the issue of papal infallibility. A reporter of the New York *Herald* called on Gibbons in Richmond to ask his views. The bishop recalled that the Vatican Council had created no new doctrine, "but confirmed an old one." He likened the decree of papal infallibility to decisions of the Supreme Court when it decided constitutional questions. The decision of the justices embodied no new doctrine but rather a new form of words, since the judgment was based on the letter and spirit of the Constitution. Similarly when the Catholic Church defined a new dogma of faith, the definition was nothing more than a new form of expression given to an old doctrine, "because the decision must be drawn from the revealed word of God, and based upon the constant tradition of the Church." Gibbons stated that he found it singular that Gladstone was frightened by the tyranny of the Pope whereas he was completely silent on the tyranny being practiced just then by Bismarck against the Church in Germany. The *Herald* of November 29, 1874, carried the Gibbons interview, along with a sympathetic editorial note that closed with a reference to the bishop's surprise at Gladstone's silence regarding Bismarck's policies: "this surprise," said the *Herald,* "most persons are obliged to share."

The following year President Ulysses S. Grant caused a stir by his message to Congress in December, 1875, when he recommended a constitutional amendment forbidding the teaching of "sectarian" matters in any school supported wholly or in part by public funds and excluding from school funds and taxes any school conducted by a religious denomination. Grant likewise recommended a tax on church properties. Again a reporter from the *Herald* interviewed Gibbons. The bishop said that if the amendment proposed by Grant were enacted, it "would reduce our American Republic to the condition of things existing in pagan Rome." The bishop commented on the dangers of a more centralized government to individual liberty and to education. He championed the rights of the family and of the states in matters of education and added that if education were handed over to the federal government, it would "give the administration an overwhelming patronage, which would destroy all balance of power and reduce minorities to a mere cipher." Gibbons said he could not see how both religion and paganism could be excluded from the schools, "for if an education excludes all religion it is necessarily pagan, there being no medium between the two terms." He was equally vigorous in opposing Grant's proposal to tax church property; to him such action would put a premium on infidelity and avarice while making "religion and philanthropy odious by imposing a penalty on those who maintain Christianity and support charitable houses." The bishop closed the interview by saying that he did not believe the American people would ever be found advocating or even endorsing "such novel legislation."

When the young bishop went South in 1868 to assume his episcopal duties, he had entered upon a renewal of his previous experiences with poverty, steady toil, and uncertain economic status among those with whom he lived. He knew at close range the lot of those who toiled for a living, and his sympathies were with them. Preaching in Richmond in 1876, Gibbons counseled his flock on the topic: "Man Born to Work: or, Necessity and Dignity of Labor." He paid tribute to the useful and beneficent role of the laborer: "I would rather grasp the soiled hand of the honest artisan, than touch the soft, kid-gloved hand of the dandy." He stated that he had three admonitions to give to the men who composed his congregation: avoid idleness as they avoid theft; take an active personal interest in the business of their employers; and be content in the state and city where Providence had placed them, not moving from place to place since, as he said, "a strolling family gather very few coins or greenbacks in their perambulating wheel of fortune."

As time passed, the health of Archbishop Bayley showed further deterioration, and this prompted him to reopen the question of the coadjutorship for Bishop Gibbons. Early in 1876 Bayley told John Cardinal McCloskey of New York that his (Bayley's) doctor said he must either resign the See of Baltimore or get a coadjutor. He said that it did not seem necessary to him that three names should be submitted to the Holy See. "Bp. Gibbons of Richmond would be 'the right man in the right place.' " Of Gibbons the archbishop remarked: "He is clear headed — sensible — a good administrator — is very popular in Baltimore, and would be most aceptable to Clergy & People." Bayley asked McCloskey to second his efforts in Rome by writing to the Prefect of Propaganda. Meanwhile James Gibbons maintained silence.

For a long time Bishop Gibbons had been turning over in his mind a book that, by a clear exposition of Catholic truths, would serve both uninstructed Catholics and those outside the Church who were seeking further information on its teachings and practices. Gibbons had felt keenly the need of books of instruction from his earliest days on the missions in North Carolina, where there were so few Catholic schools and such a pitifully small number of priests and Sisters to help with instructions. At the urgent insistence of Father Gross, he started to give serious consideration to writing a book. Pursuing this task with the same measured pace that marked most of his understandings, he took a long time. By the early months of 1876, however, the greater part of the manuscript had been completed. John B. Tabb, a teacher in St. Peter's school, Richmond, checked the work for style, and then Gibbons sensibly submitted the manuscript to the trained eye of Father Camillo Mazzella, S.J., professor of theology at Woodstock College, Maryland. Mazzella read the work and then sent it on to John Murphy, the publisher in Baltimore. Toward the end of the year, James Gibbons' first and most famous work appeared under the title *The Faith of Our Fathers*.

This first literary effort of James Gibbons proved to be an immediate success. Letters poured in upon him from all directions, many of the American hierarchy sending their congratulations. Bishop Louis de Goesbriand of Burlington, Vermont, for example, said he found it much more readable than other books of its kind. Father Charles J. Croghan, pastor of St. Joseph's Church in Charleston, told the bishop that he had distributed fifty copies of it among his Sunday school children: "You hit upon the right matter; the style is admirable. . . . Everything in the book is as clear as a sunbeam." Since it was especially for groups such as Croghan's that the bishop had intended his volume, this letter doubtless brought him more than ordinary satisfaction. A letter from a Protestant woman in Baltimore said that while she had reverence for many Catholic practices, she had viewed others "as the empty, meaningless ceremonies I had been taught to consider them." Recently she had come on the bishop's book. "I was charmed with it, and discovered that my predilection for the Church was because I was a Catholic at heart." She was now under instructions to become a Catholic and she wanted the author to know of her gratitude for *The Faith of Our Fathers*. Pope Pius IX expressed his pleasure at learning of the book's success and his special joy that "the bishops were taking up their pens in the defence of Mother Church." He sent the Bishop of Richmond "a special blessing with the hope that he will continue the good fight."

A year and a half after its publication the Swiss house of Benziger Brothers brought out a translation in German, and eventually the book was translated into all the principal European languages including Swedish and Bohemian, and in 1896 it was put into Braille for the use of the blind. Late in 1892 word reached Gibbons from a missionary in Japan who proposed to translate it into Japanese; he asked for permission to make certain changes in the text in order to render it more suitable for Japanese readers. In reply Gibbons stated: "I freely consent that you should make slight changes and thus accommodate it to the habits and customs, the genius and temperament of the country." These various transactions over *The Faith of Our Fathers* took place before the international copyright law of March, 1891, had won general recognition and enforcement. Regardless of the question of copyright, Gibbons was not interested in profits but in the use to which his book might be put for the good of souls.

The Faith of Our Fathers was by all odds the most popular work in apologetics ever published by an American Catholic. At the present time, eighty-five years after publication it is an active item in religious bookstores, an estimated two million copies in 110 editions having been distributed. Because of this tremendous circulation and the enlightenment the book has brought to so many readers on the teachings of the Catholic Church, it deserves to rank among the most effective apologetic works in Christian history.

At the time that the details of Gibbons' book were being worked out, the rumor of the Baltimore coadjutorship recurred constantly. In the spring of 1876 the Coadjutor Archbishop of St. Louis, Patrick J. Ryan, said that he would do his best to get a group of Sisters for Gibbons' missions, although he thought Gibbons should not be planning so far as a year in advance. "Suppose," said Ryan, "you should be *translated* in the interim? Suppose you should be found in the quiet, respectable rank of the Coadjutors of the Country. . . . But I must not joke or hint even." That winter Michael A. Corrigan, Bishop of Newark, wrote Archbishop Bayley from the Eternal City that there would not be "the slightest difficulty" about a coadjutor as soon as the necessary documents were forwarded to the Holy See. As much as James Roosevelt Bayley wished to expedite the appointment he found he must comply with Propoganda's demand that a *terna* of three names be sent for the coadjutorship. He told Archbishop John J. Williams of Boston that besides the *terna* of himself and his suffragans Rome wanted letters from the other American metropolitans. Would Williams, then, please write to Rome and, "if you can, urge the appointment of Dr. Gibbons who is the right man."

At length the appointment of James Gibbons as Bishop of Jonopolis and Coadjutor Archbishop of Baltimore with the right of succession was made. The first news of the action of Rome reached him on May 15, 1877, in the form of a telegram from James A. McMaster, editor of the New York *Freeman's Journal,* which read: "You are preconized coadjutor of Baltimore cum jure successionis. Accept my congratulations." Within twenty-four hours the news was flashed over the country and congratulations began to come in. Bishop Corrigan, with whom Gibbons was destined to have many interesting, if not always tranquil, relations, wrote: "May God be praised for his appointment which has been so earnestly prayed for, and may His Holy Spirit be always with you to guide and direct you for our common good!" Denis J. O'Connell, just after his ordination in Rome, wrote to his superior: "God has great designs upon you, and his finger is most strangely apparent in the course of your life. Whatever else awaits you here, the government of many cities certainly awaits you hereafter." O'Connell said that following dinner that day the new priests were received by Alessandro Cardinal Franchi. O'Connell remarked that Franchi had taken away his bishop. "How so?" Franchi asked. "You have given him to Baltimore." "Oh, si si," he exclaimed laughing, "Monsig. Gibbons, for they all wanted him." Father Edward McGlynn of New York was present, and at this point he entered the conversation:

"And cum jure successionis, too, Eminenza," interposed Dr. McGlynn who stood near. "Yes," replied the cardinal, "all the Bishops were in favor of him, and the people of Baltimore were most eager to obtain him." "And he is young," added the Dr., "not much above thirty." "Thirty four" his Eminence responded. Then Dr. McGlynn continued: "He is most amiable and learned and has written some very valuable works, especially one on the Faith." "Si, si," said the cardinal, "io so," [I know it] "e molto bravo."

The Prefect of Propaganda and Father McGlynn had missed Gibbons' age by almost ten years!

In April of 1877 Archbishop Bayley had undertaken a trip to Europe in the hope that the waters of Vichy might restore his health. In June Archbishop James F. Wood of Philadelphia brought him the bulls of appointment for Gibbons as coadjutor of Baltimore. Bayley asked Wood to reconvey them to Gibbons with the request that he enter on the administration of the Archdiocese of Baltimore as soon as possible. Bayley himself wrote to Gibbons and granted all the faculties he could, instructed him as to where he would find the keys and the important documents he might need, and explained how he might secure money from the cathedraticum fund in the bank. Gibbons' faculties arrived in Richmond on August 1, and the next day Gibbons had a letter from the Vicar-General of Baltimore saying the bulls had been forwarded to him by Archbishop Wood. Gibbons noted in his diary: "May God give me light to know my duty & strength to fulfill it."

In August the Archbishop of Baltimore returned from Europe, but his condition grew so critical that late in the month Gibbons hurried to Newark and anointed him. These were trying days for the bishop who was expected to wind up his affairs in Virginia and North Carolina and at the same time attempt to keep the administration of the Archdiocese of Baltimore in some kind of order. On September 5 he wrote his acceptance of the Baltimore assignment to Pius IX. One of the last important public appearances of James Gibbons in Richmond came on September 19 when he preached in St. Peter's Cathedral at the Mass celebrated during the convention of the Irish Catholic Benevolent Union. He told the delegates that he had daily commingled and conversed with peoples of all religious creeds,

and unless I have very much mistaken the character and disposition of those people, I can say to you with confidence, that you will here seek in vain for social ostracism or religious animosity. Prejudices indeed there may be & are among us, but they are relegated to the private family & to the churches. You will find in the public walks of life, a broad religious toleration & a social fraternal spirit. And the friendly smile you will see before you on Richmond's face, will reflect the warm & generous feelings of Richmond's heart. . . .

Ten days after this sermon Bishop Gibbons received a telegram telling him that Archbishop Bayley was reported to be dying. He made another hurried trip to Newark and remained with the archbishop until his death on October 3. The funeral in Baltimore, the burial beside the grave of the late archbishop's aunt, Mother Elizabeth Seton, at Emmitsburg, and the many details attendant on these events took all of Gibbons' time during early October. Three days before the funeral the new archbishop began to exercise one of his functions as metropolitan when he sent telegrams to the suffragan bishops of the Province of Baltimore announcing the approaching nominations to the vacant See of Richmond and to the Vicariate of North Carolina. Within a few days Gibbons was asked by Archbishop Joseph S. Alemany of San Francisco to fulfill another duty of the metropolitans of the country, namely to express his views to Rome on the proposed names for the coadjutorship of San Francisco.

Following the funeral of Archbishop Bayley and the transaction of the most pressing business in Baltimore, the new archbishop returned to Richmond to take final leave of his people. On Sunday, October 14, he preached his farewell sermon in the cathedral to a large congregation, among whom there were many Protestants. The clergy of the diocese gave a farewell dinner in his honor and gave him a beautiful chalice as a token of esteem and gratitude for his services in the Diocese of Richmond. While Gibbons naturally felt regret at departing from Virginia where he had spent five happy years, he left with the satisfaction that he had done a great deal to advance the cause of religion in the state. In the five years since 1872 the number of churches had been increased by seven to a total of twenty-two, nine more chapels and stations had been added to the fifteen of 1872, and eight more priests were included in the total of twenty-five scattered over the towns and country stations of Virginia and West Virginia. In 1872 there had been five so-called "female academies" and eight parochial schools for boys; by the time Gibbons left the diocese, there were fourteen parochial schools each for boys and girls and six academies for the latter. Even the Vicariate of North Carolina was able to boast of four parochial schools in the year Gibbons went to Baltimore; nine years before there had been none.

At length on October 19 James Gibbons took his farewell of Richmond. Three months beyond his forty-third birthday, this man who had now completed nine years in the episcopacy found himself the archbishop of the premier See of Baltimore, his native city. At this early age he was placed in the seat of a Carroll, a Kenrick, and a Spalding, a position that, although not by official act of Rome, carried with it the practical primacy of the Catholic Church of the United States. From all the indications given of his wisdom, virtue, and ability through the years up to 1877 there seemed every reason to believe that the choice for this high post had been a happy one.

Chapter 3

First Years as Archbishop of Baltimore

By reason of his vigorous young manhood and his relatively simple administrative problems, Gibbons found no difficulty during the early years in looking after the spiritual needs of his new flock. The Archdiocese of Baltimore embraced the District of Columbia and the entire state of Maryland with the exception of the eastern shore, the 7000 square miles being far smaller than either of his previous jurisdictions. Except for Baltimore and Washington, the new archbishop's responsibility was again confined chiefly to small towns and rural settlements. In 1881 about 268 regular and diocesan priests cared for a total of about 210,000 Catholics at 168 churches and chapels. The visitation tours throughout the archdiocese, with its relatively good transportation systems, were simple in comparison to those in the South. Moreover, Baltimore, the oldest see in the country, had known a large and devoted Catholic population for many years; as a result, Gibbons fell heir to highly developed, mature religious institutions.

In the city of Baltimore there were twenty-one parishes, five designated as German and Bohemian. Four years after his arrival Gibbons dedicated a church for the 500 permanent Italian residents and for the numerous Italian seamen coming and going in the port. Washington had eleven parishes, two for Germans and one for colored Catholics. That Gibbons enjoyed a reputation for kindness to Negroes became evident several years later when Father Augustus Tolton of Illinois, the only colored priest in the United States up to that time, told him of the esteem he had won as "such a lover of our poor down trodden race." The archdiocese numbered sixty-six elementary schools; some parishes maintained separate schools for girls and boys. The academies for boys and novitiates for religious numbered nine, and the academies for girls totaled thirteen. Higher education was well served by St. Mary's Seminary, Mount Saint

Mary's College in Emmitsburg, St. Charles College, and the three Jesuit colleges, Georgetown, Woodstock, and Loyola. Organized Catholic charity took care of the less fortunate in the House of the Good Shepherd, conducted by the Little Sisters of the Poor for the aged, the Saint Mary's Industrial School for homeless boys, and six hospitals.

Before an archbishop can exercise the full powers of a metropolitan or perform certain episcopal functions, he must receive the symbol of his jurisdiction, the pallium, from the Holy See. The new Archbishop of Baltimore lost no time in asking Rome for this insignia. But pallia were conferred only in a consistory, and there was no telling when one would be held, for Pius IX's health was not good. For the interim, the Congregation de Propaganda Fide granted him ordinary power for confirming and extraordinary power for ordaining.

Meanwhile there were a number of tasks that he could perform without delay. The day after Archbishop Bayley's funeral he held a meeting of the suffragans of his province to fill the See of Richmond. Some days later, on the third Sunday of Advent, he preached the first sermon in the cathedral since his appointment. Gibbons followed the practice of Sunday preaching in his cathedral all through his forty-four years as Archbishop of Baltimore. Although business often took him away from the city, he managed to preach at least once a month at the Sunday high Mass. These sermons ultimately became occasions to which Catholics of the city looked forward with considerable pleasure. Nothing he ever said from the pulpit gave evidence of careless preparation. Of majestic eloquence and elegant diction he knew little. But he was a master of clear, simple language, rich illustration (especially from the New Testament), and unmistakable tone of earnestness.

Gradually the administration of the archdiocese became more familiar to the new ordinary. In his first months he was served by Joseph P. Dubreul, S.S., vicar-general, William E. Starr, chancellor, Thomas S. Lee, rector of the cathedral, and Alfred A. Curtis, secretary, all of whom had been on the scene in Baltimore for some time.

In Rome, the young Father Denis J. O'Connell, whom Gibbons had named his proxy at the Holy See, gathered items of Roman news and gossip. In November, 1877, O'Connell reported that Rome was virtually certain that there would be no American cardinals. He repeated this reference to an American cardinal often enough to create the impression that he was teasing Gibbons with the prospect of the red hat coming to Baltimore. In the last weeks of 1877, O'Connell chronicled his ups and downs in the matter of the pallium. Then at length on December 28 Pius IX assembled the cardinals, and the pallia for the new archbishops were postulated for and given out.

Now Archbishop Gibbons could make definite plans for the formal bestowal of the pallium in his cathedral. The date was set for February 10, 1878, and invitations were soon dispatched to the American hierarchy. Archbishop Wood was first invited to confer the pallium on Gibbons, but his health made it impossible. The archbishop then turned to his senior suffragan, Bishop Lynch of Charleston, who consented to perform the ceremony. A pressing invitation to Bishop Corrigan in Newark told him that Gibbons would be "more than disappointed by any excuse." Corrigan replied that he would be present. On January 22 Denis O'Connell arrived in Baltimore with the long-sought pallium. The plans were temporarily halted when news came that Pius IX had died on February 7. On February 8, however, Gibbons received a telegram from Cardinal McCloskey of New York that read: "Don't postpone ceremony." He decided to go ahead, omitting some of the external pomp. Besides Archbishop Gibbons and Archbishop Williams, eleven American bishops were in attendance, besides George Conroy Bishop of Ardagh and Apostolic Delegate to Canada. Lynch celebrated the pontifical Mass and preached, after which Gibbons himself responded, explaining the significance of the pallium and the advantages Catholics in large centers enjoyed in having an opportunity to witness the grandeur of solemn church ceremonies. Gibbons mentioned his experience in the South in receiving converts into the Church who had never seen a celebration of this kind since "their worship was in a place no better than a log cabin."

Gibbons had already settled into the routine of his archdiocese. There were constant calls relating to the parishes, their pastors and people, in addition to the maintenance of good relations with the many religious communities of men and women. As he never embarked upon a serious undertaking of national import without first consulting his fellow bishops, so in questions of a parochial character

Gibbons sought the advice of his pastors. His relations with his priests were on the whole very easy and friendly. He observed no formality about appointments; whenever he was at home they were free to call and to transact business. With a few of these men he had been on terms of intimate friendship even before his own consecration as a bishop. With others the naturally mild-mannered archbishop occasionally found his patience sorely tried, and at times he felt compelled to deal resolutely with them. When he had occasion to rebuke a Washington pastor for intemperate outbursts in the pulpit and in correspondence, Gibbons called to the pastor's attention the pain he was inflicting by his letters:

> . . . your letters betray a spirit calculated to alienate from you your brother priests. I pray you to meditate on the life of our Lord before committing your hand to paper. I have been always anxious, as you know, to befriend you, but your letters, I grieve to say, have added to my burden & increased my sorrows.
>
> I pray you to read this letter in the spirit of charity which has dictated it.

A reasonable man could scarcely show a more conciliatory tone in offering correction to an erring subject.

With the various religious orders and congregations within his jurisdiction, Gibbons maintained the most cordial relations. The Archbishop of Baltimore was proud to have the Jesuit scholasticate at Woodstock College located in his jurisdiction, and he took pride, too, in the learned publications of its faculty. It was a distinct advantage to him to have these theologians close at hand for consultation. At the time that Georgetown University, the oldest Catholic college in the United States, celebrated its centennial in 1889, Gibbons likened the Jesuit teachers at the college to soldiers of the Cross who were enlarging the bounds of the great republic of letters and religion. Of all the religious communities in the archdiocese, however, the Sulpicians were nearest to the archbishop's heart. Under their direction he had pursued his priestly studies for six years, and from 1877 to his death the Sulpicians were his confessors, and among his most intimate advisers. At the celebration of the centennial of St. Mary's Seminary in 1891, he said:

> I have been acquainted with the Sulpician fathers for nearly forty years. I have observed them closely, I have studied their character

and spirit, and I solemnly declare that the more I have seen them the more I have admired and loved them.

Even among the Sulpicians he reserved a special place in his affections for Alphonse L. Magnien, the sixth Sulpician superior in the United States. In 1879 Magnien was made a member of the archbishop's council, and as time passed Gibbons came to rely more and more upon this wise French priest for advice. When Magnien died in 1902, his close friend insisted upon celebrating the requiem in the cathedral and giving the absolution. When a volume in memory of Magnien was published, Gibbons contributed a preface in which he described all that the abbé had meant to him:

> I had been so much accustomed to consult the Venerable Abbé on important questions, and to lean upon him in every emergency, that his death is a rude shock to me, and I feel as if I had lost a right arm. He was indeed *dimidium animae meae*. . . . My chief consolation in my bereavement is found in the consciousness that his brethren inherit his virtues, and will perpetuate the good work which he had prosecuted for the glory of God, the service of his church, and the welfare of our beloved country.

Gibbons also had a hand in the formal establishment of an independent American branch of the Society of St. Joseph. The Mill Hill Fathers had come originally to Baltimore from England in 1871 to work among American Negroes. Finding the connection with the English superiors of the Society unsatisfactory, the American members expressed a desire for a separate group in the United States. For Gibbons, this involved a willingness to sponsor and supervise the new group. The independent American branch of the Society of St. Joseph was established in 1893, and Gibbons acted as their canonical superior from this time until his death twenty-eight years later.

The need for more nursing Sisters in Baltimore had been felt for some time, and Gibbons, in Europe in the spring of 1880, sought the services of the Bon Secours Sisters in Paris. In October of that year he informed the superior that a residence was ready for them, and in July, 1882, a larger and better house was blessed by Gibbons for these women whose services to the sick proved so beneficial to the city's unfortunate. Further facilities for the care of Baltimore's orphans were likewise provided when on December 28, 1881, Gibbons installed four Sisters of St. Francis from England, all of them converts, in their new home on St. Paul Street where they assumed charge of a foundling asylum and a school for colored children. The growing foreign-born population of the city prompted the archbishop in July, 1882, to request the Redemptorist provincial in Vienna to send him several priests who could help care for the Bohemians who were crowding into St. Wenceslaus Parish.

From his earliest years in Baltimore, Gibbons maintained cordial relations with Mount Saint Mary's College at Emmitsburg. He induced his brother and sister in New Orleans to send their sons there. In 1881, when the college found itself in one of the most severe financial crises of its history, the archbishop wrote an appeal to the alumni to aid the college. In the emergency it seemed wise that Father William J. Hill retire from the presidency. At length, William Byrne, Vicar-General of the Archdiocese of Boston, whom Gibbons had recommended, was selected to replace him. An advisory board was appointed to assist with the college finances, and Gibbons agreed to take the chairmanship and treasurer's post on this board. Within seven months he received $15,625 in donations. At the same time, he told Byrne: "My own donation is available at any time." As a result of the efforts of the advisory board and the loyalty of the alumni, Byrne could report by March, 1882, that the court had released the college from the custody of a receiver.

Gibbons' help to the Emmitsburg college was typical of his response to demands upon his purse from worthy causes. When the yellow-fever epidemic broke in the South in the fall of 1878, the archbishop within three weeks sent off checks varying from $100 to $500 for a total of $3,000. He directed his charities mainly to New Orleans, Tennessee, and Mississippi with requests that they be given to the particular missions or orphanages most in need. Bishop William Henry Elder of Natchez told Gibbons: "The liberal contributions that you and others have sent have been a great service already." During the epidemic word reached Baltimore that Elder had died of the yellow fever; thereupon a requiem Mass was celebrated and a sermon preached on Elder's sacrifice. The Bishop of Natchez wrote of this false report: "And what shall I say in acknowledgement of the Requiem Mass & the funeral sermon! Well — if the Mass did not get me out of Purgatory, it helped to get me out of my sick bed. And for the sermon — I cannot say much about that, until I see it or hear it." Gibbons continued his help to the yellow-

fever victims well into the autumn, and as late as November 4
Elder was acknowledging an additional check of $500.

Among the charities that the Archbishop of Baltimore patronized
in these years was an annual donation of $100 to the support of
Dr. Levi Silliman Ives, the convert Protestant Episcopal Bishop of
North Carolina. He likewise used the collections taken up throughout his archdiocese by the Society for the Propagation of the Faith
to assist less favored missionary areas of the Church in the United
States. And when in 1879 bankruptcy overtook Archbishop John
B. Purcell in Cincinnati, Gibbons contributed $4,460 to the fund
being raised by the American bishops, in addition to writing Purcell
several letters of encouragement and sympathy. Shortly thereafter
word reached the United States of the great suffering in Ireland as
a consequence of the war over the Land League. In this crisis for
the Irish peasants, Archbishop Gibbons directed that nearly £3,000
be sent for relief purposes with £400 earmarked for Archbishop
MacHale of Tuam and a like sum for his old schoolmate, Bishop
McCormack of Achonry. These various sums were but a small
amount of the benefactions that he gave to a wide variety of charities
all through the time that he was Archbishop of Baltimore.

Gibbons visited the various institutions in the archdiocese as
frequently as time permitted. On one visit to St. Charles College
in Ellicott City, William H. O'Connell, a student there who later
became Cardinal Archbishop of Boston, wrote his impressions of
Gibbons. The archbishop struck him as

a very holy man, and withal very keen, too. He is almost emaciated.
. . . His face is thin — his features, large and bony. His eyes are
lanterns; they transform his whole face — very bright and keen if
rather small. He bears himself with simple dignity, and one sees at
once the genuine priest and gentleman. . . . His voice is very pleasant
and he speaks in a clear-cut manner. I should think he was a very
careful, orderly painstaking man in everything; and then his face, not
handsome, but very pure and noble, as if he had known great difficulties and had patiently worked them out.

Gibbons always showed a strong inclination to demonstrate his
regard for the civil authorities and for the nation's customs. When
the time neared for the celebration of Baltimore's sesquicentennial
in 1880, the archbishop sent out a circular to his clergy instructing

them to have the various parish societies prepared to march in the parade on October 14. Moreover, the *Te Deum* was ordered to be sung in all the churches after vespers on Sunday, October 17, and the priests were urged to preach on the event. The Catholic people should be told to enter into the spirit of the occasion with their fellow citizens, but to avoid "all sinful excess" during the days of the celebration. The following year when President James A. Garfield was shot on July 2, 1881, by an assassin, Gibbons at once wrote a circular letter to the clergy in which he urged prayers for the stricken chief executive,

> . . . at once entreating God to spare his life and also as making an act of expiation for a crime which appertains to us as a nation and not only concerns but tarnishes us all.

That fall, when he issued an order for public prayers on Thanksgiving Day, he told Bishop Richard Gilmour of Cleveland: "We should not let Protestants surpass us in our expression of loyalty & devotion to our country."

In 1883 the archbishop suffered the loss of his mother, but the speedy burial of the dead in New Orleans and the great distance between the two cities did not permit him to attend the funeral. A week later he extended his thanks to Archbishop Francis X. Leray of New Orleans for, as he put it, "your great kindness and charity in presiding at the funeral service of my dear Mother. I beg you also to thank for me your devoted clergy who were present on the same occasion."

Amid his varied duties Gibbons managed to find time for writing. One of his first publications after his appointment to Baltimore was a pastoral letter on "Christian Education." In it the archbishop gave a fairly lengthy description of the evil effects of a purely secular education. He said that from the evidence submitted, "the conclusion is forced upon us, that Catholic Parochial Schools must be established and fostered, if we would preserve the faith of our children." He ended with a strong exhortation to parents to heed their duty to see that their children were given the benefits of a religious education. Some months after the appearance of the pastoral letter Gibbons made a visit to St. Joseph's Academy in Emmitsburg where he complimented the Sisters on their work for the education of young girls. On this occasion he took the opportunity to urge them to work for the canonization of Mother Elizabeth Seton, their American foundress, adding,

> I would myself very gladly take the initiative, if I had any encouragement from here; the first movement must naturally begin here. . . . You remember too that American canonized Saints are very rare birds, and Mother Seton's name would add another to the very short list.

One of the principal duties of a metropolitan is to serve as a counselor to the suffragan bishops of his province. In the early years of Gibbons' tenure as Archbishop of Baltimore a number of matters in the province demanded his attention. After a long delay in filling the See of Richmond, occasioned in part by the bulls being misdirected and sent to the dead-letter office in New York, the bulls arrived in Baltimore on August 1, 1878, with the name of John J. Keane as the new bishop. The ceremony of consecration was fixed for August 25 at St. Peter's Cathedral in Richmond. Keane chose Gibbons to consecrate him, the first of twenty-three such ceremonies that the archbishop was to perform in the years ahead. Gibbons found real satisfaction in installing Keane as the fifth Bishop of Richmond and his own successor in that see, for he had taken a liking to the thirty-nine-year-old prelate and had been impressed by his fine work at St. Patrick's in Washington. He had a special admiration for Keane's exceptional ability as a preacher.

Both as ordinary of Baltimore and as an American metropolitan, Archbishop Gibbons was called on constantly to give his judgment to the Holy See on the qualifications of men for the episcopacy. While it was a simple matter to name men suitable for the episcopal office from among his acquaintances, it was at times anything but simple to give an informed judgment on the filling of vacancies in distant dioceses. When in 1878 the question of a coadjutor for Archbishop Alemany in San Francisco was raised and Bishop Elder of Natchez was prominently mentioned, Gibbons wrote to Rome, "exposing reasons why Bp. Elder should be permitted to remain in Natchez or that his departure for San Francisco should be delayed." Meanwhile, however, the financial disaster in Cincinnati prompted the proposal that the aging Archbishop Purcell have a coadjutor, and the suffragans of Cincinnati drew up a new list on which Elder was placed first. Gibbons, heartily in favor of Elder for the Cincinnati position, warmly recommended the choice to Rome. In 1880 Elder went to the See of Cincinnati. Three years later Alemany was given Patrick W. Riordan as coadjutor.

One episcopal vacancy introduced Gibbons to the intensity of the conflict of nationalities among Catholics in America. In 1878 the aging Archbishop John M. Henni asked Gibbons' support for a *terna* of three bishops, all with German names, for the post of coadjutor archbishop of Milwaukee. Gibbons had already in his hand a petition from some priests in the archdiocese begging him to use his influence to end the excessive nationalism in the Church in Wisconsin. A pastor in Fond du Lac warned that "the principal and ulterior object" of the German clergy in the Archdiocese of Milwaukee was "to perpetuate a young Germany here." One of the immediate goals, this priest said, was to secure a German successor in the See of Milwaukee.

For the new Archbishop of Baltimore this was a novel problem. In North Carolina and in Richmond, few immigrants had settled, and of these only a handful were Catholic. In Baltimore, the several nationalities lived in peace. The Germans, who constituted about 60 percent of the foreign born, had established a thriving parochial life long before the advent of James Gibbons as archbishop. Their parishes, mainly under the direction of the Redemptorist Fathers, had shown steady growth, and since 1859 the German-speaking Catholics of the city had their own weekly newspaper, the *Katholische Volkszeitung*. The German Catholic community of Baltimore gave no cause for uneasiness to the archbishop, and his relations with both priests and people were friendly. Nor was any other group disgruntled.

But elsewhere the problem was more acute, especially where there were concentrations of Germans and Irish. The Catholic Germans held tenaciously to their mother tongue. Wherever they settled in any numbers the familiar pattern of church, parish school, parish clubs and societies, and the German language newspaper soon appeared. Confronted by hostile forces that resented their foreignism and their religion, the German Catholics quite naturally clung all the more closely to their German priests, schools, and press as the best media through which to preserve their faith. However lofty the motives or undoubted the merit of many features of the life of these Catholic Germans, their adherence to the German language appeared to many non-German Catholics as excessive fondness for Old World customs, as well as lack of appreciation for the language and customs of the country that had given them a haven. In the torrent of national feeling in the last quarter of the nineteenth century, many American Catholics became more sensitive about their German coreligionists' attachment to their native language, for the charge of "foreignism" had been one of the most constant refrains against Catholics in former times. Some of the most vociferous Catholic critics of the Germans were themselves either born in or were only one generation removed from Ireland. Still their exclusive use of English gave them, or so they thought, at least the appearance of belonging.

Added to the difference of language were profound differences in temperament. To the phlegmatic German his mercurial Irish neighbor often appeared fickle and unstable, while the somewhat volatile Irishman viewed the more somber and plodding German as respectable but generally dull. These differences, of course, showed up among the clergy as well as the laity; when the two groups were thrown together in Church government, the result frequently was friction. Resentments were also fired by the comparative number of each group in its hierarchy. In 1886, the extraction of American bishops was: Irish, thirty-five; German (including Austrian and Swiss), fifteen; French, eleven; English, five; and Dutch, Scottish, and Spanish, one each. Many German Catholics felt with considerable justification that their numbers and strength warranted a higher proportion of bishops. Furthermore, the fiery advocacy of the Catholic temperance movement by prelates of Irish blood aroused little besides ridicule and resentment among the Germans; they felt that they knew how to use liquor with moderation, something they believed the Irish had yet to learn. If the growing differences had remained in the hands of moderates in both camps, most of the trouble could have been avoided. But, unfortunately, a minority of extremists among the Irish were intent upon compelling the Germans to step into line with the increasing tempo of Americanization, and they did not scruple to resort on occasion to abusive language that left behind wounds long in healing. On the other hand, a minority of leaders among the Catholic Germans were extremely tactless in urging what they regarded as their rights in the matter of their parishes, and especially of their parish schools. The great majority of both groups, who deplored the bitterness and the damage being done to Catholic fraternal sentiment, was powerless to check the extremists before the storm had run its course.

Alarmed by the situation in Milwaukee, Gibbons decided to consult the Archbishop of Boston before he wrote to Rome. He told Williams that while he wished to gratify Henni by recommending his selection, he felt the memorial of the Milwaukee priests was worthy of some consideration. To this Gibbons added that perhaps Bishop John Lancaster Spalding of Peoria, who knew German well, might be placed second or third on the list. Williams advised Gibbons to put the case clearly before the Holy See so that someone would be appointed coadjutor who would be satisfactory to the Germans, but who would likewise "take an interest in others not German."

Rome refused to consider Henni's nominations for the coadjutorship until he consulted his suffragans. Henni held a meeting with his suffragans for this purpose in the early autumn of 1878. Shortly thereafter Gibbons learned that Spalding's name now appeared second on the list. Another petition from four Milwaukee priests followed within two weeks. They earnestly begged Gibbons to use his influence to have Spalding chosen, since in their opinion, "he would be just the man for the place." In writing to Giovanni Cardinal Simeoni, Prefect of the Propaganda, Gibbons yielded to their advice and backed Spalding. But Spalding refused to be considered for the coadjutorship. Rome took its time in making the appointment, but when it finally came in the spring of 1880, the first choice of Henni, Michael Heiss, Bishop of La Crosse, was named. Thus one of the earliest contests between the German element and their coreligionists resulted in a victory for the Germans.

During the following summer Cardinal McCloskey of New York appealed to Gibbons for assistance in getting a coadjutor of his choice. The New York case moved more rapidly, and within two and a half months McCloskey got as his coadjutor with the right of succession Bishop Corrigan of Newark, the third name on his list. Corrigan told Gibbons that he had hoped to "avert this fearful load." Now that it had happened, he said, he could "only humbly commend myself to your prayers — amazed at the thought that I am bidden to carry a cross which your Predecessor told me, years ago in your room, that even he would not dare to carry."

Much of this type of business, to be sure, fell to the lot of all the archbishops of the United States, but the amount reaching the Archbishop of Baltimore was especially great since, in the absence of an apostolic delegate, he exercised many functions normally performed by such an official.

The archbishop had not been long in Baltimore before he began to make frequent trips to Washington to be the guest of government officials or to confer with them about problems in which they had a mutual interest. In 1879 Alexander H. Stephens, the former Vice-President of the Confederacy who was then serving in the House of Representatives from his native Georgia, stated that he was anxious to make the archbishop's acquaintance, but that in consequence of his physical infirmities he had not been able to call. Gibbons accepted Stephens' invitation to dine and on this occasion met a number of other congressmen. He always took these contacts with public men very seriously. Nor did he fail to inform the Holy See when he believed they had made a contribution to the cordial relations between Church and State. In early July, 1879, he wrote Cardinal Simeoni telling him "of the good feeling which now subsists between the civil authorities and the Church," and he instanced the attendance of President Rutherford B. Hayes at the commencement of Georgetown College and the recent action of the Governor of Maryland in signing a law which remitted "to a great extent" the tax on Church property. The knowledge that the archbishop was acquainted with and esteemed by public men brought its annoyance, too, in the form of increasingly heavy demands for his intervention in behalf of office seekers. Whenever the archbishop felt that he could in good conscience recommend a person for an appointment, he did so.

In the fall of the same year Archbishop Gibbons gave his support to a project of national scope when he subscribed for five shares of stock at $100 each in the recently organized Irish Catholic Colonization Association, which had been formed to colonize the western states with Catholic settlers who would strengthen the Church in rural areas. Bishop John Ireland of St. Paul, one of the founders, wrote him enthusiastically of the plans of the association for settling Irish Catholic farmers in Nebraska and Minnesota. He closed with a typical flourish: "The one name of the Archbishop of Baltimore on our list did more than fifty discourses from little bishops of the West."

In his capacity as Archbishop of Baltimore, Gibbons was made a member of the executive board of the American College in Rome; as secretary of its board, he handled the correspondence about the college. When in 1878 Pope Leo XIII requested that the student body of twenty-one at the college be doubled, Gibbons was asked by the board at its meeting in New York on July 17 to communicate this wish to the metropolitans of the United States.

In February, 1880, the Archbishop of Baltimore had printed a circular letter to his clergy informing them that shortly after Easter he was going to Rome where he would inform the Pope of the fidelity of his priests and people. He asked them to be generous to the collection for Peter's Pence on Easter Sunday. Less than two weeks before sailing, Gibbons wrote Simeoni discrediting the rumors that the German Catholics in the United States were unjustly treated by the Irish bishops, and protesting against the removal of women from church choirs which in his judgment would be "impracticable & inexpedient."

Gibbons and his party sailed for Rome on the *City of Chester* on April 22. It happened that Henry Cardinal Manning was in Rome when Gibbons arrived, and Gibbons invited him to dinner at the American College. The meeting with Manning gave Gibbons an opportunity to discuss problems that the American and English Churches had in common with the Holy See. During his three weeks' stay in the Eternal City the Archbishop of Baltimore had two private audiences with Leo XIII and several conferences with Cardinal Simeoni and with Lorenzo Cardinal Nina, the Secretary of State.

Gibbons used the occasion of his visit to Rome to express deep hostility to the establishment of an apostolic delegation, a resident representative of the Holy Father in Washington similar to those in Paris, Vienna, and Madrid. It was Rome's preference that this official have the rank of an apostolic nuncio enjoying diplomatic recognition from the American government and possess full faculties from the Holy See to settle on the spot troublesome cases within the Church itself. To the overwhelming majority of the American hierarchy, however, this was not an acceptable arrangement, and from the earliest rumors of such an appointment it was vigorously resisted by many of the bishops. The precedents were not favorable.

An incident in June, 1853, had left a lasting memory in the minds of men of both Church and State. The Apostolic Nuncio to Brazil,

Archbishop Gaetano Bedini, who had been commissioned by Pius IX to investigate serious troubles in Buffalo and other American sees, had arrived in this country just as the nation had been in a state of serious agitation over the Know-Nothing movement against Catholics and foreigners. Before the termination of his visit in February, 1854, he had been made the victim of numerous unfriendly demonstrations in various cities. The American bishops had not been consulted in advance; if they had, they might have spared the nuncio his painful experiences by advising the Holy See of the inopportuneness of sending a representative to the United States when the Know-Nothing bigotry was at its height.

Nearly a quarter of a century later the Church in America received a visit from another papal envoy when Bishop Conroy had come to this country in 1878. Conroy had met with no such vicious attacks as Bedini. After an extensive tour of many of the American sees, the bishop had expressed his astonishment at the progress of the American Church and his thought that an apostolic delegate should be appointed to the United States. Suggestions of this kind naturally increased the alertness of American Catholics about having a papal envoy in their midst, and the presence in this country from time to time of minor prelates from Rome who had no official standing but who, nonetheless, conducted themselves in an imprudent and officious manner did not improve matters.

In the absence of a regularly established apostolic delegation, the business of the Church with Rome had from the beginning of the hierarchy been channeled principally through the occupants of the See of Baltimore. From the very outset of his tenure as Archbishop of Baltimore, Gibbons received a constant stream of inquiries from Rome. The archbishop's handling of these situations was generally successful. Most bishops saw no need for any other official representative of Rome in this country.

Gibbons, and many others in the hierarchy, believed that any other need for a direct contact with the Vatican could be met by having a strong representative stationed in Rome. England, with a much smaller Catholic population, wielded more influence than the United States by reason of powerful representation there. In a report to Archbishop Elder in June, 1880, Gibbons set forth a clear statement of the motives which governed his policy:

I spoke freely to one or more of the Cardinals & other officials on the inexpediency of sending us a Delegate. I would have mentioned the matter to the H. Father, if I were not assured that there is no danger of such a step being taken at least soon. I agree with you, & I believe that one of the certain results of such a step would be to create a school of service diplomacy, & another would be to retard the healthy progress of the Church & arouse complications with our government. If the danger is renewed, the Archbishops would do well to send a joint strong but temperate remonstrance.

He also reported to Elder that there was a plan underway for increasing the Peter's Pence from the United States. It involved designating two bishops who would go from one diocese to another, or, as an alternative, setting up confraternities, "presided over by distinguished ladies," under the supervision of the pastors. He concluded: "I gave the Card. a lengthened opinion in writing condemning in strong terms the two plans proposed, & adding that the plan already in vogue among us was the only feasible one. The H. F. not only approved of my suggestions, but incorporated them in a letter to the Abps. of the U. S. of which I am the bearer."

After a return journey through northern Italy, Austria, and Germany, where he witnessed the Passion Play at Oberammergau, the archbishop stopped at Amsterdam, Brussels, and Paris and then crossed to England. He visited Lulworth Castle where Archbishop John Carroll had been consecrated in 1790 and then went on to Birmingham where he called on John Henry Cardinal Newman for breakfast. After a month in Ireland he sailed from Queenstown on the *City of Chester* on August 25. Ten days later he told the congregation in his cathedral that he was "proud to own that whatever be the faults and drawbacks of our own system & they are not a few, still I would infinitely prefer to live under our own flag than any Gov. of Contin. Europe, for with us liberty is not a name but a living reality."

After Gibbons' return from Europe, the problem of secret societies, a perennial one for the hierarchy, drew his attenion. As organized media for easy social intercourse, secret societies spread widely in the large industrial areas. They served, also, the egoistic impulses in many obscure Americans who delighted in belonging to groups to which all could not belong and which encouraged the romantic extravagance of elaborate regalia on occasion. In the more practical order, most secret societies provided sickness and death benefits for their members, a service that held a strong attraction for many. While the older and still flourishing secret societies, such as the Freemasons and Odd Fellows and the Ancient Order of Hibernians, had been imported from abroad, the trend in the late century was toward indigenous groups. Between 1880 and 1900 approximately 490 new native-born secret lodges were established in the United States. Large numbers of American Catholics found their way into one or other of these secret groups.

The American bishops, of course, had long followed the directives of the Holy See forbidding Catholics to join the Freemasons. But what complicated the matter was the periodic emergence of secret societies on which Rome had not given a decision; the nature and purpose of these groups were often so hidden that it was almost impossible to gain an exact knowledge of their character. The Holy See showed caution before condemning societies by name, and the American hierarchy likewise moved slowly, prudently, lest it be guilty of an injustice and of a consequent injury to souls. For example, the bishops of the United States hesitated over the Fenians for a long time until the Holy See in January, 1870, finally condemned them. A bewildering variety of secret Irish groups intensified their activity during the 1870's, and the rising tempo of violence in places like Schuylkill County, Pennsylvania, where the Molly Maguires led the campaign for redress of their very real grievances against the coal operators, became a source of acute anxiety to those responsible for the spiritual guidance of the Catholic laity. The Ancient Order of Hibernians itself did not escape the suspicion of many of the Catholic clergy.

All during these years provincial and plenary councils of the American bishops repeatedly condemned secret societies in general. Yet their handling of the issue frequently created confusion and even scandal. A pastor here and a bishop there periodically thundered against a particular society while their neighbors in nearby parishes or dioceses often remained silent.

The earliest evidence of Gibbons' attitude toward secret societies came as a result of the activities of the Ku Klux Klan in North Carolina. Gibbons' friend, Edward Conigland, drew the bishop's praise for a lengthy speech in which he detailed the outrages committed by the Klan and the dangers to society that arose from secret associations. Gibbons moved slowly in his own jurisdiction. In Richmond, he confessed he was unwilling to take any overtly hostile action against the Ancient Order of Hibernians until he had consulted more experienced bishops; but meanwhile he was trying to freeze them out quietly.

In the fall of 1881, Gibbons made his own view clear in a letter to Archbishop Elder of Cincinnati. He was disposed to be very indulgent toward Catholic societies since they were generally actuated by a proper spirit of loyalty toward the Church, he said. He knew the current trend to belong to some organization; so long as Catholic men belonged to authorized societies, it would help to keep them secure from the dangerous and condemned groups. He elaborated on this view when Catholic membership in the Grand Army of the Republic, the organization of Civil War veterans, was at issue. He agreed that efforts should be made to eliminate objectionable ceremonials in the G.A.R., but then added:

> I may be wrong, & too liberal, when I say that I would not hastily make the saying of a prayer by a non-Catholic before exercises a cause for excluding Catholics from the society, provided the obligation of assisting at them were not forced as a sine qua non. Such prayers are said in Congress & other deliberative assemblies in this country. The presence of a Catholic congressman is not considered, I think, a communicatio in divinis. It is looked upon as a civil function. To refuse to allow a Catholic to be present at these exercises would involve our exclusion from all participation in our legislative assemblies.
>
> I hope I do not shock you by these remarks which are hastily made.

With a conviction very deeply rooted, James Gibbons reacted against harsh and unnecessary condemnations of any kind at any time. It was Gibbons' way to win men through persuasion and kindliness, not to alienate them through hasty and unsympathetic use of ecclesiastical authority. Comfortable in the atmosphere of conciliation, he felt estranged when the discussion of differences lost that spirit and assumed the air of uncompromising dogmatism. This trait invited accusations of vacillation, lack of courage, and even false liberalism. It was true that he did at times waver and hesitate; but beneath his uncertainty of action there lay fundamental strength.

One other problem, the relations between bishops and their clergy, was showing the need of attention on the highest level. In the last quarter of the nineteenth century the number of appeals reaching the Holy See from American priests who were in trouble with their bishops grew steadily, and so did the annoyance of the Roman officials. In a considerable proportion of these cases Rome gave its judgment against the bishops. This in turn caused irritation in the American hierarchy, which felt that Rome's leniency was detrimental to episcopal authority. The answer of the Holy See to prelates' complaints was frequently that the bishops did not keep Rome fully informed and that in some instances decisions had to be made without complete documentary coverage from the bishops. Moreover, some officials of the Roman Curia thought that American bishops had on occasion shown an arbitrary disposition in dealing with their priests. While an instruction from the Holy See of July 20, 1878, on the removal of priests from pastorates settled some aspects of this problem, a number of ill-defined points remained, such as the extent to which the bishop's council could exercise judgment in cases of removal of pastors. Several particularly difficult cases in the early 1880's pointed up the need for clarifying legislation and strengthened the view of some bishops that the Church of the United States should hold another plenary council.

Though Archbishop Gibbons alluded vaguely in 1880 to a forthcoming plenary council, it was characteristic of him not to initiate action, for all through his life he showed a marked disinclination to launch ambitious projects of any kind. The initiative for a council came not from him, but from some insistent demands from a half dozen bishops in the West, especially Thomas L. Grace, O.P., Bishop of St. Paul, who considered the council not only "most useful" but in some respects "even necessary." Gibbons did not share this view. Late in 1881 he consulted Cardinal McCloskey and Archbishop Corrigan in New York, and he wrote the latter to say: "The more I think on the subject of the council, the more I incline to the Cardinal's view — that it is undesirable for years to come to hold a Plenary Council, & if his Eminence has not yet written, he might if he think proper express my views in connection with his own." Nevertheless, the more venturesome western sentiment finally prevailed. Bishop Richard Gilmour of Cleveland told Gibbons in 1883 that he had advised Rome "that a Plenary Council was necessary but should not be held for at least three years to come, & before holding it that at least five Bishops should go to Rome & there with

Rome prepare a schema to be submitted to all the Bishops here after which the Council should be called with profit."

Faced with these conflicting opinions, the Holy See decided by the spring of 1883 that a plenary council of the American hierarchy should be held. Late in May Cardinal Simeoni addressed a letter to the heads of most of the ecclesiastical provinces in the United States inviting them to come to Rome the following November for preliminary conferences with the officials of the Propaganda. The task that lay ahead was, of course, an arduous one. Gibbons asked Denis O'Connell, then pastor of Sacred Heart Church in Winchester, Virginia, to come to see him. Since O'Connell knew Rome so well, the archbishop found his assistance invaluable in making the preliminary preparations for the meeting, and when the time came for Gibbons to depart that fall for Rome, he had the young priest accompany him.

Fortunately for Archbishop Gibbons, one of his closest friends and most trusted advisers was in Rome that summer of 1883 — Bishop Keane of Richmond. Keane wrote him two very lengthy letters in an effort to describe accurately the background to the Holy See's summons of the American bishops for consultation. After conferences with Simeoni and an audience with the Holy Father, Keane reported that he found among Roman officials, even Pope Leo XIII himself, "a sort of suspicion or dread that there was not a perfect disposition of concord & union on the part of the American Hierarchy towards the Holy See." The Roman officials had noted that some American bishops appeared to lack politeness in not observing the proper style in their correspondence with the Holy See; to this Simeoni had added that often when he wrote American bishops for information, he did not even receive an answer. Keane agreed that this last, of course, was inexcusable, but the style in writing might be explained by ignorance of the proper forms and by brusqueness in the American character. Neither indicated insubordination to the Holy See. Keane stated that the Holy See had grown weary of receiving appeals from American priests against their bishops and that the Roman officials had likewise complained that the bishops often did not submit evidence to Rome for their side of these cases; consequently, curial officials, "to their great regret," sometimes had to decide against the bishops. There was a grave need, therefore, for more personal consultation between the American prelates and the Holy See.

Keane's second impression dealt with the question of personal representation. Simeoni told Keane that when Leo XIII had spoken to a certain American bishop of sending a delegate to the United States, the bishop had replied: "Oh we are independent, and would rather not have any one coming over to settle our business for us." Once more Keane contended that either the bishop had expressed himself poorly or that the Pope had misunderstood him. He then explained that the American hierarchy shrank from the idea of a stranger who would be immediately besieged by a crowd of malcontents and who would be unable to appreciate the real nature of the cases laid before him. Simeoni's answer at this point was that the delegate would not be a tribunal for deciding cases at all, but only an envoy to investigate, gather information, and report to Rome.

Keane again returned to the attack with a strong plea for an accredited American prelate in Rome who could perform the functions for the American Church that Edward Cardinal Howard did for the English Church. To this Leo XIII had replied that he desired this himself.

Summarizing his impressions, Keane wrote:

> After my conversations with all these, it is perfectly clear to my mind that the summons has been issued in a spirit of the most entire friendliness towards the American Hierarchy, and through the desire to have all their relations with their priests & with the Holy See placed on the footing that will be the most advantageous & agreeable to our Hierarchy.

Pope Leo XIII, Keane reported, had spoken most kindly to him about the Church of the United States; he had said that through the conferences and the plenary council that would follow "the perfect unity of action which I desire among the Bishops & between them & the Holy See will be secured." For this reason, said Keane, it was important that the American bishops "should come *cheerfully,* as any objections would surely be misunderstood."

With these two lengthy explanations of the mind of Rome at hand, Gibbons was in a better position to assume the leadership that would be expected of him when he reached the Holy See. The uncertain health of Cardinal McCloskey of New York precluded his attending the conferences; in his absence the American prelates would naturally look to the Archbishop of Baltimore to take the lead.

Archbishop Gibbons left Baltimore on October 8 and sailed from

New York two days later on the *Gallia*. He reached the Eternal City on November 1, about two weeks in advance of the opening of the conferences. Since the Church of the United States was still regarded in a canonical sense as missionary territory, its business was conducted through the Congregation of the Propaganda, headed at this time by Cardinal Simeoni, the prefect, who had as his associates Giovanni Cardinal Franzelin and Lodovico Cardinal Jacobini with Archbishop Domenico Jacobini, secretary, and Bishop Luigi Sepiacci, O.S.A., consultor. At the first meeting held on November 13 the American bishops were presented with thirteen headings as a suggested agenda for discussion. Simeoni made clear at the outset that the American bishops were to feel entirely free to offer their observations on the subjects proposed by the Propaganda and to suggest additional items. This opportunity for free discussion was fully employed by the Americans; as a result, a thorough canvassing of opinion took place before decisions were reached on the various topics. Archbishop Gibbons took the lead for the Americans in debating practically all the more important points; on a number of occasions the record revealed his speaking "in the name of all his other colleagues."

At the opening meeting on November 13 Gibbons took exception to the recommendation that summer villas for seminarians be instituted in the United States. The summer vacation offered a good time to test the vocation of students for the priesthood, he said; if a student were to change his mind about his vocation, it should happen before ordination. The Roman officials finally agreed that the coming council not make the institution of villas obligatory, although it should strongly recommend them.

On a second topic, that of erecting cathedral chapters in the Church of the United States, Gibbons argued that chapters would not conform to the customs of the American people; that qualified priests could not easily be convened in chapter meetings because of the great distances and the expense involved in traveling; that some priests given the dignity of canons might become haughty in their attitude toward their bishops; and, finally, that the system was conducive to strife between a bishop and his canons. The objection of Gibbons and his associates finally carried, and, as an alternative, the system of diocesan consultors was to be made mandatory for all American dioceses.

At a subsequent meeting the question arose whether a bishop should seek the consent, or merely the counsel, of the consultors on diocesan business. Gibbons and his colleagues were anxious to set limits to the consultors' authority. Although the cardinals gave their assent to all of Gibbons' suggestions, a number of aspects of this problem remained unsettled and provided material for one of the most closely debated subjects in the council itself.

On two other matters the suggestions of the Archbishop of Baltimore were adopted. Agreeing at the outset with the Roman suggestion that a certain number of priests in each diocese be named irremovable rectors, he felt that their selection should be governed by the bishop's judgment as to the fitness of a candidate, by an examination, and by a test of ten years of praiseworthy work in the ministry. Once more speaking for all the Americans present, he gave his approval to the system outlined by the Propaganda for obtaining the votes of priests of a diocese in the case of a vacant see. The archbishop merely suggested the substitution of the metropolitan or one of the suffragan bishops instead of the administrator of the vacant see to preside at the priests' balloting.

On November 22 Archbishop Gibbons again spoke for his associates in giving full assent to the instructions of the Propaganda forbidding the collection of money at church doors, and ordering that space be provided for the faithful who were not able or who did not wish to pay for the seats they occupied. Gibbons did not agree, however, that picnics and fairs held for the purpose of raising money for church purposes need be entirely abolished as the cardinals had recommended. The archbishop preferred to have rules governing these affairs in such a way as to remove the causes of scandal and sin.

Archbishop Gibbons accepted fully the general regulations proposed for secret societies. But when Archbishop Charles J. Seghers of Oregon City, seconded by Bishop Silas M. Chatard of Vincennes, mentioned the danger of labor unions (*societates operariorum*) because of the secret oaths, the predominantly non-Catholic personnel, and the tendency to use violence to prevent others from working, Gibbons and Archbishop Patrick A. Feehan of Chicago immediately came to the defense of the unions by saying that many of them offered no reason for ecclesiastical authority to prohibit Catholics from belonging to them. The conclusion reached was that in the case of a doubtful society of any kind the bishop would have recourse to the Holy See if he could not clearly decide about its forbidden character.

In the conference on November 29 Gibbons promptly gave his approval to the strong stand of the Propaganda for parochial schools in the United States. Before the close of this day's meeting the discussion turned to the subject of the improvement of religious facilities for the Negroes in the United States. Gibbons here gave his ready assent to an annual collection to further the Negro apostolate, and he added the suggestions that the Society for the Propagation of the Faith be instituted in all American sees, that bishops in prosperous circumstances who had no Negroes in their charge contribute to the missions in dioceses where Negroes lived in great numbers, and finally that the Prefect of the Propaganda be asked to help supply missionaries for work among the American colored population. These ideas of Gibbons met with general approval.

In the meeting of December 1, Gibbons agreed with the cardinals' proposal of American commitees for religious aid for Italian immigrants to the United States; he added the idea of similar committees in Italy to work in conjunction with those in the United States. Gibbons also suggested similar committees for other nationalities that were then emigrating in large numbers from various countries in Europe. The St. Raphael Society for German immigrants was singled out for special praise as a model. On the final major topic of this session, forms of holding Church property, Gibbons favored the bishop's holding temporal possessions of a diocese, not absolutely in his own name, but in the name of all the Catholics of the diocese. The archbishop stated that this method conformed more closely to American customs than the others.

One of the most delicate questions to arise in negotiations related to the choice of an apostolic delegate to preside over the council. The choice for the post fell first on an Italian, but, in the face of opposition from the American bishops, the Pope dropped this idea and appointed Gibbons. The appointment pleased most Americans involved, but Ella B. Edes, a journalist who was the unofficial agent of Archbishop Corrigan in Rome, was greatly annoyed. Speaking of Archbishop Gibbons, Miss Edes told Corrigan: "At the risk of scandalizing you I say of His Grace 'Il est capable de tout' where his own vanity or self-aggrandizement come in. It is provoking to see such intriguers succeeded in their plans." Later on she added:

I hope he is not going to be suffered to interject at will and have all the say. He is an intriguer and an ambizioso of the *first water* for all his pretended sanctity and he has fully conveyed that impression here. . . .

But the irritation of Miss Edes did not at the time seem to affect adversely the friendship between Gibbons and Archbishop Corrigan. Before leaving Rome, the Archbishop of Baltimore was accorded a special honor when Pope Leo XIII appointed him to officiate on Christmas Day in the Basilica of St. Mary Major. Abbé Magnien was encouraged by this news. "I hear many say," said the Sulpician, "that this is an omen of something else. I fondly hope it is."

At length Archbishop Gibbons completed his business in Rome and left for home by way of the British Isles. After an absence of over five months he returned to Baltimore on March 13, 1884, to face the most important and difficult task that had yet been assigned to him. He confided to his diary that he reached home in good health and that Denis O'Connell, who had accompanied him on his journey, had been of great service and comfort to him. On the Sunday following his return Gibbons preached in the cathedral. The archbishop paid a tribute to the simple living and hard-working habits of the Roman cardinals, spoke of his three private audiences with Leo XIII, and added that the large standing armies of Europe had made him feel grateful to be back in peaceful America. He remarked: "The oftener I go to Europe, the longer I remain there, and the more I study the political condition of its people, I return home filled with greater admiration for our own country and more profoundly grateful that I am an American citizen."

Archbishop Gibbons had been at home less than a week when he began to prepare for the council by issuing the formal letter of convocation to the American hierarchy. Gibbons explained the purposes for which the council was called, set the date of opening for November 9, and explained to the prelates that because of the illness of Cardinal McCloskey he had been named apostolic delegate. Gibbons also exerted a serious effort to obtain the best theological talent in the United States to come to Baltimore in the late summer to work on the preliminary schema of decrees. He hoped that they might be properly drawn up and submitted to the bishops in advance of the council's opening.

All through the spring of 1884 Archbishop Gibbons kept in close touch with Archbishop Corrigan on almost every important matter that arose. He also consulted one or more of the other archbishops frequently. For example, when it came time to select the conciliar officers, he sought the approval of several of these leaders of the Church. From the consensus of their answers he was able to frame a judgment that met with the approval of a majority of the hierarchy.

By agreement among the archbishops, each metropolitan and his suffragans made themselves responsible in advance for commentary on one or more sections of the projected decrees. These were analyzed in the respective provinces, then forwarded to Baltimore where they were printed and distributed. The bishops of the Province of Chicago suggested the importance of some uniformity of textbooks in the schools in each diocese, "and especially the need of a Catechism, to be used everywhere." This suggestion appealed to Francis Janssens of Natchez, and he, therefore, sent along further suggestions about a catechism. There was enough demand to warrant Gibbons' appointing a committee of bishops to report on a uniform catechism. Thus began the project that eventually led to the *Baltimore Catechism,* still so widely used in revised form in the United States.

By mid-October the schema of the decrees, fresh from the printer, went off to the bishops. By getting the document into their hands three weeks in advance, Gibbons believed they would have ample time to examine it before the council met. Corrigan congratulated Gibbons on the successful completion of his labors. He thought that the proposed decrees showed throughout "marks of great zeal, good judgment and enlightened wisdom," and that the distribution of matter was "remarkably good, logical and judicious. . . ." While the actual work on the schema had been done by the consulting theologians, the responsibility for its overall preparation belonged to Gibbons, and it was reassuring to receive the approval of so exacting a critic as Archbishop Corrigan.

By the last days of October all was in readiness. In the first week of November the bishops and their theologians began to arrive in Baltimore and to settle themselves in various residences. The throng to be accommodated — fourteen archbishops, fifty-seven bishops, seven abbots, thirty-one superiors of religious orders, eleven superiors of major seminaries, and eighty-eight theologians, to say nothing of other minor officials — taxed every available bit of space in religious houses, parish rectories, and the private homes of Catholic families during the month the council was in session. On November 7 at St. Mary's Seminary on Paca Street the apostolic delegate greeted the prelates formally for the first time. Exceedingly nervous at first, Gibbons spoke simply of the need for harmony and good will:

> God grant that our deliberations may be marked by mutual for-bearance, & good will & genuine charity. May we keep in view the golden maxim of St. Augustine: In necessariis unitas, in dubiis libertas, in omnibus caritas. May God bless our labors, & may His Holy Spirit so shape our thoughts & words that all our decisions may contribute to His glory & the exaltation of our Holy Religion.

The New York *World* described the formal opening in the cathedral at some length:

> Venerable princes moved along, their long trains supported by bright-faced boys; keen-faced and intellectual-looking men in the prime fit to rule and ready to obey, walked with modest mien. . . . Occasionally among the crowd of clean-shaven faces could be seen one with pa-triarchal beard and venerable look seeming as though he had stepped out of a stained-glass window. Slowly swinging his censer, and spread-ing round an odor of frankincense walked the censerbearer, and then bringing up the rear walked the Apostolic-delegate, Archbishop Gibbons.

When the bishops and theologians began the real work on Monday, November 10, a document of nearly 100 pages entitled *Schema decretorum concilii plenarii Baltimorensis tertii* furnished the basis for debate. The role of the apostolic delegate was that of presiding officer who, in the parliamentary rules drawn up to govern the debates, had the power to break a tie with his vote, to recognize each speaker who wished to enter the debate, to appoint all special committees in the council, to call members to order in case the rules were being violated, and to settle any doubts that might arise con-cerning the rules.

The private edition of the *Acta et decreta,* which is the only extant record of the debates in council, indicates that Gibbons used his powers as apostolic delegate very sparingly. On the more im-portant questions, however, he interjected his opinion. When debate started on the subject of irremovable rectors, Bishop Ireland asked the apostolic delegate to tell the assembly his mind on the subject. Gibbons stated that it was the fixed opinion of the cardinals in Rome that there must be irremovable rectors in the Church of the

United States, and that if the council failed to pass legislation on this point it would only invite action from Rome that would not be without embarrassment to the bishops in this country. The apostolic delegate, therefore, indicated his view that the decree should be passed as it stood. That was done. In the extended and rather heated debate on secret societies, the voice of Gibbons was heard again on the side of moderation. He warned the bishops that it was the mind of the Holy See that, as he expressed it, "we condemn no society hastily."

Gibbons permitted the maximum of freedom of debate among the bishops, and his natural inclination to take the judgment of older and more experienced men contributed to his silence. Although he had passed his fiftieth birthday and had been an archbishop for seven years, he felt a certain reserve in the presence of men who were much his seniors both in age and in their years as bishops.

As the council neared its close and the newspapers found little in the realm of fact to report from Baltimore, speculation began about a red hat. The New York *World* of November 30 settled the question to its own satisfaction:

> It can be stated now as an absolute fact that Archbishop Gibbons, of the metropolitan see of Baltimore and delegate apostolic to the third Plenary Council, will be a cardinal before the adjournment of the present council, or at least before January. This was determined upon at the Council of American Bishops held at Rome last November. After his elevation to the cardinalate it is likely that he will be given a coadjutor, on account of the increase of work in this archdiocese.

One unexpected item was added to the business of the council. For years eloquent advocates, of whom Bishop Spalding of Peoria was the most active, had proposed a national university for the Church in the United States. The friends of the university had been hopeful when the archbishops went to Rome in November, 1883, to prepare for the plenary council; but their hopes were disappointed, for the project of a university found no place in the conversations of the American prelates with the cardinals of the Propaganda. In fact, no concrete progress was made until four days after the formal opening of the council, when Miss Mary Gwendoline Caldwell, a young heiress of New York City, gave written expression of her intention to donate $300,000 toward the beginning of a university.

The Caldwell offer, followed three days later by a powerful sermon for a university delivered by Spalding in the cathedral, definitely put an old idea in a new light. A committee of bishops studied the problem and on December 2 reported to the council that Miss Caldwell's offer should be accepted and the plans begun for a university. The council embodied the plan in the decrees to be sent to Rome for approval, and when the Holy See approved the decrees with a few minor changes, the American hierarchy was committed to a university for the American Church. At the request of Miss Caldwell, Gibbons had been named chairman of the committee for the university.

The solemn closing of the council took place on Sunday, December 7, in the cathedral with Archbishop Corrigan of New York the celebrant of the Mass, Bishop Spalding the preacher, and Gibbons presiding as delegate. After the Mass there followed the customary *acclamationes,* the bestowal of the *pax* by Gibbons on each of the bishops, and then two brief speeches by Archbishop Peter Richard Kenrick of St. Louis and Archbishop Gibbons. With the chanting of the *Te Deum* the ceremony came to an end. The Third Plenary Council had finished its long and difficult work.

In all, the council passed 319 decrees, grouped under eleven major titles, that ranged over practically every problem touching on the Church in the United States. After a brief chapter on the Catholic faith the bishops defined the rights and authority of various classes of ecclesiastical persons; framed laws governing feasts, fasts, and the administration of the sacraments; devoted a very lengthy section to Catholic education with provision for a university; passed decrees on diocesan newspapers, secret societies, work for the Negroes and Indians, ways of holding Church property, clerical trials; and, finally, added a brief chapter on Christian burial. The chapter on immigrants contained words of praise for the German and Irish immigrant societies and emphasized the need for priests in the seaboard cities to care for the newcomers, the necessity of special protection for women immigrants, and the desirability of directing foreign-born from the cities to the rural areas. On secret societies, the council finally adopted a decree that took judgment entirely out of the hands of the individual bishops and gave it to a committee composed of all the metropolitans of the United States. A unanimous decision of the American archbishops would settle the fate of a given society insofar as the Catholic Church was concerned; if they could not reach unanimity, then the case was to be referred to the Holy See for judgment.

Before the decrees framed at Baltimore in 1884 became law, they had to be approved by Rome, and that, of course, took further time and effort on the part of Gibbons and the bishops whom he appointed to represent the hierarchy at the Holy See. Yet so thoroughly had the council done its work that the decrees remained as the law of the Church of the United States practically unchanged down to 1918 when the *Code of Canon Law* went into force for the Universal Church, and even after that date many of the decrees continued in effect.

In the last days of 1884 Archbishop Gibbons prepared the many documents that had to be transmitted to the Holy See, and after having dispatched them, he wrote a glowing overall account of the council to Cardinal Simeoni. In this letter Gibbons commented on the harmony that had marked the meetings, the generally friendly attitude of the public and the press, and the fact that the Post Office Department had established a special postal service for the bishops. He told Simeoni that the president would have liked to have been present for the opening of the council but the pressure of urgent business kept him away. He concluded his description by saying:

> It is evident that everyone in our free America appreciates the important influence of the Catholic Church for the grandeur and prosperity of the nation and we can be only very grateful for the manifestations to which this sentiment has given rise. I am certain that your Eminence and His Holiness will be happy to learn this.

To win the formal approval of the Holy See for the legislation of the Third Plenary Council, Gibbons as apostolic delegate decided to send Dr. O'Connell to Rome. O'Connell possessed the double advantage of having worked on the legislation from the outset and of having had considerable experience in the conduct of business with the Roman Curia. In addition to O'Connell, Gibbons chose John Moore, Bishop of St. Augustine, one of his own suffragans, and Joseph Dwenger, C.Pp.S., Bishop of Fort Wayne. The choice of Bishop Moore seems to have been prompted in good measure by the fact that he had studied in Rome and could speak Italian fluently. In the case of Dwenger, his German extraction made him a suitable candidate to represent the German Catholics of the United States, and he was thought to enjoy cordial relations with a number of the Propaganda officials.

The uneasiness of Gibbons and other American bishops centered on the diocesan consultors' rights. Gibbons was anxious that the American bishops' freedom of action should not be fettered by having to get the consent of their consultors for the purchase and sale of property, and he was determined that the substitution made in the language of the decree in Baltimore should stand. Cardinal Franzelin, on the other hand, was holding out for "consent" in the place of "counsel." Worried, Bishop Gilmour suggested to Gibbons the necessity for strengthening the American delegation at Rome. He said he did not feel confidence in the ability of Dwenger and Moore to stand up to Franzelin and others, and at the risk of obtruding he suggested that he and Bishop Bernard J. McQuaid of Rochester go to Rome after Easter. Gibbons, fearful of Rome's reaction to the arrival of so many Americans, sought to meet Gilmour's proposal, and at the same time safeguard his own position, by a countersuggestion that Gilmour and McQuaid announce that they were going to Europe for reasons of health and relaxation; Gibbons believed that

> This and some other motives that may suggest themselves to you, while saving you from any suspicion of exercising any pressure, will not interfere with the exercise of your zeal and your aid in Rome. The authorities even will be glad to have you then for consultation.

McQuaid rejected this suggestion indignantly. He told Gilmour that if he did not know what kind of a man Gibbons was he would feel disposed "to resent his proposition as an insult." McQuaid would be no party to any unofficial visit to Rome; either they would go as the accredited representatives of the apostolic delegate, or he would not go at all. The Bishop of Rochester's annoyance did not abate; two weeks later he told Gilmour: "His Grace would be pleased if you could go to Rome on your own 'hook,' and save the American Church, without the possibility of his incurring any displeasure." He suggested that Gibbons seek the cooperation of the other archbishops. "Thus united," he continued, "he need not fear adverse criticism for himself. But he will get plenty of it should there be radical changes through his default." Meanwhile disquieting news over Franzelin's opposition continued to reach Baltimore from the Eternal City. Fears mounting, Gibbons still could not bring himself to commission the Bishop of Cleveland to go as his official representative. He limited himself to saying: "You can draw yr. conclusions about going. I cannot take the responsibility of advising you to go, but I wish you were there. You must decide for yourself & quickly."

The plain truth of the matter was that Archbishop Gibbons was sorely confused by contradictory advice. Dwenger was by all odds the most optimistic, but O'Connell informed the archbishop that he should take with some reserve what Dwenger wrote to him since the Bishop of Fort Wayne showed a tendency to overrate his own ability to convert the Propaganda officials to his views. To add to Gibbons' discomfort O'Connell, his most trusted adviser, disapproved of Gilmour's coming to Rome. He told the archbishop he could not see "what other interpretation could be put upon it by the Propaganda than an intention to coerce." Archbishop Elder of Cincinnati strongly advised Gibbons to issue the credentials for Gilmour. "If you feel a delicacy about assuming it," he wrote, "you might consult some of the Archbishops & some of the older Bishops; and I think their answers will reassure you." Fortunately, the opportunity was at hand, a meeting of the Bishops who composed the committee for the proposed Catholic university scheduled in Baltimore on May 7. At this meeting Williams, Ryan, Corrigan, Ireland, and Spalding all agreed Gilmour should be sent officially.

Just before Gilmour's departure, Gibbons warned him that talk of an apostolic delegate had begun again. When Gilmour arrived in Rome, he called on Cardinal Manning who was then in the Eternal City. He reported Manning as "very clearly and openly opposed" to the idea of sending a delegate to the United States. Bishop Moore had, on two or three occasions, spoken to Archbishop Jacobini about having an American bishop living in Rome; the last time the Propaganda secretary had, according to Moore, "let the cat out of the bag" when he replied that the Americans wanted to tie Rome's hands. Jacobini had asked about appointing one or two American bishops, either permanently or temporarily, to receive appeals in the United States and to treat matters there for Rome. Moore was agreeable to this proposal, providing there was also a prelate in Rome from the United States who could put matters into shape for the Propaganda and who could inform the officials of the value to be attached to testimony that came from this country.

Just a week before Moore wrote his letter to the Archbishop of

Baltimore there occurred an appointment which, to the mind of Gibbons, gave promise of solving the difficulty. On June 15, 1885, Denis J. O'Connell was named fourth rector of the American College in Rome. O'Connell had been Gibbons' favored candidate for the post, and the archbishop succeeded in adding endorsements from other members of the hierarchy as well — Williams, Ryan, Corrigan, Ireland, and Spalding. Ryan attached great significance to the post: "Unless some regular representative of the American Bishops shall be selected, the Rector of the College will have to act — more or less — in that capacity and the Propaganda will consult him." For this very reason, Gibbons was all the more anxious that the man selected be O'Connell. When Leo finally approved O'Connell's nomination, the news rejoiced the heart of the new rector's patron in Baltimore. He told Gilmour: "I regard his selection as not only a great blessing to the College, but also as a signal advantage to the American Bishops who will find in him a wise and discreet intermediary between them & the Holy See. He will discharge with zeal & ability whatever commission may be entrusted to him." O'Connell, confirmed as rector, thus began a decade of service during which he served many of the American bishops as their Roman representative, although he never received any formal appointment nor any official recognition from the Holy See. With his intimate friend in that role, the Archbishop of Baltimore had every reason to believe that the questions in which he took a special interest would receive from O'Connell the attention they deserved. In this he was not disappointed.

While the nomination of O'Connell was working its way through the Curia, the Italian government was threatening to sell the property of the American College. Word of this danger reached McCloskey by cable from Simeoni the first week of March, 1884, while Gibbons was still on the high seas returning from Europe. Corrigan, acting for McCloskey, approached President Chester A. Arthur to use the good offices of the United States government in preventing the seizure of the property. The confiscation was to be made under the law of 1866 ordering the sale of all Church property held in *mortmain* throughout Italy, and a second law of 1873 that had applied the former measure to the city and district of Rome. Although the deed to the college property was held by the Propaganda, the cost of its upkeep had been borne for years by the American hierarchy. The bishops could, therefore, legitimately protest against the seizure of property upon which they had expanded so much money. The favorable reception given to Cardinal McCloskey's appeal by the president, Secretary of State Frederick T. Frelinghuysen, and the American minister in Rome, William W. Astor, saved the property. Astor energetically appealed to the Ministry of Foreign Affairs, and by March 25 the property of the American College was excepted from confiscation.

The months of waiting for the final word on the conciliar decrees were anxious ones. Dwenger related that the arrival of Gilmour had aroused the suspicion of coercion in the mind of Simeoni, as Gibbons had feared. He said: "Two weeks ago I felt sure that Bp. Moore and myself would obtain all we asked. I can give no such assurance now, in fact I feel a great deal discouraged." To add to the troubles Moore bluntly told Gibbons that neither he nor Gilmour could get along with Dwenger because of what Moore called Dwenger's "vanity and selfishness."

Yet, on the whole, progress seemed fairly steady. By mid-September O'Connell could inform Gibbons: "The Council work is done, nothing remaining but the Pope's approval. I feel as if a mountain had been lifted off my mind." On September 10 Leo XIII gave his approval to the legislation. The troublesome question of the "consent" and "counsel" of diocesan consultors was settled by a special brief giving the American bishops permission for ten years to proceed with property transactions without first winning their consultors' consent.

The German question led Bishops Moore and Gilmour to one more chore. In August, 1883, there had arrived in the United States Peter Paul Cahensly, the secretary-general of the St. Raphael's Society for the Care of German Catholic Emigrants. Cahensly spent several months visiting the German Catholic centers, conferring with both priests and lay leaders. After Cahensly's visit, though not necessarily because of it, a German Catholic monthly journal in St. Louis, the *Pastoral Blatt,* published an article called "Clerical Know-Nothingism in the Catholic Church of the United States." The article criticized the system of maintaining German Catholic churches under the jurisdiction of English-speaking parishes. While the German Catholics could fulfill all their religious duties in such succursal churches, their priests did not enjoy the full privileges that were accorded to other pastors. The system led to friction, and the

Pastoral Blatt called for a grant of full autonomy to these German congregations. By the summer of 1884 the German priests of St. Louis had framed a protest to the Holy See.

The attention of Archbishop Gibbons had been drawn to the situation in St. Louis by a letter from Cardinal Simeoni in which the latter transmitted the views of the St. Louis priests and suggested that the matter be made a subject for discussion at the Third Plenary Council. In his reply, the Archbishop of Baltimore deplored the publicity that this question had received in the German-language newspapers. It would have been better, said Gibbons, to have the Propaganda informed and the matter then referred to the bishops in council so that a remedy might be applied without exciting odium and spite. He feared that quarrels of this kind in public would aggravate the situation and make a peaceful settlement all the more difficult. Gibbons promised to do all he could to have the council deal justly with the Germans and with Catholics of other nationalities. Actually the question of independent parishes for the Germans did not arise during the council, nor did the bishops of German nationality make any effort to introduce it.

Aware that the agitation still existed, Moore and Gilmour now prepared a memorial on the subject for the Propaganda. They charged the German Catholics with egotism in resisting the request that they attend church with other nationalities. This attitude, the bishops maintained, threatened to lead to a conflict between the German and Irish Catholics in the United States; if it were not stopped, scandal to religion and injury to souls would ensue. For the time being, Rome took no action on their memorial.

Its business completed, the Third Plenary Council redounded to the personal fame of the Archbishop of Baltimore, for his management of its affairs during and after the sessions contributed greatly to its ultimate success. In fact, so generally favorable had been the impression created in Rome, that when Archbishop Elzear A. Taschereau of Quebec contemplated a provincial council, Cardinal Simeoni advised him to delay the meeting until after the Baltimore decrees were published. Similarly, the Archbishop of St. Andrews and Edinburgh told Gibbons that the Scottish bishops were making plans for their first provincial council and that "Rome recommends to us your last Council of Baltimore as the best model for our imitation." Archbishop Gibbons felt a natural gratification at this approval by the Holy See and other hierarchies. With pardonable pride he concluded: "Thus are they all marching into line."

The completion of the work of the council released Gibbons for a variety of other assignments from Rome, such as resolving the ticklish administrative difficulties of the Archdiocese of New Orleans, and assignments from the hierarchy, such as getting affairs of the Bureau of Catholic Indian Mission in Washington straightened out. At the same time, the Archbishop of Baltimore managed to carry on the business of his own archdiocese and to respond to the increasing calls for his services from men in both Church and State. On December 28, 1884, he dedicated the new church for St. Patrick's parish in Washington. A week later he traveled to Philadelphia where he invested his friend, Archbishop Ryan, with the pallium. Shortly after Grover Cleveland was inaugurated as president, the archbishop called at the White House for about half an hour. The president expressed the hope that the visits would be renewed from time to time during his administration. President Cleveland was the first chief executive with whom Gibbons enjoyed close personal friendship; during the next four years the archbishop was a fairly frequent caller at the White House.

That fall Cardinal Simeoni, in a confidential letter, asked Gibbons' judgment on the propriety of Leo XIII's sending a note of greeting and goodwill to President Grover Cleveland. The Archbishop of Baltimore replied after a few weeks, laying before Simeoni a detailed explanation of why such a letter would do more harm than good. The United States, he said, was largely a Protestant country with Protestant traditions. Catholics were still a minority of eight out of fifty-five millions. Prejudices, however much buried at present, could easily be aroused again. American Catholics were in a position like that of the Catholics in England; only by the exercise of prudence could they remain strong. The American people, though opposed to religious persecution, were quick to resent favor to any particular religion. A letter from the Pope to the president would make Catholics suspected of ambition, intrigue, and even of disloyalty.

Moreover a letter from the Pope would embarrass President Cleveland. Most American Catholics were identified with his party, and their opponents, the Republicans, would surely make the papal letter a weapon against the Democrats. In these circumstances Cleveland might not make a reply in keeping with the dignity of the Sovereign Pontiff and in accordance with the veneration with which Catholics surrounded his person. In the United States the real force, public opinion, would not be favorable to an exchange of letters even if Cleveland responded as fully and courteously as he should. At the moment both political parties were favorably disposed toward the Catholics. It would be unwise, said Gibbons, to do anything that might change these good dispositions. He was happy to assure Simeoni, however, that personally the Holy Father was held in the highest esteem in this country, as was demonstrated by the universal admiration shown by serious and intelligent Americans for his encyclicals like *Immortale Dei*. The point of view outlined in this lengthy reply contained the sentiments that motivated Gibbons all through his life in opposition to the establishment of diplomatic relations between the two governments.

As James Gibbons came to the close of 1885 and his eighth year as Baltimore's archbishop, he could look back with considerable satisfaction at the generally prosperous growth of the archdiocese, the finished work of the Third Plenary Council, and the increasing stature that he was gaining with American people of all faiths. He was easily among the three or four top leaders of the Church in the United States, not only by virtue of his office as Archbishop of Baltimore but, also, through the exercise of talents and natural virtues that recommended him strongly to the affection of his associates. To his friends and admirers the rumors of greater honors that were in store for him seemed altogether fitting, and when in October, 1885, the only cardinal of the United States died, the speculation about a red hat for Gibbons took on more immediate significance.

Chapter 4
The Red Hat

The highest honor that can come to a Catholic churchman, aside from the Papacy itself, is membership in the College of Cardinals. A great personal distinction for the recipient, the cardinalate also often signifies the Holy See's favorable opinion of a particular nation and attests the maturity of the branch of the Universal Church thus honored.

The growth of the Catholic Church in the United States — well over six million members by 1880 — led, not surprisingly, to repeated rumors of a second cardinal for this country. Furthermore, the relations between the government and the Church, although entirely unofficial, were cordial; there was every prospect that the Church's progress in the republic would continue unimpeded by any hampering action of the civil power. With the first American cardinal, John McCloskey, Archbishop of New York, in poor health, Archbishop Gibbons' skill as apostolic delegate at the council, together with his position in the premier see of the country, focused attention on him as the most probable candidate. When Denis O'Connell arrived in Rome in the early spring of 1885, he had an audience with Leo XIII in which the Pope inquired about McCloskey's health and closed the audience with a reference to Gibbons:

> He spoke of you with an air of great acquaintance and affection, and tho he did not say so in so many words, I am satisfied that he intended to convey to me the impression that he intended to create a cardinal in Balto. to succeed the one of New York, and I think you know from experience with me that I am not disposed to commit myself to the promises of hope.

After Cardinal McCloskey died in the autumn of 1885, the rumors quickened. O'Connell heard from Archbishop Jacobini at the Propaganda that the red hat would come to Baltimore. Then in February

77

of 1886 Archbishop Gibbons received a telegram from the Archbishop of New York: "It is authentic. Biglietto will arrive about the twenty second." Corrigan, convinced of the authenticity of a cablegram he had received from Rome, released the news in New York. Within a few hours Gibbons began to receive congratulations from many friends and admirers. The Baltimore *American* of February 11 promptly picked up the Associated Press dispatch from New York. A reporter on the *American* rushed to the archbishop's residence that night and was told by John Foley that private telegrams received by the archbishop confirmed the authenticity of the news.

Later that day Gibbons noted in his diary: "Should the report be verified may God give me as He gave to His servant David a humble heart, that I may bear the honor with becoming modesty & a profound sense of my unworthiness. . . ."

Meanwhile he acknowledged Corrigan's telegram; he hoped the day was not far distant when he would be "sweetly revenged" by communicating a similar message to the Archbishop of New York. "Then what a hurricane there will be! The present storm will be mild in comparison to it." Just at this time Corrigan fixed March 4 as the date for receiving his pallium, and Gibbons gladly agreed to confer it.

During these days of mid-February, 1886, Archbishop Gibbons received hundreds of congratulatory messages. Their authors ranged through all the ranks of the hierarchy and priesthood, officials of the United States government, officers of the state and municipality, on down to little children in the parochial schools.

Yet amid all these notices in the public press and the numerous letters received by the archbishop from his admirers, no official word came from the Holy See. Two weeks passed, and then a registered letter to Archbishop Corrigan from Ella Edes in Rome revealed that he had unwittingly committed "an awful blunder." With the approach of Lent the Archbishop of New York and his consultors had discussed the subject of permitting the Catholic people the use of meat on Saturdays of the Lenten season. Corrigan knew that Gibbons had requested a similar indult. With that in mind he asked Miss Edes to inquire of Propaganda if Gibbons' request had been granted; if time pressed she was to cable the answer. Following out Corrigan's orders, Miss Edes cabled him on February 10 in these words: "Granted, Official Letter Baltimore, Feb. 8th." Corrigan, having meanwhile entirely forgotten about the Lenten indult, jumped to the conclusion that the cablegram pertained to Gibbons' red hat. The episode proved painful, of course, to the two principals. Corrigan told Gibbons that he was "mortified beyond measure," but that if the information were kept secret probably no harm would be done. The mistake would hasten the consummation if Corrigan himself could wield any influence, he said, and meanwhile the goodwill of the entire community had been made manifest. The Archbishop of New York craved the forgiveness of Gibbons for his error; as he put it, "I *meant* to do a kind act, and on the contrary have only covered myself with confusion."

Archbishop Gibbons replied promptly:

> Your letter came just as I was going down to breakfast with Bp. Kain & Bp. Dwenger. You may well realize its effect on me. I tried with great difficulty to maintain my composure at the table. It has of course unnerved me. But I am praying earnestly to God to give me grace & strength to bear the humiliation & drink the chalice. I am sorry also my Dear Friend, for your sake. I know how distressed you must feel & all on my account, in your friendly eagerness to send me what you naturally supposed would be a joyful message. I will keep the secret, but I cannot stop the congratulatory messages that are coming in every day. I can only say to them in reply, as I have been saying, that I have no communication from Rome on the subject. . . .
>
> Pray my Dear Friend that I may have grace to bear this confusion, & may joyfully do God's will, & I beg you not to be distressed on my account.

The tension of these days must have been exceedingly trying. The excitement died down in Baltimore, but, as Gibbons confessed to Corrigan, he dreaded the gauntlet he would have to run in New York when he came for the conferring of the pallium. He was fearful that the strong emotion under which he had written his first letter to Corrigan would convey the impression that he was thinking more of himself than of his friend in New York, for as Gibbons expressed it, "You needed more sympathy than I did." He was especially uneasy lest the Roman correspondent of some American secular or religious paper seek authentication of the news at the Vatican. In that case Rome might well cable an official contradiction to the United States. For this reason, Gibbons remarked, it had occurred to him that Corrigan might forestall such a contingency by sending to Rome an explanation of what had really happened.

Corrigan did communicate to the Secretary of the Propaganda, Jacobini, the story of his blunder. He added a statement — in the name of the entire American hierarchy — that if the Pope should see fit to confer the hat on Gibbons it would be gratifying to all the American bishops. Jacobini informed Leo XIII of Corrigan's error. The Pope received the report good-naturedly and said that no harm had been done. Gibbons told his friend in New York that he never dreamed Corrigan would carry his atonement "for a most pardonable & magnanimous mistake to such a length of noble generosity."

At length the official silence was broken in May when a cablegram arrived from Lodovico Cardinal Jacobini, Secretary of State, informing Gibbons of his designation by the Pope for the cardinalate in the forthcoming consistory. In Rome, O'Connell was plainly elated: "Gibbons 'are trumps' now, and everyone will try to play them."

Even as Gibbons rejoiced in his new honor, he shared the general horror provoked by the riot caused by the explosion of a bomb in Haymarket Square, Chicago, on May 4. Eleven persons, including three policemen, died as a result of the tumult. On the following Sunday, the new cardinal seized the opportunity of the dedication of Holy Cross Church for the German Catholics in Baltimore to utter a strong cry of warning to foreign born of his own faith. Gibbons emphasized that the United States welcomed foreigners, but he lashed out against the turbulent minority of anarchists who preached the gospel of socialism and nihilism and whose favorite weapon was dynamite. He said: "Instead of strengthening the hands of the government that upholds and protects them, they are bent upon its destruction. Instead of blessing the mother that opens her arms to welcome them, they insult and strike her." In this salutary warning Gibbons joined his voice to those of responsible citizens everywhere in deprecating the tragic events in Chicago that had implicated a number of the foreign born.

Even as Gibbons waited for the arrival of the red biretta, he showed that, though he was at all times respectful of pontifical authority, he did not respond to every hint that emanated from circles close to the Roman Curia. Robert Fulton, S.J., provincial of the Maryland province of the Society of Jesus, told Gibbons that he had been instructed by Rome to take an active interest in raising a special collection in the United States for the golden jubilee

of Leo XIII's priesthood. Gibbons frankly opposed the collection.
The bishops had pledged themselves in the Third Plenary Council
to take up a collection for the Pope sometime before the summer
of 1887; there was also the annual Peter's Pence. In Gibbons' judgment three collections in one year for the same purpose would
fatigue the people. The fact that Fulton mentioned pressure from
Rome did not disturb the cardinal, for he remarked to Archbishop
Williams of Boston: "I replied that I would wait for the pressure." He
proposed to the Archbishop of Boston that at the proper time the
hierarchy join in a letter of felicitation to the Pontiff and make his
jubilee the occasion for increasing the Peter's Pence. "I think it is
very important," he said, "that we should act in concert on this
matter, and agree on a basis of action." In the end the proposals
made by Gibbons were carried out.

The cardinal-elect chose June 30 for the imposition of the red
biretta in Baltimore. It was the silver jubilee of his ordination as a
priest by Archbishop Francis P. Kenrick, the brother of the man
who had now been appointed to confer upon Gibbons the symbol of
his new rank. On the afternoon of June 29 the official letter of
notification and the red zucchetto were presented to Gibbons in
the parlor of his residence. On the following morning the Cathedral
of the Assumption was filled to overflowing. The solemn procession
into the cathedral found twenty-four bishops and ten archbishops
in the line of march. Archbishop Williams said the Mass, Archbishop Ryan preached the sermon, and at the end of the Mass
Archbishop Kenrick of St. Louis imposed the biretta on the new
cardinal. Monsigneur Germano Straniero, the papal ablegate, made
a brief speech. The long, unusual ceremony was concluded by three
brief addresses by Gibbons, the first to Kenrick, the second to
Straniero. The third address, directed to the prelates, clergy, and
laity, afforded Gibbons an opportunity to pay a special tribute to
the high moral influence exercised by the reigning Pope. The new
cardinal also struck a favorite note in praise of his own country:

> In no country of all the nations of the earth does he [Leo XIII]
> find more loyal and devoted spiritual children than among the clergy
> and laity of this free republic. And I am happy to add that our
> separated brethren, while not sharing in our faith, have shared our
> profound admiration for the benevolent and enlightened statesmanship
> of the present Supreme Pontiff.

The American press's reaction to the ceremonies found favor in Rome where the tokens of respect expressed by the American newspapers for Leo XIII and the new cardinal were contrasted to the antipapal attitude of the Italian government and press. The *Osservatore Romano,* the Vatican newspaper, paid high praise to the United States for the friendly reception given to its new cardinal, then went on: "To those proud republicans, citizens of the greatest and best constituted republic the earth has ever known, the Pope is something higher than any other man, and they laugh at and scorn and cannot understand those who seriously pretend to consider the Pope a simple citizen of Italy."

For Cardinal Gibbons the principal ceremony was yet to come — the consistory at Rome at which he would receive the red hat itself. In the meantime, the new cardinal attended to certain formalities, such as addressing letters of greeting to all other cardinals in the world, and to the Catholic sovereigns which, in turn, brought him the felicitations of the King and Queen of the Belgians, the Emperor and Empress of Austria-Hungary, the Emperor and Empress of Brazil, and the Queen of Portugal.

The fall and early winter of 1886 found Gibbons preoccupied with diocesan business and with increasingly serious problems facing the Church in the United States.

Since the Third Plenary Council, Gibbons had not exerted himself for the proposed new university. In 1885 Bishop Ireland of St. Paul, restive at the long delay, pointedly reminded him that two members of the original committee had already died and that further delay would endanger interest in the project. The strong pressure of Spalding and Ireland finally led Gibbons to make a new start; he set May 7, 1885, for a meeting of the university committee in Baltimore. On this occasion the leading item of business was the selection of a site. When Bishop Spalding put the motion for Washington, it carried without difficulty. The choice was not to the liking of Gibbons but he yielded to the strong preference of Spalding and Ireland and the wish of Miss Caldwell. The news of the selection of the nation's capital was greeted with favor by both the Catholic and the secular press.

In the fall of 1885 the Holy Father addressed a private letter to the Archbishop of Baltimore in which he expressed gratification over the plans for a university. The arrival of Leo XIII's letter in time for a committee meeting on November 11 enabled Gibbons to read it to members as an encouragement to their efforts. On that occasion Bishops Spalding, Ireland, Keane, and Martin Marty were authorized to collect funds throughout the dioceses of the United States; Gibbons was to write a letter to the American hierarchy explaining the authorization and inviting the support of the bishops. When three months passed and no letter appeared, Bishop Keane, on the job collecting in New York for some time, prodded the archbishop: "Does it not seem time for Baltimore to speak out & act?" Archbishop Gibbons' caution found support in the spring of 1886. While Denis O'Connell was personally enthusiastic about the university, his correspondence suggested that the idea had not taken too well with a number of the officials of the Roman Curia. More alarming was the resignation of Archbishop Heiss from the university committee. Heiss pleaded his many duties in Milwaukee, the great distance he would have to travel to meetings, and the little he could contribute to the university's work. His resignation removed the leading representative of the German Catholics in the United States, and O'Connell reported that the Heiss resignation was made to look "ominous" in Rome.

At a meeting in Baltimore May 12, a special subcommittee named to select a rector chose John Lancaster Spalding. When he refused the post, the archbishops turned to John J. Keane, Bishop of Richmond. After expressing his reluctance to undertake a position for which he had no training or experience, Keane at length accepted. The appointment was to be kept confidential until it received the approval of the Holy See. The subcommittee also decided that Bishop Keane should personally go to Rome in the autumn. John Ireland was going at that time to make his *ad limina* visit; the committee planned to have the two bishops travel and work together. In the meantime, Keane begged his friend, Denis O'Connell, to be on his guard and to protect the university project against "petty undermining."

In the autumn of 1886, the university committee convened to draw up two lengthy letters for Leo XIII and Cardinal Simeoni. Five other archbishops, in Baltimore on other business, also signed. The letters thus bore the names of nine of the twelve archbishops in the United States. Armed with these documents, Bishops Keane and Ireland sailed on the *Aurania* three days later to lay the plans before the officials of the Curia.

Meanwhile, quite unknown to Gibbons, Cardinal Simeoni asked Archbishop Corrigan for a confidential opinion on the university. Corrigan had recently sought the judgment of Father Fulton, who had opposed the university strenuously in the Third Plenary Council. Fulton complied with detailed objections; these the Archbishop of New York made the substance of his reply to the Propaganda. When Keane and Ireland arrived in Rome, they easily spotted the source of the opposition to the university that had been reaching the Holy See. Seriously concerned, they composed a very strong answer to all the objections made to them by the Propaganda officials. A copy of this lengthy document, along with private letters from Keane and O'Connell, kept Gibbons posted. Still he said little, even though his failure to speak out strongly proved to be a source of embarrassment to the Americans in Rome. When the Secretary of the Propaganda, Archbishop Jacobini, told the two bishops that the whole question was to be laid aside until Gibbons' arrival and then "laid on the table indefinitely," that proved too much for the Americans. They demanded and received an audience with Leo XIII the next day. During this interview the Holy Father told them he had not yet made up his mind about the university. He asked the two bishops to remain in Rome until Gibbons arrived. Until then the matter lay dormant.

That same autumn Cardinal Gibbons received a letter that began a chain of events that would involve him deeply in the conflict among nationalities. In this letter, Father Peter M. Abbelen of Milwaukee stoutly defended the right of the Germans to enjoy full parochial rights and just as strongly condemned the undue haste with which some people were trying to Americanize the Germans. He correctly pointed out that the Germans — unlike the Irish — were surrounded by fellow countrymen who were often infidels and members of secret societies who did everything in their power to lure the Catholic Germans away from the Church. If these non-Catholic Germans could taunt their Catholic countrymen with being only second-rate Catholics, the Church would suffer serious consequences. The Milwaukee priest admitted that in the course of time Americanization would come through a gradual amalgamation. But he did not appreciate the danger that other American Catholics saw, that the tenacious holding to the German language might end in his country-men's being considered not second-rate Catholics but second-rate citizens. At any rate, Abbelen was going to Rome to lay the matter before the Holy See. He asked Gibbons to recommend him to Simeoni as "a trustworthy person and sufficiently Americanized not to be a one-sided partisan in this question." The cardinal gave him the letter.

Before long, Cardinal Gibbons had reason to regret his act. In Rome, Bishops Keane and Ireland soon got wind of the Abbelen mission and even secured a copy of the Abbelen document — "a more villainous tissue of misstatements I have seldom read," Keane said. Abbelen's petition, which bore the approval of Archbishop Heiss of Milwaukee, dwelt particularly on the succursal parishes for the Germans in St. Louis and on unfair treatment in Albany and New Orleans. While Abbelen praised Cardinal Gibbons personally for his fairness to the Germans in the Archdiocese of Baltimore, he added that Gibbons' kindness did not prevent "Irish rectors from acting against the letter of the law, and meddling in various ways with the rights of the Germans." The language of the Abbelen peti-tion was, on the whole, judicious, the claims substantially just. Nevertheless, Keane did not hesitate to tell Gibbons of his and Ireland's amazement that "this secret emissary of a clique of German Bishops among us" had come with a letter of recommendation from the cardinal: "No wonder the Propaganda is puzzled."

Unduly excited, Ireland and Keane sent cables to a number of American prelates urging them to write to Rome in protest. The cables at once alerted the American bishops, and Cardinal Gibbons began to receive urgent pleas for action. Corrigan advised him to call a meeting of the Archbishops of Boston and Philadelphia, him-self, and Gibbons right away so that they could draft a letter in time to reach Rome before the next meeting of the Congregation of the Propaganda.

Meeting in Philadelphia, the four archbishops denied any unfair treatment of any national group in the American Church. They acknowledged some trouble in the succursal parishes for the Ger-mans in the Archdiocese of St. Louis, but they emphasized to Simeoni that there had been ample opportunity in the Third Plenary Council for discussion of this question when a special committee for "new material" was appointed with Archbishop Heiss himself a member; yet the German bishops had remained silent. Therefore, the archbishops asked, in what way had they offended? The eastern metropolitans recognized, too, the folly of trying to uproot customs in a sudden and violent manner, and for that reason they had made provision for non-English-speaking Catholics in their respective sees. Their efforts had not led to the results that Abbelen envisioned. In Gibbons' jurisdiction, St. Joseph's Church of Washington had been tried as a mixed congregation for Germans and non-Germans; but when sermons were delivered in German, the second-generation Germans got up and left, although they remained for the English sermons. The Prefect of the Propaganda was warned that any precipitous action by the Holy See on the Abbelen petition would endanger the welfare of Catholicism in the United States.

The day following the meeting in Philadelphia the Cardinal of Baltimore gave an account of the conference to Archbishop Elder:

> If they [the Germans] get what they ask, other nationalities will claim similar privileges [sic], & we will have a war of races, the charges of our enemies that we are a religion of foreigners will be vindicated.

Gibbons also explained to Rome that he had written the letter for Abbelen under the impression that the priest was going to Rome to resolve some local conflict between German- and English-speaking missions. "My letter simply recommended him as a priest who had rendered us good and faithful services at the Plenary Council," Gibbons said, "I did not make any allusion to any other subject."

Despite Gibbons' show of vigor once he understood the grave issues involved, Bishop Keane was plainly alarmed for Gibbons' reputation. Other issues were also calling for the utmost care lest a blunder be made. The naturally cautious temperament of Gibbons, combined with his desire to give satisfaction to the many conflicting elements that sought his support, convinced Keane that Gibbons' seeming vacillation was endangering his reputation in Rome. With this thought in mind, he wrote the cardinal a letter in every sense admirable for its candor and genuine bravery. He begged the cardinal to pardon him if he now mentioned painful truths that only his high regard for Gibbons personally and for Gibbons' exalted office could induce him to write. Keane then proceeded:

I find, to my intense regret, that an impression has taken shape
in Rome to the effect that your Eminence is changeable in views,
weak and vacillating in purpose, anxious to conciliate both parties on
nearly every question; that it is hard to know, therefore, upon which
side you stand concerning any important question, or what weight
to attach to your utterances. Hence I find a growing inclination to
look elsewhere than to your Eminence for reliable information &
judgments, — a tendency, not only here but among the Bishops of
the United States, to look to New York rather than to Baltimore for
the representative & leader of our Hierarchy.

As Keane explained, the accusations against Gibbons' integrity were
not always made in so many words, but in "shrugs, and smiles, and
insinuations." Even Leo XIII had intimated he had a kind of apprehension about the cardinal. Bishop Keane acknowledged Gibbons'
kindness of heart, his anxiety to be gracious and yielding. Yet Keane
reminded the cardinal that lack of determination would lead to a
widespread mistrust of his strength of character and capacity for
leadership. Keane closed his remarkable letter with these words:

Let me hope that you will not be offended, that you will appreciate
the affectionate devotedness which, next to my desire for the Church's
best welfare, has been my only motive in thus writing; and let me
hope that henceforth your Eminence will more than regain the lost
ground, by showing such singleness, such consistency, such firmness,
such nobleness, in every word and act, as to fully realize the grand
ideal of your position in the forefront of the foremost Hierarchy of
the world.

A letter such as this could have been written only by a man
possessed of the forthright, transparent honesty of John Keane; it
could have been received with profit and equanimity only by a man
whose lofty position had not robbed him of the spirit of humility that
permitted him to view these criticisms in their true light. The friendship between the two prelates was in no way impaired by Keane's
candor, and it may have had a salutary effect, indeed, upon the
cardinal's stamina.

By the late summer of 1886, the failure of the American archbishops to take definite action for or against some of the secret
societies prompted certain parties to lodge pleas for action with the
Holy See. Monsignor O'Connell informed the Cardinal of Baltimore
that Bishop Chatard of Vincennes was again trying to get a condemnation of the Ancient Order of Hibernians and — an even more

disquieting fear — perhaps a condemnation of the Knights of Labor as well.

An all-inclusive labor union founded in 1869, the Knights of Labor had used secrecy as protection against blacklists and ritual as bait for prospective members. After Terence V. Powderly, a Catholic, became head of the order in 1879, he succeeded in diminishing the secrecy and in chipping away at the ritual. But even these reforms did not altogether quiet criticism from some of the clergy, for the order retained secrecy regarding the private work of the various assemblies and prohibited members from revealing the name of any fellow member without his permission. In the meantime, of course, the hostility of the managers of industry did not abate, and this opposition, coupled with the criticism of churchmen, prompted Powderly to tell one correspondent: "Between the men who *love* God and the men who don't believe in God I have had a hard time of it." Regardless of the difficulties, the organization continued to grow. The depression of the years 1883–1885 swelled the ranks of the Knights, and by September, 1884, the membership rolls showed a total of 71,326.

Just three weeks before the Third Plenary Council, the Holy Office, in response to an inquiry from Archbishop Elzear A. Taschereau of Quebec, sent out a directive that the Knights were a society that "ought to be considered among those prohibited by the Holy See." The adverse action against them in Canada soon became known among the bishops in the United States of course, and before long the more conservative prelates were pointing to it as a precedent that the American hierarchy should follow. At the Third Plenary Council, on the other hand, the decrees on the prohibited societies repeated word for word the exception made in favor of *bona fide* labor unions in the legislation of the council of 1866.

In the midst of the discussion aroused by the decree of the Holy Office for Canada, it became known that Gibbons had examined the ritual and the constitution of the Knights and had raised no objection. The sudden and almost startling growth of the K. of L. in Gibbons' see city, an increase of over 11,000 members for the year 1886, brought the Knights in Baltimore to a total of 13,052 in 111 local assemblies.

That spring when the disastrous strike of the K. of L. on the

Southwest Railway System of Jay Gould was in progress, the *Catholic Review* of New York for April 3 reported that the Archbishop of Baltimore directed his secretary to assure the laborers that Gibbons gave "cordial approval" to every movement consistent with fair dealing toward employers that had for its end the amelioration of the conditions of the laboring class.

While these cautious but sympathetic indications of Gibbons' attitude were appreciated by the Knights, and by the same token probably reprobated by conservative ecclesiastics, they did little to clarify the status of the American branch of the order. Gibbons attempted to clarify his own position in a letter to Archbishop Elder:

> With regard to the Knights of Labor it is not easy to determine what action if any should be taken. A masterly inactivity & a vigilant eye on their proceedings is perhaps the best thing to be done in the present junction. If the Holy See has disapproved of the society in Quebec, as has been represented — the decision was *juxta exposita*. My impression is that the metropolitans of the United States will be almost, if not unanimous in not condemning them. The society cannot be held responsible for the acts of individual members. There are however some features of this organization that ought to receive an official rebuke:
> 1. Their persecution of non-unionmen, forbidding employers to employ them &
> 2. The custom of boycotting. . . .
> It has occurred to me to propose to the Abps. that a formula of paternal exhortation (calling attention also to the irregularities which I have referred to) be drawn up, that the draft be submitted to each of the Abps., published in the name of all the metropolitans after they have approved of it.
> But we should be careful not to be too hard on them, otherwise they would suspect us of siding with the moneyed corporations & employers.

Later in the year Gibbons moved forward a step on his own. He was aided by a communication from the pastor at Carbondale, Pennsylvania, which included not only a copy of the constitution of the Knights but a letter from Powderly that breathed, as Gibbons told Elder, "a truly Catholic spirit of obedience and respect for the voice of the Church, and a willingness to amend the constitution if anything faulty is found out." With these documents in his possession, and with an outline made up for him by Aloysius Sabetti, S.J., of Woodstock College, the cardinal sent O'Connell a letter for Simeoni in which he set forth his reasons against a hasty condemnation of the K. of L. The cardinal explained that the purpose of the Knights in the United States was in no way evil, that their sole aim was to strengthen themselves by united effort within the law so that they could better protect their members against what he termed "the tyranny with which many very rich corporations, and especially those controlling the railroads, inhumanly oppress the poor workers." He pleaded against a condemnation that would expose the Catholic Church of the United States to serious losses, and he was at pains to explain that the secrecy of the K. of L. was in no sense intended to hide its aims from legitimate authority. Furthermore, the Knights had made frequent offers to institute whatever changes the Church might recommend. Near the end of his letter Gibbons emphasized that a condemnation would prove a detriment to religious growth. Since the government did nothing to protect the workers, the latter — in good part Catholics — looked to the Church for sympathy and counsel. If instead of sympathy they encountered penalties and condemnation, they would naturally give a willing ear to agitators who babbled about the Church's favoring the strong and leaving the weak to their fate. Referring to the K. of L., Gibbons stated that as far as he knew all the American archbishops were "entirely of the opinion that it should not be condemned." This opinion was advanced without evidence, and on this point the cardinal was wrong.

The Knights, from their side, were alert to win ecclesiastical approval. When the order held its annual convention in Richmond, Bishop Keane, just prior to his departure for Rome, arranged for Powderly to confer with Gibbons in Baltimore at the end of that month.

The morning of October 28 found nine of the twelve archbishops of the United States gathered at the cardinal's residence. The cardinal opened the meeting by noting that there were about a half million Catholic members of the Knights of Labor and that Powderly had declared against the boycott and the refusal to allow nonunion men to work. He most likely had these facts freshly in his mind from the conference he held that morning with the grand master workman.

After the metropolitans had been given ample opportunity to air their opinions, Gibbons restated his benevolent attitude toward the organization. The rough draft of the minutes revealed his position:

Labor has rights as well as capital. We should not condemn labor and let capital go free — would regard condemnation of K. of L. as disastrous to the Church — We should send documents to Rome and if objectionable features are eliminated K. of L. should be tolerated, should not be condemned — We have controlling influence over them; if they are condemned, a secret organization will follow in their wake and over that we will have no control.

On the final vote all but two of the archbishops — Kenrick of St. Louis and John B. Salpointe of Santa Fe — gave their judgment against condemnation, but since the vote lacked unanimity, the canonical procedure laid down by the Third Plenary Council demanded that the case be referred to Rome for ultimate decision.

The second major social question in which Cardinal Gibbons was destined to play a prominent, if somewhat reluctant, role was the controversy that centered on the economic theories of Henry George and the advocacy of those theories by Dr. Edward McGlynn.

In 1879 there had appeared from the pen of the self-made economist and reformer, Henry George, a volume entitled *Progress and Poverty.* George contended that men were entitled to their fair share of land in the same manner that they were to water and air. In order to eliminate the inequalities of landholding, George proposed a land tax adjusted in such a way that the gain, or what was termed the "unearned increment," accruing by reason of advantageous location in a growing community, would be taken away. To the young reformer economic rent was a form of robbery. George would, therefore, siphon off this economic rent in taxation and then abolish all other taxes. Land would not have to be distributed, he said; only its economic rent would be taken away. In the end the single tax would, in his judgment, yield so much revenue to government that it could take over the railroads and telegraphs and inaugurate a vast program of social services. The book enjoyed a tremendous vogue, and the energetic crusade of its author in the United States, the British Isles, and elsewhere served to spread its message to an immense audience.

Although many American Catholics doubtless read *Progress and Poverty,* the author and his economic doctrines would never have become a problem to the Church had it not been for George's stanch ally Edward McGlynn, pastor of St. Stephen's Church in New York City, then one of the most populous parishes in the entire country. Daily brought face to face with the problems of unemployment, McGlynn studied economic problems and ultimately accepted the single-tax doctrines of Henry George. The occasion that brought on a crisis was the bid made by Henry George in the autumn of 1886 for the office of mayor of New York. When Archbishop Corrigan learned that McGlynn intended to address a rally of the Labor Party, which supported George, the archbishop forbade him to do so. The priest refused to obey, and as a consequence he was suspended from his priestly functions for a period of two weeks. Several weeks after the election Archbishop Corrigan, in pursuance of what he regarded as his duty to guide the faithful of his jurisdiction, issued a pastoral letter especially defending the right of private property. Although it did not mention any names, the archbishop's pastoral was obviously directed against the teaching of Henry George.

Though aware of the trouble in New York, Cardinal Gibbons took no cognizance of the matter, since it was entirely outside his jurisdiction. When the pastoral letter of the Archbishop of New York appeared, the cardinal told Corrigan that he felt that the remarks on land and private property were well timed and would go far to counteract the evil effects of loose utterances on the subject.

Meanwhile matters were going from bad to worse in New York. When McGlynn refused to cease his public addresses on the single tax, he was suspended a second time, and on December 6 there came a summons to Rome, a command that he likewise refused to obey. McGlynn maintained that nothing in George's teaching or his own was contrary to the Church's doctrines. Until his suspension was lifted he would not comply with the orders of his archbishop or of the Holy See; in obeying, he would be tacitly admitting the correctness of his superiors' action in penalizing him for views that he insisted were not erroneous. After discussing the matter with his consultors, Archbishop Corrigan on January 14, 1887, removed McGlynn from the pastorate of St. Stephen's Church.

At just this point, a cablegram from Cardinal Jacobini arrived, informing Gibbons that the consistory would be held at the end of February or in early March and that the Pope desired him to come to Rome.

A week before leaving Baltimore the cardinal received a letter from Secretary of State Thomas F. Bayard that enclosed a circular to the diplomatic and consular offices of the United States in Europe requesting "official aid and courtesies" for Gibbons. The cardinal decided to pay a farewell visit to President Cleveland, and, since the day fixed for the appointment coincided with a reception that Mrs. Cleveland was giving, the president suggested that possibly the cardinal might wish to attend and to meet the first lady.

Up to this time Cardinal Gibbons had taken no part in the controversy over Henry George and Edward McGlynn. About a week before his departure, he told Corrigan: "I hope that God will give Your Grace strength to pass through the present trying ordeal." A week later Gibbons was in New York where he received a visit from Father Richard L. Burtsell, close friend and legal adviser of McGlynn. According to Burtsell's own account of the interview, the cardinal advised Burtsell to urge McGlynn to go to Rome and to explain his views to the ecclesiastical authorities. The cardinal was quoted as saying that he would see to it that if McGlynn consented to answer the summons of the Holy See as soon as he was again in good health, he would not go on trial except to unfold a principle.

With all preparations finally attended to, Cardinal Gibbons set out from New York on Saturday, January 29. He sailed on the *Bourgogne,* where he had as a fellow passenger Cardinal Taschereau of Quebec, who was also to receive a red hat in the consistory. On his way to Rome Cardinal Gibbons stopped in Paris, Genoa, and Pisa and finally arrived in the Eternal City on February 13. There he found a warm welcome awaiting him at the American College from his trusted friend, Denis O'Connell, then in his second year of his rectorship, and from Bishop Ireland and Bishop Keane.

Having arrived a month before the secret consistory scheduled for March 17, Gibbons immediately plunged into a busy round of audiences and conferences. Three days after his arrival he had his first private audience with Leo XIII in which the Pope immediately expressed his anxiety about the McGlynn matter. Leo XIII instructed Gibbons to write to McGlynn and urge him to obey the summons. All this the Archbishop of Baltimore explained later to Corrigan, and he added:

In obedience to the H. Father's command, I will send a brief letter today detailing without note or comment the H. Father's conversation. As I do not know Dr. McGlynn's address, I will send the letter to the care of Dr. Burtsell.

Whatever may be the upshot of his visit, I am sure you need have no fears of his being sent back to St. Stephen's. I told Canon Sparetti [*sic*] that this was out of the question, & said the same to the Cardinal [Simeoni], & if it were necessary I would say the same to the H. Father himself. His return to St. Stephen's would simply destroy your moral influence, & destroy Episcopal authority. Before I leave Rome, I will see to it that there is no fear on this score. But I have no apprehensions at all in the matter.

True to his word, Gibbons sent the letter to Burtsell. He refrained from adding any comment to the summary of his conversation with Leo XIII except to say in conclusion, "I may add that the Holy Father's and the Cardinal's words were expressed with paternal kindness."

At home, meanwhile, the affairs of Archbishop Corrigan and Father McGlynn were growing progressively worse, creating a grave scandal and a serious threat to ecclesiastical discipline. Not only did the laity take sides, but the clergy themselves were divided with the great majority supporting the archbishop but a strong and articulate minority favoring McGlynn. McGlynn's own public statements became more and more intemperate.

Burtsell explained many of the recent details of the controversy for Gibbons in a letter that dealt harshly with Archbishop Corrigan for what the writer stated was unfairness in his dealings with his unruly subject. The cardinal was probably a bit disconcerted in learning that his letter of February 18 to Burtsell was regarded by the canon lawyer as gratifying proof of what he termed "your earnest sympathy with Rev. Dr. McGlynn in his troubles." Three days after writing this letter, Burtsell cabled the cardinal asking what prospect there was of McGlynn's reinstatement, saying he would proceed to Rome if reinstated and remarking: "State of affairs here intolerable." The following day Gibbons cabled in reply: "No prejudgment possible but immediate compliance with Holy See's call necessary." The Archbishop of Baltimore had no intention of lending encouragement beyond what the instructions of the Holy See warranted. Later on, revealing his sympathetic feeling for the Archbishop of New York, the cardinal told Corrigan: "The strain on you would try a younger man."

While this issue hung on, Gibbons moved on promptly to the

threatened condemnation of the Knights of Labor. Several days in advance of Gibbons' coming, Keane had sought the support of Cardinal Manning in order that the English prelate might help the Americans prevent a hasty decision. Knowing that Cardinal Taschereau would exert all his influence to prevent a rescinding of the decree against the Knights, Gibbons availed himself of all the help his colleagues could lend in the supreme effort that was before him. He called upon all the key officials in the Congregations of the Holy Office and the Propaganda, and in what an earlier biographer described as a "heated interview" with Archbishop Vincenzo Sallua, O.P., commissary of the Holy Office, he went so far as to say he would hold Sallua responsible for the loss of souls in the United States if the Knights were condemned. He determined to fortify his position with an elaborate statement for Cardinal Simeoni, the Prefect of the Propaganda, and for this he turned to Keane and Ireland for assistance. Keane and Ireland made a major contribution to the memorial. Nonetheless, the only signature it bore was that of James Gibbons, and, more important, the responsibility before the Roman Curia for the arguments it advanced was his alone.

The memorial, dated February 20, 1887, proceeded in orderly fashion to outline the case against condemnation. First Gibbons insisted that the American Knights could not be classed as a society condemned by the Church since they were free of any oath, extreme secrecy, or blind obedience. As evidence that they were not hostile to the Church the cardinal cited Powderly's pledge of devotion. Nor was the order of the type that intrigued against the State, since President Cleveland had told Gibbons of a long conference he had had with Powderly. As for the laborers organizing themselves, this was only "natural and just," and if Catholic workingmen avoided, as Powderly had stated, the protection afforded by Masonry because it was banned by the Church, were they now to find themselves hindered from what the cardinal called "their only means of defense" by a condemnation of their organization?

To the charge that Catholics would suffer by contact with Protestants in organizations like the K. of L., the Archbishop of Baltimore replied that to suppose that the faith of the Catholic laborers was endangered by this contact was to reveal ignorance of the Catholic workingmen of the United States. Admitting that Catholics were thrown in with radical elements at their work, Gibbons maintained that this was merely another test of their faith, and he stated that Powderly and the press were agreed that they had stood up well under this trial to their religious beliefs. Gibbons then spoke with pride of the happy relationship in the United States between the Church and its faithful; the only serious danger he would fear would be a cooling of this affection, which, he added "nothing would more certainly occasion than imprudent condemnations."

He quoted Cardinal Manning to the effect that the Church had no longer to deal with parliaments and princes but rather with the masses, and from this he educed a warning: "To lose the heart of the people would be a misfortune for which the friendship of the few rich and powerful would be no compensation." There would follow from a condemnation of the Knights, in the judgment of Gibbons, a threat to the Church's right in popular estimation to be called a friend of the people, a danger of incurring the hostility of the political power in the United States and of having the Church regarded as un-American. Gibbons added the danger that the American Catholic laboring class might not obey a condemnation, for "it is necessary to recognize that, in our age and in our country, obedience cannot be blind." If this were to happen, the revenues of the Church, emanating entirely from the free-will offerings of the people in the United States, would suffer; so would Peter's Pence. Furthermore, many keen observers predicted that the Knights would not endure long and if the Church now condemned them it would embitter the faithful without accomplishing any lasting good. Alluding to the suspension of McGlynn by Archbishop Corrigan, the cardinal instanced the "sad and threatening confusion" that had arisen over the case of a single priest who was regarded as a friend of the laboring people.

Cardinal Gibbons made it plain that he was speaking solely for the Church of the United States. Insofar as the United States was concerned, out of seventy-five archbishops and bishops only about five desired the condemnation of the Knights. To this reminder, Gibbons added a pointed counsel:

> And, to speak with the most profound respect, but also with the frankness which duty requires of me, it seems to me that prudence suggests, and that even the dignity of the Church demands that we should not offer to America an ecclesiastical protection for which she does not ask and of which she believes she has no need.

In every respect the Gibbons memorial on the Knights of Labor was a remarkable document. Not only did it display a deep sympathy with the just claims of the workingman to organize and of Catholics to join such organizations, but it showed as well that the cardinal understood thoroughly the temper of the age. His shrewd observations about the strength of the masses — even if he did exaggerate the power that the laboring class then wielded at the polls — his keen insight into the psychology of the American people in their dislike for orders given by simple fiat, his correct judgment that the Knights had already shown signs of a short life, and his skillful link between these observations and the future welfare of the Catholic Church in the American Republic stamped Gibbons as a man with admirable understanding of his country. No less remarkable was his courage in practically telling the highest officials of the Holy See that he did not wish to see repeated in his country the mistake they had made two and a half years before in condemning the Knights in Canada.

As a result of the memorial and of Gibbons' subsequent conference with the principal officials of the Holy Office, Keane sensed that the cardinal had already produced "an evident change of front." Gibbons, too, was breathing a more confident air when he forwarded a copy of the memorial to Bishop Gilmour in Cleveland:

> I feel strongly on this subject. We must prove that we are the friends of the working classes; if we condemn or use them harshly we lose them, and they will look on us with as much hatred and suspicion as they do in the Church of France. They commit excesses now and then. Let us correct them, but they have also real grievances. Let us help them to redress them. I would regard the condemnation of the Knights of Labor, as a signal calamity to the Catholic Church of America.

Gibbons' confidential memorial to Simeoni soon leaked to the press, probably because the New York *Herald's* man in Rome bribed some secretary in the Vatican. Once published in the United States, the memorial drew generally favorable reactions, though the *Nation* referred to the cardinal as "partaking freely of the labor beverage" and sarcastically lamented the loss sustained by politics when he entered the Church.

While preparing the memorial on the Knights, Gibbons learned of a disposition in some circles of the curia to put the writings of

George on the *Index of Prohibited Books*. The cardinal was decidedly opposed to such a move as neither opportune nor useful. With that in mind he prepared a memorial on this question, too. Gibbons contended that ideas similar to George's had been expressed by Spencer and Mill. The world would judge it rather singular if the Holy See were to attack the work of "a humble American artisan" instead of condemning the writings of his masters; and if the Holy See thought it had a duty to condemn Spencer and Mill, it would seem prudent to consult first with Cardinals Manning and Newman. The cardinal also pointed out that George's theories differed from those of communism and socialism; in proof of his point he quoted the definition of communism given by Valentino Steccanella in a work published by the Propaganda press five years before. Only in the matter of land, explained the cardinal, did George set a limitation on ownership by an extension of the *supremum dominium* of the State, and in this case he did not teach that the actual proprietors should be dispossessed but that the system of taxation should be changed so that taxes should come from the land only and not from the fruits of industry.

The relation of the State to the right of land ownership and to the taxation of land would not admit of solution by a trenchant sentence from ecclesiastical authority, Gibbons warned. Moreover, the question was already before the American public in the political arena and there it would speedily find its end. Gibbons alluded, without mentioning names, to the recent excitement in New York. He told Simeoni that even if there was a certain need for a condemnation of the works of Henry George, this was not the time to do it. Finally Gibbons held it as certain that a condemnation of George's work would excite the curiosity of readers so that thousands of additional copies would be sold. Prudence suggested that absurdities be allowed to perish of themselves and that the tribunals of the Church not run the risk of giving them an artificial life.

In both these memorials, Gibbons used similar devices. In both he revealed his distaste for measures of a harsh and negative character, in both he correctly guessed that the phenomena were of a transitory nature. Likewise evident in both documents was the keen awareness of the American mind that served to give the Roman officials pause and to afford them a sorely needed enlightenment in American affairs.

When Gibbons consulted Ireland and Keane about the progress of the university and heard from Simeoni about Corrigan's secret opposition, he became so discouraged that he proposed to Keane that they abandon the enterprise and let the responsibility for its failure fall where it belonged. Keane, wearied by the trying ordeal, readily consented. But then Ireland, who had been out of Rome for a few days, returned. Thoroughly aroused, the Bishop of St. Paul protested that he would be no party to what he termed "so cowardly a surrender to so unworthy an opposition." Ireland's energy galvanized Gibbons and Keane into the preparation of a lengthy document designed to meet all the objections that had been raised by Corrigan.

In this letter to Leo XIII the cardinal reviewed the story of the university from the time of the Third Plenary Council: the support it had won in that body, the favorable reaction of the laity, and the work that had thus far been done by the university committee. He proposed that the time had now arrived for formal approbation by the Holy See. In granting approval the Pope would be giving cause for joy to the American Catholics who regarded the projected university as in harmony with the various instructions on Christian education that the Holy Father had more than once given to the world.

On Easter Sunday Leo XIII signed the papal brief giving his hearty approval to a Catholic university for the United States.

Once within reach of the Curia, the Cardinal of Baltimore also exerted every effort to prevent the appointment of a nuncio to the United States. As an alternative Gibbons submitted to Leo XIII a formal request for the recognition of Dr. O'Connell as the representative of the American hierarchy. He was convinced, said Gibbons, that of all the churchmen in the United States no one knew both the civil and ecclesiastical conditions of this country more intimately than Denis O'Connell. He asked the Pope, therefore, to accord the rank of counselor to the Propaganda to O'Connell. Despite this plea, no official action was taken by the Pope, although the Roman rector continued to serve the American hierarchy without official status.

In their anxiety over this question, a number of American bishops urged Gibbons to consent to fill the office himself. Bishop James O'Connor of Omaha suggested that the Archbishop of Baltimore might secure a coadjutor or an auxiliary bishop for the work of his see; this would enable him to spend five or six months of the year in

Rome. McQuaid, on the other hand, opposed an Italian nuncio or delegate, but he was hopeful that if the Italian delegation must come, it would put a stop to "the growing nonsense about Baltimore, *alias* the Sulpitians [*sic*], being the head of the Catholic Church in the U. S." Gibbons as nuncio or delegate would have been too much, indeed, for the Bishop of Rochester.

In addition to his numerous conferences, Gibbons also found time to fulfill a large number of social engagements. Then on St. Patrick's Day the colorful ceremony of the consistory was held in which the seven new cardinals went through the ceremony of the sealing and opening of the lips, the reception of their red hats, the assignment of their places on the various congregations, and the designation of their titular churches. Gibbons was appointed to places on the Congregations of the Propagation of the Faith, Religious, Indulgences, and Studies. The Pope also assigned to Cardinal Gibbons as his titular church the ancient Basilica of Santa Maria in Trastevere, which dated in its original foundation from the time of Julius I (337–352). On March 25, a week after the consistory, Gibbons took possession of the church in a memorable ceremony which found him surrounded by a large gathering of friends, among them some colleagues in the American hierarchy. For this occasion, Denis O'Connell advised him to go beyond the expression of polite generalities and to deliver a major address that would carry a serious message, not only to his Roman audience but to the United States and to the world at large. The cardinal decided to adopt the suggestion.

The present prosperous condition of the American Church, the cardinal maintained in his sermon, was owed under God and the vigilance of the Holy See "to the civil liberty we enjoy in our enlightened republic." He then continued:

> For myself, as a citizen of the United States, without closing my eyes to our defects as a nation, I proclaim, with a deep sense of pride and gratitude, and in this great capital of Christendom, that I belong to a country where the civil government holds over us the aegis of its protection without interfering in the legitimate exercise of our sublime mission as ministers of the Gospel of Jesus Christ. . . .
>
> But, while we are acknowledged to have a free government, we do not, perhaps, receive due credit for possessing also a strong government. Yes, our nation is strong, and her strength lies, under Providence, in the majesty and supremacy of the law, in the loyalty

of her citizens to that law, and in the affection of our people for their free institutions.

There are, indeed, grave social problems which are engaging the earnest attention of the citizens of the United States. But I have no doubt that, with God's blessings, these problems will be solved without violence, or revolution, or injury to individual right.

For naming Gibbons to the cardinalate, the prelate thanked Leo XIII not only in the name of the hierarchy, clergy, and Catholic laity of the United States:

I presume also to thank him in the name of our separated brethren in America, who, though not sharing our faith, have shown that they are not insensible — indeed, that they are deeply sensible — of the honor conferred upon our common country. . . .

If European Catholics, so accustomed to union of Church and State, were surprised at the forthright approval of the harmonious relationship based on separation, Americans themselves were delighted with Gibbons' pronouncement. Bishop John J. Kain of Wheeling expressed what was in the minds of many when he said that a native American cardinal, "voicing with clarion tones beneath the very shadow of the Vatican the sentiments so dear to all lovers of our free institutions, is the strongest refutation of the grievous charges by which our loyalty has been so long impugned." The New York *Herald* of March 26 carried the text of the sermon, a news article on the ceremony, and an editorial on the address, which, the paper said, would be "read with interest by Catholic and Protestant alike." The New York *Independent,* a Protestant weekly, called the address "one of singular spirit and tact"; it was especially gratified at Gibbons' references to American non-Catholics as "our separated brethren."

Gibbons also received a heartening reaction to his efforts on the German issue. After some weeks he wrote encouragingly to Elder that the American bishops had "gained immensely lately in Rome." Not only were their petitions granted, but the Propaganda officials had conceded that in the future nothing would be decided on vital matters affecting the American Church until the bishops had been heard from. Furthermore, after Gibbons presented his case on the Abbelen petition to his colleagues of the Propaganda, they yielded a few details to the Germans, then rejected the rest of it. When the question of a possible softening of the decision arose, Gibbons let O'Connell know privately that he was opposed to the least sign of backing down or weakening of the decision since he believed this "would only make the Germans more insolent & aggressive."

At last his official business with the Holy See was concluded, and on April 18 he left Rome. From Florence Gibbons advised O'Connell to urge Jacobini, Secretary of the Propaganda, to make another effort to get McGlynn to Rome. If he once more failed to obey, then, said Gibbons, it would be the Holy See's business to determine whether and to what extent he should be punished for contumacy.

The view in newspapers that Gibbons sympathized with McGlynn, indeed that he was McGlynn's defender, caused the cardinal considerable chagrin. Finally the leading Catholic newspaper of New York, the *Freeman's Journal*, carried an unsigned statement under a Roman dateline that expressed astonishment at the "absurd rumors" about Gibbons' sympathy with the priest; it was authoritatively stated that the cardinal was amazed that any Catholic would believe he would countenance disobedience of this kind. Gibbons himself, genuinely apprehensive of the effect that all the garbled press reports might have on Corrigan, wrote to Corrigan from Paris:

> I have been sorely distressed by the continuation of your troubles, and deeply wounded by the insinuations thrown out in the papers that I was championing the cause of Dr. McGlynn. I most solemnly declare that my constant & prayerful desire has been to see an end to the trouble with honor to yourself and with the full maintenance of your Episcopal authority.

He confessed to "one error of judgment" in communicating with McGlynn through Burtsell, and he revealed his embarrassment at the possible misinterpretation of his reference to the McGlynn case in his memorandum on the Knights of Labor. Gibbons' misgivings were not without foundation, for Corrigan's aggrievement at what he regarded as an interference in the business of his archdiocese continued to grow.

From Paris the cardinal traveled to London where he visited with Manning and exchanged notes on the struggle they had just come through at Rome. It gave Gibbons an opportunity to thank the Archbishop of Westminster in person for the splendid support he had given to the cause of the American workers and to talk over in further detail the case of Henry George in which Gibbons was again to appeal for Manning's assistance.

Although Gibbons had originally planned to go immediately to a private home upon his arrival in New York, he cabled Corrigan that he would come directly from the steamer to Corrigan's residence. By this time McGlynn had received a letter from Cardinal Simeoni in which he was told that if he did not appear at Rome within forty days after receipt of the letter he would be excommunicated. Through one channel or another Gibbons was fully aware of the more critical turn that events had taken. Virtually every communication reaching him in these days suggested supreme caution. From Baltimore Father John Foley warned the cardinal to watch his step in New York, where any demonstration in his favor would be made use of by the followers of McGlynn. While in New York, Gibbons received a detailed written explanation from Burtsell, who denied that he had implicated Gibbons in defense of McGlynn. In reply the cardinal very briefly assured the canon lawyer that his explanation was quite satisfactory. But beyond the demands of politeness Gibbons did not go.

After a day or two in New York, the cardinal and his party left for Baltimore on the morning of June 7. At the railroad station there, they were greeted by an immense throng headed by an official committee. Mayor James Hodges and Charles J. Bonaparte, prominent Catholic lawyer, made the speeches of welcome to the cardinal. The Catholic societies of the archdiocese then formed in line and marched to the cathedral where the cardinal expressed his gratitude for the enthusiastic welcome. Speaking of the sentiments that had been expressed to him by various groups, he said: "They will bind me still more strongly, if that is possible, to my fellow-citizens, and to this city of Baltimore, where I was born, where Providence has cast my lot, and where I hope to die."

Finally the forty days of grace expired without McGlynn making any move to comply with the Roman command, and on July 8, 1887, Archbishop Corrigan, following the instructions of the Holy See, issued a statement explaining that the priest had incurred excommunication. The cardinal clearly did not believe that this extreme measure would remedy matters. He forwarded a copy of the New York *Herald* covering the announcement to Denis O'Connell, and he said:

> I hope I am mistaken, but my impression is that it will lead to the loss of many souls, & to a weakening in some places of the reverence due to the Holy See. It was prudent not to require the reading of the excommunication in the churches; for, I dare say, there would have

been a commotion, judging from the temper of the people as exhibited in the journals.

Though Gibbons scrupulously resisted all attempts to draw him into the McGlynn case again, Corrigan remained disgruntled. A few months after Gibbons' homecoming the papers carried a report that Archbishop Williams of Boston would be named a cardinal. Corrigan told his friend, Bishop McQuaid, that Williams was deserving of any honor Rome could give him; he added that the report of a cardinal for Boston made him wonder if it was not intended to save the Roman purple from falling into discredit "by conferring it on one whose head would not be turned by the compliment."

Corrigan's hostility made itself felt in his withdrawal of support from the university. Just after Gibbons' arrival in New York, the Archbishop of New York told his friend in Rochester that he was disposed to resign from the university committee since he had lost confidence in the good faith of some of the members. The charge was not apt. The Archbishop of New York had been present at all the meetings and could, if he chose, have presented his objections to the body. The fact that he remained silent and concealed his own plans for a Jesuit university in New York naturally put the committee at a disadvantage in knowing the archbishop's real mind.

At a committee meeting in September, 1877, the cardinal emphasized that Leo XIII was really enthusiastic about the project and had taken several occasions to speak of it, with the result that his words had been quoted all over Europe. He also reported that a large majority of the bishops who had replied to his inquiry favored Washington as the site. Plans had now advanced far enough so that the next meeting could be scheduled to coincide with the laying of the cornerstone of the university's first building in May, 1888. Another item of business was the formal announcement of the appointment of Bishop Keane as the first rector, and from this time on, the active management of affairs passed almost entirely into his capable hands. Keane kept closely in touch with Gibbons in all matters of importance, and the cardinal gave his active assistance to the rector by writing a letter to the hierarchy begging its support for the bishops who would come into the dioceses to collect.

Later that fall Gibbons received the woeful intelligence that Archbishop Corrigan would not permit the collectors to enter the Archdiocese of New York and that he was resigning from the university committee. It was a major blow. Gibbons was deeply affected by the news, and he asked Corrigan to reconsider. Corrigan replied, reaffirming his resignation. To this Gibbons answered in a restrained manner, dismissing the subject with the words, *"Fiat voluntas Dei."* The following year Corrigan's resignation became known, and the Chicago *Tribune* carried a sharply critical editorial, imputing the archbishop's action to jealousy of Gibbons, Ireland, and Keane. Writing to Gilmour, the cardinal revealed to the Bishop of Cleveland his personal attitude on the university:

> If I were to consult my feelings & personal comfort I would have the project abandoned. It has been to me a source of anxiety and care since the close of the council. If the enterprise succeeds, as I hope it will, it will redound to the glory of God & of our faith in this country.

By midsummer of 1887 the decline in the Knights of Labor had become a source of alarm to its leaders. To bolster the order's falling fortunes, the Knights sought and received an encouraging word from Gibbons to be read before their annual convention scheduled for Minneapolis in early October. In this instance the cardinal referred to his defense of the laboring man's rights when he was in Rome; now that he was at home he wished to speak in a friendly spirit of the workingmen's duties. Gibbons warned of the evil effects of strikes and the danger to the good name of the order that would come from any association with anarchists and nihilists. In all probability the K. of L. would have appreciated a stronger emphasis on their rights, but on this occasion they did not get it.

That fall Henry George was defeated in his effort to become mayor of New York, and his defeat was looked upon by some as a rout of the Knights. With this in mind Bishop McQuaid gleefully asked Archbishop Corrigan:

> How does his Eminence feel now about his pets, the Knights of Labor?
> They are evidently breaking to pieces and are getting many more kicks than kisses. . . . For the countenance his Eminence gave them, he will have to suffer. He exceeded his instruction and must bear his burden.

Far from feeling any burden, His Eminence was just at this time concluding a triumphal tour across the continent.

As the ranking American prelate, Gibbons received numerous invitations to represent the Catholic Church at important public functions. Just after his return from Rome, one invitation caused him some concern. In September, 1887, the United States government was scheduled to celebrate the centennial of the federal Constitution at a three-day affair in Philadelphia. Hampton L. Carson, secretary of the Constitutional Centennial Commission, wrote to Gibbons to request the kind of offices of the cardinal "for one of the services of prayer, to form part of the exercises on the 17th of September." From the outset the cardinal wished to accept the invitation, but the novelty of his position as a member of the College of Cardinals and the sensitiveness of the Holy See about Catholic prelates participating with ministers of other faiths in public exercises having a religious significance made Gibbons uneasy. For that reason he sent off a hurried note to Archbishop Corrigan, asking for his advice. The same day Gibbons wrote to Denis O'Connell telling him to inquire of the Holy See if there would be any objection. After advancing all the arguments in favor of his acceptance, he concluded with a postscript: "My presence on the occasion would, I am sure, give great joy to the Catholics of this country; they wd. rejoice to see our Church represented."

The results of these precautionary moves were, in the main, reassuring. Corrigan believed that the invitation could be accepted and that genuine good would come from Gibbons' presence at the celebration, providing that ministers of other religions did not offer prayers on the same occasion. The Archbishop of New York believed that the exercise of prudent precaution would avert a mistake, and in the end "only good results would follow from your attendance."

It was not so easy for Denis O'Connell to give an answer. The well-known opposition of Rome toward the participation of Catholic churchmen in mixed religious gatherings was born of the teaching that Catholicism was the one true religion; to make it appear that it was only one among a group of equal religious bodies was, in the Catholic position, to run the danger of religious egalitarianism and ultimately of religious indifferentism. Neither Cardinal Simeoni, Prefect of the Propaganda, nor Raffaele Cardinal Monaco, the head of the Holy Office, would approve. Finally, Monaco agreed to ask Leo XIII. The Pope assented.

The celebration in Philadelphia in September, 1887, was the type of ceremony, honoring the finest traditions in American history, that Cardinal Gibbons thoroughly enjoyed. The Catholic Club of Philadelphia gave a reception in his honor on the evening of September 15, an affair brilliant beyond the anticipation of those who had planned it. The distinguished guests who came to honor the cardinal were headed by President Cleveland and Secretary of State Bayard and Secretary of the Treasury Charles S. Fairchild, ex-President Rutherford B. Hayes, several justices of the Supreme Court, a large number of senators and representatives from Congress, and the governors of seventeen states. On September 17, the final day of the celebration, Cardinal Gibbons entered Independence Square, extended his greeting to President and Mrs. Cleveland, and then met the Protestant Episcopal Bishop of New York, Henry C. Potter. The churchmen shook hands, the New York *World* reported, "while fully fifteen thousand people looked on at the unusual sight of the meeting of the two American heads of the Romish and Anglican churches." At the close of the program, the *World* went on:

> Silence came over the assemblage as Cardinal Gibbons raised his hand and opened the words of the closing prayer. He, too, had been cheered until he found it necessary to step to the front and quiet the people with a bow.

Gibbons chose as his prayer a combination of Archbishop Carroll's prayer for civil authorities, the Our Father, and a final general blessing.

Any misgivings about Rome's reactions were quickly dissipated when word reached Gibbons from Monsignor O'Connell and others. O'Connell told the cardinal: "They feel proud in Rome now of your presence at the Philadelphia feast, seeing how imposing it became."

As the date of the golden jubilee of Leo XIII's priesthood approached, Gibbons received a letter from President Cleveland in which he asked if Gibbons "could without impropriety on your part, convey to him my congratulations and felicitations." The president's suggestion prompted the cardinal to visit Cleveland and, in turn, to suggest that he send the Pope a copy of the Constitution as a souvenir of his jubilee. Cleveland was pleased with the idea and requested Gibbons to write for him the inscription to accompany the document.

The news about President Cleveland's letter gave Leo great

pleasure, and he told O'Connell that he could bring along a small delegation so that the president's letter would be presented with some solemnity. The episode was closed when Leo XIII wrote to Cardinal Gibbons and charged him with thanking President Cleveland for his letter and gift. In this letter the Pope paid tribute to the American Constitution when he said:

> In fulfilling this duty We desire that you should assure the President of Our admiration for the Constitution of the United States, not only because it enables industrious and enterprising citizens to attain so high a degree of prosperity, but also because under its protection, your Catholic countrymen have enjoyed a liberty which has so confessedly prompted the astonishing growth of their religion in the past and will, We trust, enable it in the future to be of the highest advantage to the civil order as well.

In the fall of 1887, Gibbons agreed to cross the country to confer the pallium on his old friend, William Gross, the new Archbishop of Oregon City. Gross, delighted, felt that Gibbons' visit would do good for the Church in that region; the Catholics, who were few in number and without social standing, would be heartened by his presence. As he expressed it: "The visit of Your Eminence will give a tone to Catholicity."

When the trip was announced, invitations to receptions in various cities along the route led to plans for four principal stops between Baltimore and Portland. After gala receptions in Chicago and Milwaukee, the editor of the *Catholic Mirror* glowed with pride at the attentions shown to Baltimore's cardinal. In a flamboyant editorial on October 1 he wrote: "Reports from points *en route* indicate that the beloved head of the Church in America has been everywhere received with the strongest tokens of affectionate respect and esteem by all classes of citizens without regard to creed." The reception in St. Paul outdid Chicago and Milwaukee. The resourceful mind of John Ireland had seized upon the occasion to show off the cardinal of the United States to the best advantage and to the largest number of prominent citizens. After the party left St. Paul, it traveled on to Portland where on Sunday, October 9, the ceremony of the conferring of the pallium on Gross was held in the Church of the Immaculate Conception. After a few days in Portland the cardinal went on to San Francisco, where he was the guest of Archbishop Riordan, and then to Los Angeles. By the first week in November Gibbons reached

New Orleans, and at a reception for him in Grunewald Hall he had the pleasure of meeting again old Mr. Raymond in whose grocery store he had worked as a clerk over thirty years before. On the following Sunday Gibbons presided at the high Mass and preached at St. Joseph's Church, the parish wherein he had heard the sermon that had set his feet on the path to the priesthood.

By the middle of November the cardinal returned to Baltimore. This first visit of Gibbons to the West aroused a great deal of enthusiasm among the Catholic people of those regions. For many, this was their first glimpse of a prince of the Church, and their pride in playing host to a member of the College of Cardinals was heightened when they observed the generally friendly manner in which their non-Catholic neighbors greeted the visitor. For Gibbons himself, the outpouring of respect and affection was a bracing experience. The cardinal, quick to sense the value of these demonstrations for the Church, had shown care in each of the cities to pay courteous tribute to the local bishops, to the governors and mayors, as well as to make special calls at the leading Catholic institutions. The effect of his gracious presence was not lost upon his hosts. And the experience helped to fit him for the larger role that he was destined to play as the acknowledged leader of American Catholicism in the years ahead.

Chapter 5

In the Midst of Controversies

Many times during the last twenty years of the nineteenth century the Archbishop of Baltimore longed to concentrate on the affairs of his archdiocese. As it was, one question affecting the welfare of the Church of the United States was hardly settled before another appeared. Not until the opening of the twentieth century did there emerge a period of relative peace.

Before the establishment of an Apostolic Delegation in Washington in 1893, Gibbons was called upon to act as the official agent of Rome in a number of disputes in the American Church. In the spring of 1888, he received a distasteful assignment to act as arbitrator between Bishop Richard Gilmour of Cleveland and the Sisters of Charity, or Grey Nuns, of St. Vincent's Orphan Asylum in Toledo over the title to the asylum's property. Archbishop Ireland reflected something of Gibbons' frame of mind about what lay before him: "I assure you he was more afraid of Richard, than Richard was of James, and he started out from Notre Dame for Toledo in fear and trembling." After reaching Toledo, Gibbons gathered all the facts as presented by both sides, then returned to Baltimore. O'Connell kept him abreast of Rome's various opinions on the case, and he indicated the difficulty with which the situation was viewed by Vatican officials: "If you can succeed there, you will lose nowhere." By the first week in October the cardinal pronounced judgment. On all points except the most important, the question of legal title, the decision favored Gilmour. Gibbons had been instructed several times from Rome that he should be guided by the prescriptions of Leo XIII's constitution, *Romanos pontifices,* on May 8, 1881, which regulated the relations between bishops and religious. "Until our legislation in this subject is radically changed," he told Gilmour, "I see no possibility of obtaining the redress you have so ably contended for."

The Bishop of Cleveland, unhappy over the outcome, believed that the consequences would extend far beyond the limits of the orphan asylum. Yet in spite of his disappointment, he wished the cardinal to know that "the result in no way changed the pleasant and I hope lasting kindness that has grown up between us."

Before the year was out, Cardinal Simeoni sent Gibbons another chore in the Diocese of Cleveland, asking that he investigate a dispute of long standing between Bishop Gilmour and Father Patrick F. Quigley, a pastor in Toledo. The quarrel between Gilmour and Quigley had developed because the priest had disregarded the bishop's admonitions against abusing parishioners from the pulpit and fighting battles in the public press. The cardinal was able to remove at least part of the friction, but the differences had gone too far to enable the cardinal to head off a crisis. On March 19, 1889, the bishop suspended Quigley for a period of three months and removed him from his pastorate. Gilmour later outlined his procedure to Cardinal Simeoni, but he put himself in the wrong by giving no specific reasons for the penalties he had inflicted on the priest, a procedural form required by canon law, and Quigley won a restoration to his status as pastor with a restitution of salary from the date of his suspension. Within a very short time after Quigley's reinstatement, he and Gilmour were at odds again over the bishop's order that the orphans in Quigley's parish be moved to Cleveland. Quigley sent Gibbons a long telegram appealing for his judgment. The cardinal promptly wired back: "Obey." Some days later he told the priest that he did not feel warranted in rendering a decision on this new issue unless instructed to do so by the Holy See. He had seen more than enough of the Cleveland troubles, and he was not going to be drawn in again except on orders from Rome.

The year after Gibbons' appointment as cardinal, the Holy See entered upon a new and acute crisis in its relations with the Italian government. The radical elements that supported the Crispi regime were determined to paralyze the influence of the Church in Italian life. Individual bishops and priests denounced the new penal code, and Pope Leo XIII issued a solemn protest against it. Catholics in several European countries also made public protests, and certain officials of the Vatican let it be known that they would like to see similar manifestations from the Catholics of the United States. After consulting the other archbishops, Gibbons decided against any public demonstrations supporting the Holy See. They agreed instead on a letter to the Pope. Although the Vatican authorities doubtless found it difficult to understand this reluctance to move more decisively, the archbishops were behaving prudently. Anti-Catholic bigotry was at this time steadily on the rise in the United States because of the recently founded American Protective Association. For this reason, Gibbons and his colleagues were more than ordinarily sensitive to anything that might offer further weapons to the Church's critics. Gibbons' careful letter steered a middle course. It deplored the recent antireligious laws and the growing fury with which the enemies of God and His Church persecuted His followers. These men, it was said, were not satisfied with their victory in fraudulently occupying the lands of the Holy Father; now they defiled good morals by their attacks upon the institutes of religion. The letter stated that the Holy Father's suffering was deeply lamented in the United States. The American hierarchy also affirmed that the Pontiff could not properly fulfill his functions unless he were entirely free. On the subject of the temporal power itself, however, Gibbons spoke only in general terms. The letter pleased most of the metropolitans, and Gross told the cardinal that "in this as on so many other occasions Your Eminence has most decidedly succeeded in voicing the opinions of the entire body of the American Episcopate."

One problem, the Knights of Labor, soon ceased to occupy Gibbons' time. During the year since Gibbons had left Rome the officials of the Holy See moved slowly toward a decision. The final judgment, rendered on August 16, 1888, noted that the Knights were to be tolerated, but only on condition that

> whatever in its statutes is improperly expressed or susceptible of wrong interpretation shall be corrected. Especially in the preamble of the constitution for local assemblies words which seem to savor of socialism and communism must be emended in such a way as to make clear that the soil was granted by God to man, or rather the human race, that each one might have the right to acquire some portion of it, by use however of lawful means and without violation of the right of private property.

Gibbons had his own way of handling the attached condition. He told Ireland: "I attach little or no importance to the conditions imposed by the H. Office. . . . Something had to be done to save them from the charge of inconsistency." Gibbons emphasized to

Denis O'Connell that he did not wish the decree to be given any publicity, even among the bishops, until he had taken "the little sting" out of the document with Powderly's pledge of cooperation. The cardinal was in a contented mood: "I now breathe freely, thanks to God, & to your vigilance."

The second meeting between Gibbons and Powderly took place in a cordial atmosphere on September 24, and the following day the cardinal assured his fellow metropolitans that the labor leader had cheerfully promised to make the emendations required by the Holy Office and to comply at all times with the wishes of the Church. Powderly's promise was likewise reported to Simeoni, along with a vindication of Gibbons' prediction that the Knights would decline — of the order's 700,000 members, scarcely 350,000 were left. Gibbons had, indeed, made a deep impression on the Roman officials by his handling of the Knights' case. Speaking to O'Connell, Archbishop Francesco Satolli of the Propaganda praised the alertness and skill of the American bishops. In speaking of Gibbons as the "great statesman he is," he gave him the main credit for saving Rome from "the commission of a great mistake."

When a year later the proposal for an international conference on labor legislation was taken up by Leo XIII and Emperor William II of Germany, the aging Cardinal Manning reminisced:

> We little thought when we were writing about the Knights of Labour in Rome, a few years ago, that every word would be so soon published to the world by an Emperor and a Pope.
> This is surely the New World over-shadowing the old, and the Church walking with its Master among the people of Christendom.
> Were we prophets?

Archbishop Ireland, when he saw Manning's letter, reacted with a typical flourish:

> You were a prophet! The people are the power, and the Church must be with the people. I wish all our own bishops understood this truth!

To have taken the stand Gibbons did on the Knights of Labor in 1887 required courage of the first order. On the subject of the Knights, as on few other things in his life, this ordinarily mild man displayed an unrelenting firmness that withstood every effort, from any quarter, to deflect him from his goal. Near the end of his life

Gibbons was asked to write some of his reminiscenses for the *Dublin Review*. Referring to the Knights he said:

> I can never forget the anxiety and distress of mind of those days. If the Knights of Labor were not condemned by the Church, then the Church ran the risk of combining against herself every element of wealth and power. . . . But if the Church did not protect the working men she would have been false to her whole history; and this the Church can never be.

The danger of another condemnation had already reappeared. In the excitement over McGlynn's disobedience, a judgment on the doctrinal aspects of Henry George's writings had temporarily faded from view. But Rome had not been allowed to forget it, for Archbishop Corrigan had again suggested a condemnation to the Holy See. The cardinal had been quick to respond to the new threat. In March, 1888, he had told O'Connell that, just as he had predicted in his memorial, the book was almost forgotten, that its doctrines boasted few adherents. If the American bishops were consulted, he had said, they would unite in deploring the condemnation of a "dying book." In the ensuing weeks he had busily solicited letters from those in the hierarchy whom he knew to be friendly to his point of view so that he might furnish Denis O'Connell with weapons to be used at the Holy See. "We cannot too often & too strongly impress this thought on the H. See just now," the cardinal had said. He had also begged Cardinal Manning, who was a member of the Congregation of the *Index,* to assist in preventing condemnation.

In July, 1888, just before Rome issued its decree on the Knights of Labor, the Cardinal of Baltimore, at O'Connell's suggestion, sent a detailed account of his position on Henry George to Leo XIII. All the familiar arguments were used again: the fear of reviving George's dying popularity, the danger of criticism from the Church's enemies, and the near unanimity of the American hierarchy in opposition to condemnation of the book. He told the Pope that no light would be shed on social problems merely by putting the book on the *Index* or condemning some propositions extracted from it. In his different encyclicals the Pope had treated questions of the highest importance with a force, clarity, and wisdom that had convinced readers, Gibbons said. A similar instruction on the right of property, given with the authority attaching to his apostolate and to his person, would dissipate the shadows and would have a salutary influence in solving the great questions that disturbed modern society. From Rome O'Connell reported his deep satisfaction. "Your letter on the George question," he said, "is masterly."

The minority of prelates who supported Archbishop Corrigan likewise made their position known to the Holy See, and in the fall of 1888 they enjoyed the advantage of having a very forceful advocate when Bishop McQuaid made a trip to Rome. Rome was now confronted with a flow of documentary evidence and personal exhortation from both sides. As usual the curial officials took their time, but finally on February 6, 1889, the Congregation of the Inquisition ruled that the works of George deserved condemnation. In transmitting this ruling to Gibbons, Simeoni stated that in view of the peculiar circumstances of time and place, and by reason of the vigilance with which Rome credited the American hierarchy in guarding its people against doctrinal errors, the condemnation need not be published. It was forwarded to Gibbons, therefore, under the seal of the Holy Office.

The decision seems to have been a compromise between Gibbons' and Corrigan's positions. Corrigan could rightly feel that the decision vindicated his view that the teaching of Henry George was not reconcilable with Catholic doctrine. But his disappointment in not being able to reveal his triumph was probably reflected in the remark of his friend McQuaid to Denis O'Connell: "What's the use of it, if you can't publish it?" Certainly the Cardinal of Baltimore would have preferred no action, but he doubtless consoled himself that the secrecy of the decree gave him a substantial victory. For that much — and it was a major point in his policy — Gibbons could breathe a sigh of relief.

The Cardinal of Baltimore worried a great deal, nevertheless, about the attitude of Archbishop Corrigan toward him. Regardless of their discretion, the coolness between the two archbishops afforded a subject for comment among both their friends and enemies. Archbishop Ryan suggested direct communication between the two principals. Following this advice, the cardinal, in October, 1890, wrote a detailed explanation of all that had taken place from the time Burtsell first made his unsuccessful appeal to him for friendly intervention, including as well copies of the exchange of correspondence between him and the canon lawyer and his own letter to Simeoni. On the condemnation of George's works, Gibbons frankly told the Archbishop of New York:

> I regarded & still regard that subject as neither local nor personal, but one affecting the general interests of the Church of the U. States. And while having no sympathy for George or his doctrines, I deprecated a public condemnation as calculated in my judgment to do harm to religion.
>
> I sincerely regret that my action in this matter did not accord with your judgment; but I assure you that it was prompted solely by a conscientious sense of duty & the interests of religion.

While the correspondence of the Archbishop of New York with Baltimore continued in a polite but terse form, there was no acknowledgment that the cardinal's explanations had been found satisfactory. Time alone would calm the ruffled feelings.

While the controversy over the Knights of Labor and the condemnation of Henry George still raged, the Catholic University of America moved ahead. Cardinal Gibbons laid the cornerstone May 24, 1888, at a ceremony attended by President Cleveland, several members of his cabinet, and more than thirty bishops. In July Archbishop Corrigan returned to the university committee. In November, Bishop Keane sailed for Europe to hire professors and to win the Holy See's consent to the statutes governing the new institution. The following March, Pope Leo XIII issued his apostolic letter, *Magni nobis gaudii,* in which he placed his final approval on the university. The formal opening was scheduled to coincide with the centennial of the American hierarchy in November, 1889.

The centennial celebration was opened with pontifical Mass in the Cathedral of the Assumption in Baltimore on Sunday, November 10. On the next two days a Catholic Congress was held at the Concordia Opera House during which thirteen papers on a variety of subjects such as the Church's relations to the press, labor, social order, temperance, education, the state, and the independence of the Holy See were heard. On the opening day Gibbons addressed the delegates. The cardinal confessed his early skepticism concerning the congress, but he now saw it as an excellent means for drawing the clergy and laity closer together in a land where they needed to cooperate more than in any other on the face of the earth. He paid a generous tribute to the Catholic laity for its support of the Church in the United States, where churches and schools were built and maintained by free-will offerings, where the salaries of the clergy came not from the government, but from the "warm hands and hearts of the people themselves."

On the day preceding the four-day celebration, the Baltimore *Catholic Mirror* had defended the Pope's complete independence, but then continued:

> The Holy Father, as Vicar of Christ and visible Head of the Church, has no absolute need for extensive territory wherein to wield the power and exercise the rule of an earthly kingdom.

Gibbons did not see the editorial until someone called his attention to it a week after it was published. The editorial may well have represented the opinion of a considerable number of American Catholics, but the cardinal realized at once the painful impression it would create in Vatican circles. He instructed Monsignor O'Connell, who was then in Baltimore, to call on the lay editor to "reprimand him for his indiscretion, not to use a stronger phrase." Gibbons wished it to be known in Rome that O'Connell had charged the editor in Gibbons' name never in the future to publish anything on the temporal power of the Papacy without first submitting it to him.

The ceremonies in Baltimore were concluded on Tuesday evening, November 12, with a gigantic torchlight procession through the streets. It was viewed by thousands of onlookers headed by two cardinals, nearly twenty archbishops, over seventy bishops representing the United States, Canada, England, and Mexico, hundreds of priests and laymen from all over the country, and many more from foreign lands.

On Wednesday, November 13, the hierarchy and their guests moved to Washington for the opening of the university. Once more, as on the day of the cornerstone ceremony, it rained the entire day. In the morning Cardinal Gibbons, as chancellor, dedicated Caldwell Hall. Then followed the solemn pontifical Mass in the chapel celebrated by Archbishop Francesco Satolli, the Pope's representative, with the sermon by Bishop Gilmour. After the Mass a dinner was served to the guests, including President Benjamin Harrison and three members of his cabinet as well as the distinguished prelates headed by Gibbons and Cardinal Taschereau of Quebec. At the end of the day the original band of thirty-seven priest-students entered upon a retreat, and on Monday, November 18, the first classes were held.

This second week of November, 1889, had been exhausting for the Cardinal of Baltimore, but the general enthusiasm attendant upon the festivities repaid all his anxiety and labor. The entire program had delighted Archbishop Ireland. He felt that never before had the Catholic Church stood so well in the United States, and in one of his typically flamboyant passages he attributed it all to Gibbons:

> We have to thank you for all this. You have the ear of the American public as no other man in the Republic. Your words are heeded by all & God be thanked, they are always the words that are needed.

Mariano Cardinal Rampolla, Secretary of State, said that Leo XIII wished to extend the highest praise for the celebration and his full approval for Gibbons' prudent conduct in every endeavor.

Once the university had opened Cardinal Gibbons generally confined himself to acting at the instance of the rector on matters requiring attention between meetings of the board of trustees. He likewise made himself available at all times for counsel to the rector, the trustees, and the professors. Gibbons gave the prestige of his name to the university as chancellor, and he was always faithful in attending the principal functions of the academic year and in presiding at meetings of the trustees. It meant a tremendous amount to Bishop Keane and his successors to have the strong support of a national, even an international, figure.

Just after the celebrations, Gibbons' second book, *Our Christian Heritage,* appeared. In the introduction he made it clear that, far from despising or rejecting the support of Protestants who retained faith in the divine mission of Christ, he "would gladly hold out to them the right hand of fellowship, so long as they unite with us in striking the common foe." He wanted to reach those who, he feared, were increasing in number, persons who through association, absence of Christian training, distorted education, and pernicious reading had become estranged, not only from the teachings of the Gospel, but even from the truths of natural religion that underlay Christianity.

In thirty-five chapters running to over 500 pages the author in his customary simple language, but with the familiar richness of biblical quotations and of reference to works in theology, philosophy, history, and science, discussed such fundamental topics as the existence and attributes of God, the dignity of Christ, the relations of the Church to science, the moral and social conditions in Christian history and in pagan antiquity, and the rights and duties of the laboring classes. The concluding three chapters were devoted to the religious basis of civil society, the religious element in American culture, and the dangers that threatened civilization in the United States.

The work was widely reviewed in both Catholic and Protestant journals, as well as in the secular press, and in the main it was well received. The *Independent*, the leading New York Protestant weekly, liked the work for its defense of Christian principles, but regretted the tone of Gibbons' comments on Luther. It considered the cardinal's tone "high, bold and sound" on temperance, Mormonism, the relations of capital and labor, and the need for social and industrial reform. Though entirely opposed to his position on the school question, the *Independent* was glad to find it discussed in a frank way. The most extended and critical review came, unexpectedly, from the *Lyceum* of Dublin. The reviewer, a Jesuit of the Irish province, approached his task as a professional theologian, and as such he found the book seriously wanting. He particularly censured the omission of the metaphysical proof for the existence of God, which, he said, was almost universally admitted to be the strongest. The review was not entirely negative, however; there were words of commendation for the style, the choice and use of illustrations, and the arguments adapted to the popular intelligence.

As soon as the attention of the General of the Society of Jesus had been called to the review, he sent an apology to the cardinal; he expressed his deep sorrow that a member of his society should have written in such a spirit. In reply, the cardinal said that he was profoundly touched by the evidence of this sensitive regard for his literary reputation. Gibbons confessed that he considered the criticism in some particulars unfair and captious. As for the metaphysical argument for the existence of God, the cardinal thought the average American reader would find it too abstruse to grasp. He assured the Jesuit general that the review had left no painful impression on his mind.

In the spring of 1890, Gibbons was vividly reminded that Rome's decision on the Abbelen petition in 1887 had not ended the German question in the American Church. After Archbishop Michael Heiss of Milwaukee died on March 26, the bishops of the Milwaukee Province drew up a *terna* of three bishops all of German extraction: Frederick X. Katzer of Green Bay, Kilian Flasch of La Crosse, and Henry J. Richter of Grand Rapids. John Ireland got wind of the first choice and immediately urged Gibbons that the American metropolitans delay sending their judgments until he could be heard from. The Archbishop of St. Paul felt that Katzer was "thoroughly unfit to be an archbishop."

Gibbons, also in favor of a thorough discussion of the Milwaukee candidates, requested Simeoni to delay the appointment. When the first annual meeting of the archbishops of the United States convened in Boston on July 23–24, 1890, the name of Katzer was unanimously set aside. For his place as the first on the list they chose John Lancaster Spalding, Bishop of Peoria. Gibbons promptly sent off the choice to Simeoni. Shortly before Christmas, however, Katzer was named Archbishop of Milwaukee. The appointment was a severe disappointment to Gibbons, but characteristically he accepted defeat in good grace. He quickly sent his congratulations to the archbishop-elect, and in the interests of peace in the Church of the United States, he counseled Archbishop Ireland to do the same. The aspect of the whole affair that Ireland found most galling was the slight put upon the archbishops by the Holy See. Denis O'Connell wrote ominously of a few intransigent cardinals in the Propaganda who were determined to teach the American bishops a lesson in docility toward the Holy See. Donato Sbarretti, the *minutante* of the Congregation, did not hesitate to say that German influences in Rome were invoked to win the miter of Milwaukee for the Bishop of Green Bay. Sbarretti was quoted as having told O'Connell concerning the Germans in Rome: "There are some of them in the congregation and you have no voice there at all. We should have Gibbons here." The aptness of this advice became clearer later in the year when, despite the efforts of Gibbons and Elder, Ignatius F. Horstmann of Philadelphia, one of the German party, was named Bishop of Cleveland.

In May 1891, a new storm broke; the fierce excitement that it aroused made all other aspects of the problem appear trivial. Following an international conference of the European St. Raphael's

Society in Lucerne in December, 1890, a memorial to the Holy See recommended the creation of separate parishes for each nationality; the appointment of priests of the respective nationality to these parishes; the provision of priests who understood the language in those areas where there were foreign-born Catholics but not in such numbers as to enable them to form a parish; the erection of separate parish schools for each nationality wherever possible; equal rights and privileges for priests who served the immigrants; Catholic confraternities; mutual aid and protection societies for the immigrants. Finally, said the document, it would be desirable as often as judged feasible for the immigrant groups to have in the hierarchy some bishops of their own race.

When the so-called Lucerne memorial was published in the United States in May, 1891, indignation burst out in American Catholic circles. Ireland inquired of the cardinal if Peter Paul Cahensly, a leading layman at the Lucerne conference, was to be permitted to tell Rome how the Church of this country was to be ruled. He knew that Gibbons' "delicacy of sentiment" might tempt him not to act lest jealous minds complain; yet there were times when delicacy must yield before stern duty. "We are American bishops," said Ireland, "an effort is made to dethrone us, & to foreignize our country in the name of religion."

Gibbons communicated his views privately to Monsignor O'Connell who, in turn, made them known at the Holy See. In reply, Cardinal Rampolla stated that the Pope had instructed him to reassure Gibbons and his colleagues that the Lucerne proposal was not viewed with favor in Rome.

Early in July Archbishop Katzer informed the cardinal that he had set August 20 as the date for conferring the pallium and that he hoped Gibbons' health would permit him to fulfill his promise to do Katzer that honor. Gibbons had not been well of late, so about this time he decided to take a holiday at Cape May, New Jersey, to regain his health. On July 11 while taking a walk with Abbé Magnien, the cardinal happened to meet President Harrison, who invited him into his cottage for a visit. The president brought up the subject of the Cahensly memorial and expressed his pleasure that Gibbons deplored the movement. Gibbons had the satisfaction of being able to tell the president that on that very morning he had received the Rampolla letter in which the Holy Father had rejected the Cahensly proposal. Some weeks later Gibbons sent Rampolla a complete report on this interview.

Less than a month after this report, at the ceremony conferring the pallium on Frederick X. Katzer in St. John's Cathedral in Milwaukee, the cardinal delivered a major pronouncement. Gibbons cited the large number of nationalities represented in the Catholic body of the United States, united, as he said, by the precious bond of Christian brotherhood. Then he came to the heart of the warning he had determined to utter:

> Woe to him, my brethren, who would destroy or impair this blessed harmony that reigns among us! Woe to him who would sow tares of discord in the fair fields of the Church in America! Woe to him who would breed dissension among the leaders of Israel by introducing a spirit of nationalism into the camps of the Lord! Brothers we are, whatever may be our nationality, and brothers we shall remain. We will prove to our countrymen that the ties formed by grace and faith are stronger than flesh and blood. God and our country! — this our watchword. Loyalty to God's Church and to our country! — this our religious and political faith.

Gibbons developed the double loyalty that should motivate American Catholics, love of God and of country, and he exhorted his audience to glory in the title of American citizen. Directing his remarks to the Catholic foreign-born, the cardinal stated that when they decided to cross the Atlantic to seek a new home in this country they should be animated by the spirit of Ruth in the Old Testament when she determined to join her husband's kindred in the land of Israel. Gibbons would have the Catholic immigrant say in the words of Ruth:

> Withersoever thou shalt go, I will go: and where thou shalt dwell, I also will dwell. Thy people shall be my people, and thy God my God. The land that shall receive thee dying, in the same will I die: and there will I be buried.

Reactions to the sermon were both widespread and favorable. The Chicago *Tribune* pronounced it "patriotic in every sense," and said if it had not been delivered before the altar it would undoubtedly have been frequently applauded. Over twenty years later Gibbons himself said the Milwaukee sermon was one of the most audacious things he ever did; "When I finished they were aghast, but I think the lesson had its effect."

The animus aroused over this question pervaded the atmosphere of American Catholicism through the closing years of the century. The strife occasioned in the early years of the Catholic University of America, the "school controversy" in Minnesota, and the struggle over the alleged heresy of Americanism would have been robbed of much bitterness had not the atmosphere been poisoned by the unfortunate differences between German- and English-speaking Catholics.

The "school controversy" gave the American Church some of the most acrimonious moments in its history, exciting its most tempestuous spirits over an issue of central importance, the parochial schools. The Church was intent upon the spread of its parochial schools as a major safeguard for the religious faith of its children. At the same time the growing spirit of secularism in American society lessened its emphasis upon religious instruction and aroused resentment against any effort to offer religious training in the public schools or to give financial aid to private religious schools. When agitation over the issue of public versus parochial schools slackened, sensible compromises worked to the advantage of both sides. In Poughkeepsie, New York, and in some communities of New Jersey, Connecticut, and Pennsylvania in the 1870's, instruction in the Catholic religion had been given after the regular school hours. In the 1880's, controversy had developed. The authorities of the Church in Rome, concerned for the faith of thousands of immigrant children, yet wishing to hold aloof from an American political question such as public funds for parochial schools, had urged the construction of more parish schools as the only remedy and the Third Plenary Council had made it almost mandatory for pastors to erect parochial schools.

With the question very much in the public eye, the National Education Association invited Cardinal Gibbons and Bishop Keane to address its annual convention at Nashville in July, 1889. The cardinal's brief paper, which was read by Keane, explained why he regarded education as incomplete without religious instruction. Gibbons based his argument on man's spiritual nature and eternal destiny, and near the close of his remarks he cited the example of Canada as a way in which the public and parochial school systems could work in harmony.

The following year Archbishop John Ireland spoke to the same

N.E.A. in his see city of St. Paul. The address was entitled "State Schools and Parish Schools." At the very outset the speaker proclaimed in eloquent phrases his advocacy of the public schools, although, as he said, in the circumstances of the time he also upheld the parochial school. He wished there was no need for the latter; if he had his way, all American schools would be state schools. Nonetheless, the speaker saw no solution to the difficulty of the many varieties of the Christian religion in the teaching of a common Christianity in the schools, for "In loyalty to their principles, Catholics cannot and will not accept a common Christianity." This situation, therefore, called for a compromise in which the state could play a part. In Ireland's judgment the right of the state school to exist was beyond discussion. He maintained, however, that the primary right to educate belonged to the parents, and if they performed their obligation by seeing that their children received in parochial schools an education that would properly fit them for citizenship, then they should be free of all interference. Ireland went on to point out the chief objection of Catholics to public schools, namely, their failure to teach religion, and to state his belief in the necessity of religious instruction for the complete education of the child. In an effort to offer a compromise he made the following proposal:

> I would permeate the regular state school with the religion of the majority of the children of the land, be this religion as Protestant as Protestantism can be, and I would, as is done in England, pay for the secular instruction given in denominational schools according to results; that is, every pupil passing the examination before state officials, and in full accordance with the state program, would secure to his school the cost of the tuition of a pupil in the state school. This is not paying for religious instruction, but for the secular instruction demanded by the State, and given to the pupil as thoroughly as he could have received it in the state school.

Ireland, already disliked by German Catholics because of his opposition to the use of German in their numerous parish schools, now excited the resistance of other conservative churchmen who believed they detected the germ of European liberalism in Ireland's efforts to accommodate American Catholicism to the national spirit. Gibbons was quick to sense danger to his friend when he learned that someone had sent the text of Ireland's address to Rome for examination. Nor were his misgivings allayed two weeks later when he heard that while the archbishop would escape ecclesiastical censure this time, Simeoni was greatly troubled by the controversial speech. Uneasy, the cardinal decided upon a personal defense of his friend. He told O'Connell that Simeoni should know that not a bishop in the country had done more to advance the Catholic religion than John Ireland, that he was admired by the entire community, and that Protestants regarded him as a fearless champion of the Catholic faith, while Catholics venerated him as an eloquent exponent of their religion. Consequently, the circulation of even a rumor that he did not enjoy the entire confidence of the Propaganda would do immense mischief to religion, dampen the zeal of Ireland, elate the Church's enemies, and sadden the hearts of Catholics. "Had he been a dumb dog," said the cardinal, "no whelps would have barked at him here."

Later that year Gibbons, under prodding from O'Connell, followed up this letter with another major statement of American policy for the guidance of the Holy See. The cardinal first emphasized the efforts that American Catholics were continuing to make in behalf of the parochial schools. But he informed Leo XIII that these efforts would always have limited success, since circumstances would always make it necessary for some Catholic children to attend the public schools. Lest the Pope form a false impression of the American public schools, Gibbons was at pains to explain that

> the religious question is set aside in the schools in order not to offend the sentiments of the children who attend them and the parents who send them there. The care of providing the religious education of the children is left to the Church and the Protestant sects.

If Ireland's tribute to the public schools was read in the light of the principles set forth in the second section of the address, the cardinal could see nothing reprehensible from the viewpoint of sound doctrine. After quoting for the Pope a number of the most controverted passages of the speech, Gibbons then continued:

> It appears to me, Most Holy Father, that the various sentences in their context have no other meaning than this: The Catholics are not against state schools in principle; they recognize the great success of these schools; they desire neither their suppression nor diminution; what they ask is that the defects of the system be corrected, that religious teaching be given the place it is entitled to; in particular

that Catholics be given the guarantees demanded by their conscience in the most important task of the education of their children, then these same Catholics will be glad to patronize these schools as their conscience will no longer oblige them, in order to have their parochial schools, to take upon themselves the heavy burdens which weigh upon them in the present circumstances.

The opponents of the Archbishop of St. Paul had likewise suspected his faith because of his remarks concerning Protestantism. To the cardinal it was obvious that a religion that helped "to maintain in the public mind belief in revelation and the supernatural order" was certainly preferable to unbelief. That, too, was the meaning of Ireland when he made his appeal for Protestantism.

With these various factors in mind, it would be, said Gibbons, disastrous if the archbishop were condemned or even simply blamed. Protestants constantly proclaimed that there could be no liberty of thought in the Catholic Church. The censure of Ireland would confirm this charge since he was a living challenge to such accusations. Furthermore, Ireland's zeal for religious education was proved in his own archdiocese, where 12,000 Catholic children attended parochial schools. The campaign against the Archbishop of St. Paul was motivated not by disinterested love of truth nor pure zeal for sound doctrine, Gibbons observed acidly, but by less worthy motives.

In the interval before the next archbishops' meeting, Gibbons encouraged Thomas Bouquillon, professor of moral theology at the Catholic University of America, to publish a pamphlet, *Education: To Whom Does It Belong?* which gave vigorous support to Ireland's view of the right of the state to educate children. Even before the Bouquillon work became generally known, news of it reached the opposition. Some days before the meeting of the archbishops in St. Louis, Bishop McQuaid expressed his pleasure to Archbishop Corrigan that Bouquillon was to be answered seriously. McQuaid was doubtless referring to the effort of Father René I. Holaind, S.J., of New York, who wrote a thirty-two page pamphlet called *The Parent First.*

When the archbishops assembled in November, 1891, Archbishop Ireland explained the arrangements between the local school boards and the parish schools of Faribault and Stillwater in his archdiocese. The pastors in these towns had agreed with their respective school boards to rent their parish schools for $1 a year with stipulations similar to those in Poughkeepsie. Ireland received the explicit approval of several archbishops present, the open congratulations of Archbishop Williams, and no word of censure from his other colleagues.

With the publication of the opposing pamphlets the controversy entered its bitterest phase. Both sides supplied their European friends with letters and newspaper clippings, and the debate received wide coverage in English and continental journals. By the early days of 1892 the question had become, probably to the surprise of all concerned, a matter of international interest.

True to his nature in facing opposition directly, Archbishop Ireland sailed for Rome on January 16, 1892, armed with documentary weapons for the defense of himself and of Dr. Bouquillon. Within a month after Ireland's arrival, O'Connell reported that the Pope and Rampolla had espoused Ireland's cause. Gibbons' acknowledgment not only showed his joy, but his depth of feeling on the subject:

> God bless the Pope. Yesterday I prayed at Mass that the Lord might inspire him & that right & justice should prevail. It is not the Faribault school that is on trial, but the question to be decided is whether the Church is to be governed here by men or by children, by justice & truth, or by diplomacy & intrigue, whether the Church is to be honored as a bulwark of liberty & order, or to be despised and suspected as an enemy of our Institutions.

For one blunder the Archbishop of St. Paul was himself responsible. In his eagerness to score a point against his enemies, Ireland insisted that the editors of the *Civiltà Catolica* publish a private letter in which Cardinal Gibbons had explained the circumstances, as he remembered them, of the St. Louis meeting in which Ireland had outlined the Faribault-Stillwater school plan. The three sentences of the letter that gave rise to trouble were the following:

> The Archbishop expressed a willingness to discontinue this system, if his colleagues advised him. But he got no such advice, for the advantage is all on his side. The Archbishop answered several questions, put by his colleagues, and the result was a triumphant vindication of his course.

Although the letter was published without Gibbons' prior consent, he stood by it when challenged by Corrigan. Unsatisfied by the explanation, Corrigan launched an effort to get certain archbishops to go on record at Rome against the cardinal's interpretation. Without Gibbons' knowledge, Corrigan drew up a document that expressed an impression contrary to that of the cardinal's letter. When he found six archbishops who supported his account, he forwarded the document to the Propaganda.

Needless to say, this incident was the source of deep distress to Cardinal Gibbons, even though several of the signatories denied any thought of questioning his veracity before the Holy See. Despite the apologies Gibbons revealed to Ryan how keenly he felt: "the last few days have been to me days of intolerable anguish." Gibbons was consoled to learn from Ireland that Cardinal Ledochowski, the Prefect of the Propaganda, "emphatically impressed on me the duty of assuring you of his utter confidence in the veracity of your report."

During the public debate over Ireland's school plan, the cardinals of the Propaganda were quietly investigating, and on April 21, 1892, they reached their decision, confirmed by the Pope, that although they wished to derogate in no way from the legislation of the councils of Baltimore on parochial schools, yet, taking into consideration all the circumstances, the arrangements at Faribault and Stillwater could be tolerated. Gibbons, of course, was elated, but in this moment of triumph the cardinal had fears that the archbishop's ardent temperament might get the better of him. Gibbons therefore, gave him a sage bit of advice. "Be sure," said the Cardinal, "that no public expression will come from you which might be used by your enemies against you. Do nothing to wound or irritate. Your victory is a sufficient ground for the humiliation of others."

Archbishop Ireland concluded his Roman visit in high spirits, and when he reached Genoa, he wrote the story of his triumphs to Gibbons. Looking forward to the meeting of the archbishops in New York in the fall, he said he would be prepared to silence Corrigan. He added a word to stiffen Gibbons' firmness for the coming meeting: "Please, do not be afraid."

Hardly had Ireland arrived in St. Paul in mid-July before he was confronted with a serious revolt in the two communities; both non-Catholics and Catholics opposed continuing the Dominican Sisters as teachers in the two schools. The Stillwater school board had terminated the contract of the Sisters even before Ireland reached home, and the excitement at Faribault was only calmed sufficiently to permit a contract for one more year; but this, too, was later annulled as of October, 1893. The experiment, therefore, had proven a failure. When the fall meeting of the archbishops was held in New York, the issue was no longer a practical one.

The following year, when the Holy Father reaffirmed the compromise, even the strongest opponents in the hierarchy subsided; insofar as the bishops were concerned, the debate was over. Archbishop Corrigan received the papal decision with a spirit of resignation, and in thanking Gibbons for a copy of it, he said: "I trust the words of our Lord's Vicar will have the consoling effect of His own when He commanded the winds and the waves, and 'there came a great calm.' "

The school controversy finally brought to a head the pressure for an apostolic delegate. When John W. Foster, the Secretary of State, requested the Vatican to lend some fifteenth-century maps to the World's Columbian Exposition scheduled for Chicago in 1893, the Holy See promptly granted the request and appointed a personal representative of the Pope, Archbishop Francesco Satolli, to bring them to this country.

On October 12, 1892, Archbishop Satolli, accompanied by Monsignor O'Connell from Rome, arrived on the *Majestic*. After a brief stop in the city, during which they took dinner with Archbishop Corrigan, the ablegate and his party hurried on to Baltimore where they were the guests of Cardinal Gibbons. Two days later Gibbons accompanied Satolli to Washington for a visit to Secretary of State Foster, and on October 18, the cardinal, the ablegate, Ireland, and O'Connell left for Chicago where Gibbons gave the invocation at the ceremonies dedicating the buildings for the Columbian Exposition. From Chicago Satolli traveled on to St. Paul with Ireland, whose guest he was for nearly a month.

In one sense the visit of Archbishop Satolli was singularly ill-timed. The appearance of the papal ablegate played directly into the hands of the American Protective Association. From the outset of his visit Satolli was attacked in the A.P.A. press, and other papers were soon carrying alarming rumors about the powers with which the Pope had invested him over the lives of American citizens. The atmosphere was sufficiently charged with tension to create in the minds of the American bishops the hope that he would not prolong his stay beyond the time necessary to transact his business.

When the archbishops of the United States assembled in New

York in mid-November, Satolli presented the great desire of the Holy Father to establish with their concurrence a permanent apostolic delegation in the United States. All the archbishops, with the exception of Ireland, stated that, in view of "the serious difficulties connected with the subject," they did not feel warranted in taking action until they had first consulted with their suffragans. For the moment there the matter rested. Gibbons was instructed in a unanimous resolution to thank Satolli for the able discharge of his "special mission" and Leo XIII for sending so holy and learned a representative.

Meanwhile Archbishop Satolli returned to Washington where he took up residence at the Catholic University of America. On December 3 he received certain faculties from the Propaganda for settling disputes between bishops and their priests. Probably on the strength of these faculties, Satolli freed Father McGlynn from ecclesistical censures and restored him to the exercise of his priestly functions, an incident that, to be sure, did not endear the ablegate to Archbishop Corrigan. Other bishops also feared for their prerogatives. Bishop Keane, rector of the University, was anxious to have Gibbons impress upon the ablegate that he was to receive cases only as the Holy See did, that is, after they had passed through the court of the metropolitan. Keane added; "Were he *a court of first instance,* it is easy to imagine how much confusion & disorder would be occasioned."

The day following the mailing of this letter, there appeared in the Chicago *Tribune* of January 5 and in other American papers a story from London that the Pope was "unusually irritated by the collapse of his project to appoint a nuncio to the United States." The next day the Tribune, on the authority of the *Corriere del Mattino* of Naples, stated that the ablegate's brusque manner had caused the Roman Curia to understand that the Americans would not tolerate the arrogance of its envoy and that Satolli had, therefore, been recalled. A group of priests of the Archdiocese of New York were alleged to have signed a circular protesting against the attacks on Satolli, and stating that these attacks were instigated by certain bishops who opposed his presence here. Archbishop Corrigan indignantly repudiated any personal connection with the attacks, though Archbishop Ireland believed he had proof that the Archbishop of New York had inspired the press campaign against

Satolli. Ireland was burning with indignation. He told the cardinal: "We have fallen upon sad times. Religion is suffering; Catholics are scandalized; Protestants laugh at us." The enemies of the Church, Bishop Kain of Wheeling told Gibbons, "are chuckling over discord in our ranks."

In the midst of the discord Gibbons received a cablegram from O'Connell; it read: "American delegation established. Satolli first delegate." The gordian knot had been cut by the personal action of the Pope, and the American hierarchy was now faced with an accomplished fact.

Gibbons immediately sent his congratulations to the new delegate in Washington. Two weeks later, Gibbons forwarded to Leo XIII his thanks for the establishment of a permanent apostolic delegation. He told the Pope that his personal sentiments even more than the circumstances urged him to express his gratitude, that the cablegram had brought him one of the great joys of his life, and that he blessed from the bottom of his heart the Providence that had inspired this act of His Holiness and had induced him to execute it without delay. Nothing, said the cardinal, could have been more opportune since for some time there had been attacks upon Archbishop Satolli, directed by men who were determined to hound him out of the country. Leo's action had put an end to this disorder, checked the intrigues, reduced to silence the most bitter of Satolli's opponents. Referring then to the reaction shown toward the appointment, Gibbons said:

> Satisfaction has been very general in our ranks, and even those who have been surprised or even piqued by this exercise of your apostolic authority have already been led, or soon will be, by their personal reflection and by public sentiment to change their views and to accept with good grace the decision of Your Holiness, even to rejoice heartily in it.

Obviously the circumstances demanded a respectful acceptance of Leo XIII's action. Equally obviously, the American bishops had been confronted with a *fait accompli* that they were powerless to reverse. For reasons of prudence and common sense, therefore, they should have made their acceptance as graceful as possible. But when Gibbons stated that the news of the permanent appointment had brought him "one of the great joys" of his life, that it had been well received by Protestants as well as Catholics, and that the news had silenced all opposition against Satolli, the Cardinal of Baltimore was taking an unaccustomed liberty with the truth.

Gibbons helped Satolli get established by arranging for him to meet President Cleveland, by helping him buy a house on I Street in Washington, and, under insistent prodding from Rome, by serving — successfully — as a conciliator for Satolli and Corrigan. Since Gibbons' silver jubilee as a bishop was to be celebrated in October, 1893, he extended his peacemaking efforts by inviting Archbishop Corrigan to preach the sermon at the pontifical Mass at the cathedral in Baltimore. The Archbishop of New York accepted, and in his sermon on October 18, 1893, he referred to the affection in which the cardinal was held by his priests and people and by the very large number of prelates who had assembled to honor him, including "the venerated representative of the Holy Father," as evidences of how deeply he had engraven himself on the hearts of those who knew him. Corrigan's sermon made its contribution to setting at rest the talk about their differences over public questions, even as it excited, in certain quarters where Corrigan was not liked, misgivings about Gibbons' firmness. By the close of the year 1893, therefore, the worst of the storm was over. In the thirty years that elapsed from the appointment of Satolli to the death of Gibbons, the latter had ample opportunity to see the usefulness of the Apostolic Delegation for the Church of the United States. As subsequent delegates came and went, the Cardinal of Baltimore worked harmoniously with them.

The festivities that marked Gibbons' twenty-five years as a bishop in 1893 called forth tributes from all over the land. A dinner in Gibbons' honor for civic officials was given on October 19, and there Vice-President Adlai E. Stevenson led the distinguished audience in tributes to the guest of honor. Governor Frank Brown made known that he would be present for the celebration to show by his presence the high esteem in which he in common with all the people of Maryland held the cardinal. Another of Baltimore's distinguished citizens, Daniel C. Gilman, president of the Johns Hopkins University, expressed his congratulations that amid the arduous duties of Gibbons' high station, he had been able, beyond the bounds of his own communion, to exert "so strong an influence in the promotion of Christian charity and in defense of the political institutions of this land."

The *Jewish Exponent* of Philadelphia in its editorial of October 20 rejoiced that the Catholic Church in the United States had patterned itself after him, one of its best exemplars. The New York *Tribune* on October 22 paid tribute to the liberal views of the cardinal, but as a liberal who did not offend his conservative colleagues. "Between the extremes of both parties," said the *Tribune,* "he stands as a harmonizer, a peacemaker." The Baltimore *Sun* of October 19 hailed him editorially as one who by his life had made the world richer morally, intellectually, and industrially.

Two other issues that troubled Gibbons — secret societies and "Americanism" — showed a persistent vitality despite the apparent amity that surrounded his jubilee. The spring of 1892 brought an article in the *American Ecclesiastical Review* from Archbishop Katzer in which the more conservative point of view on the societies was set forth, and two months later Francis Janssens, Archbishop of New Orleans, in the same journal came out against the Knights of Pythias as a forbidden society, although, as he was careful to state, it was not condemned under pain of excommunication.

In this instance Gibbons' policy of "masterly inactivity" was not working to his advantage. By their forthright public stands the Archbishops of Milwaukee and New Orleans took the lead from the other metropolitans; their decisive moves were bound to attract recruits to their side. On September 14 the New York bishops adopted a unanimous resolution that in their opinion the Odd Fellows, Knights of Pythias, and Knights Templar were prohibited societies in the sense of the decrees and pastoral letter of the Third Plenary Council. Six weeks later their colleagues of the Province of Philadelphia reached a similarly unanimous decision on these three societies, to which they added an explicit condemnation of the Sons of Temperance.

The actions of these provincial meetings were taken with an eye to the approaching third annual conference of the archbishops in New York in November, 1892. In preparation for the meeting, the noted Jesuit theologian, Aloysius Sabetti, professor of moral theology at Woodstock College, sent the cardinal a copy of a study on secret societies that had been made by Salvatore M. Brandi, S.J., when he was on the faculty at Woodstock. Brandi reached the conclusion that no society except the Masons must be condemned in the United States unless it was proven that it worked against

Church or State. Thus Gibbons had support from one of the leading moral theologians of the United States. At the archbishops' meeting no unanimous judgment could be rendered on groups like the Odd Fellows and the Knights of Pythias. So all available material on the disputed lodges had to be communicated to the Holy See for a final decision. The cardinal doubtless viewed with considerable misgiving the transfer of the responsibility out of American hands. Yet there seemed to be no other course to follow.

The Roman Curia proceeded in its usual leisurely manner. On August 20, 1894, Raffaele Cardinal Monaco of the Congregation of the Holy Office forwarded a decree to Archbishop Satolli in which the three disputed societies — the Odd Fellows, the Knights of Pythias, and the Sons of Temperance — were condemned by the Church. The decree directed that the American bishops be notified of the action of the Holy Office and that their people be warned against the societies; if Catholic members persisted in the ranks after being warned, they were to be deprived of the sacraments. Rampolla told Sattoli that the carrying out of the decree should be committed to the prudence and conscience of the metropolitans.

The terse language of the official minutes of the Philadelphia meeting of the archbishops in October, 1894, gives no direct evidence of the role played by Gibbons as chairman, but in the action taken on the decree it is not difficult to detect his hand. The minutes stated:

> The Most Reverend Prelates were unanimous in their opinion that it was inopportune under the present circumstances to publish said condemnation; they moreover agreed not to communicate this condemnation even to their suffragans; and in fine they resolved that no individual Archbishop or Bishop should promulgate it, unless its promulgation were expressly ordered by the Holy See or by the Archbishops in convention assembled.

The moderates carried the day at Philadelphia principally because at the very time of their meeting the A.P.A. was growing noisier in anticipation of the congressional elections less than a month away. Even the most conservative archbishops were fearful lest the publication of the decree arm the Church's enemies.

This stay of proceeding was nullified when in early December, 1894, the Holy See ordered that the condemnation of the societies be promulgated and communicated at once to the suffragans. Archbishop Ireland was indignant, saying to Gibbons that few things in the past decade had amazed and saddened him more than this action of the Holy See; the disregard of what Ireland believed was the larger portion of the American hierarchy irritated him. Cardinal Gibbons was also annoyed, especially since the bishops would have to bear the odium and responsibility without being able to give a reasonable answer to those who would ask about their motives. Gibbons himself was not going to let the incident pass without a protest: "I wish to put myself on record. Let the responsibility rest on them that brought about the condemnation."

Several weeks later the Cardinal of Baltimore addressed a strong communication to the Secretary of State containing none of the customary thanks for the Holy See's solicitude for American Catholic affairs. Gibbons told Rampolla that it would not be opportune to publish the decree in Baltimore, since the Catholic members of the banned societies saw nothing evil in them and the Protestant members had shown no hostility to the Catholic Church. He feared the decree's publication would only irritate the Protestants and tempt the Catholics to disobedience because of the financial losses they would sustain should they abandon their membership. The cardinal pointed out that confessors could effectively withdraw Catholics from the forbidden societies in a gradual and quiet manner. Therefore, he hoped the Holy See would approve his accepting the judgment of Rome but not officially publishing it.

The reply to Gibbons came through Archbishop Satolli. The delegate had drawn up the following points as a practical guide for all concerned. Catholics were not to be allowed to join the three societies, but this ban would be lifted in the future if the societies would modify their constitutions so as to remove all grounds for suspicion; second, those Catholics who already belonged were not to be obliged to resign if their interests would suffer a serious injury. Since in practically every instance withdrawal would cause grave injury to the financial interests of Catholic members, they did not have to resign. Third, no public promulgation of the Roman decree was necessary or desirable; private instructions concerning the decree could be given to the clergy by the bishops. Gibbons was hopeful about Satolli. The cardinal told Ireland that Satolli

is fully alive to the situation & in entire sympathy with us. His interpretation of the Decree takes the sting out of it & practically puts us where we were before. He has his mind & heart set on having the whole question reopened in Rome & I strongly advised him to do so. . . .

The Archbishop of Baltimore meanwhile made preparations for a visit to Rome. Ireland was jubilant when he got word that the cardinal was going: "You are needed there. Go to conquer, and return having conquered." Still fresh in the minds of Gibbons' admirers, and in his own mind, was the triumph he had won some years before in prevailing on the Holy See to reverse itself on the ban against the Knights of Labor.

His attempt, however, failed. Several cardinals said unequivocally that the matter was settled, and even the Pope was reported to have told Gibbons to publish the decree in his archdiocese. Just before his departure from Rome, Gibbons acknowledged his failure in a letter to Keane:

> The H. Office is inflexible, & a few days before I arrived a letter was sent to the Delegate urging more explicit promulgation. Interested parties were working with H. Office before I arrived, & representing some Prelates as neglectful in this regard. But those high in authority suggest an interpretation which moderates the severity of the decision. I will have much to say to you viva voce.

Essentially the issue was settled, though the details remained to be worked out. Gibbons knew that he had suffered his first major setback at the Holy See.

In several ways this European journey proved to be an unpleasant experience, for scarcely a week after Cardinal Gibbons' arrival in Rome, he received the exceedingly painful news that Monsignor Denis J. O'Connell had been forced to resign as rector of the American College. Over the previous ten years his identification with the party of Gibbons, Ireland, and Keane damaged his prestige as liaison man for the American hierarchy with the Holy See. Criticism lodged with the Congregation de Propaganda Fide, under which the American College operated, convinced certain officials of the congregation that the rector must go. The opponents of the so-called liberals regarded O'Connell's resignation as a triumph. To the Cardinal of Baltimore, the entire affair was a cruel blow, though he accepted the decision with outward serenity. For nearly thirty years he had been an intimate friend of O'Connell's, had promoted his interests on every possible occasion, and had followed his advice on important questions. Now Gibbons threw over O'Connell the mantle of his protection; for the present, he appointed the deposed rector as vicar of his titular Church of Santa Maria in Trastevere. He assured O'Connell: "You are almost hourly in my thoughts."

The forced resignation of Denis O'Connell offered only a foretaste of what was to come. The Archbishop of St. Paul noted gloomily: "I remain most pessimistic as to Rome's general influence on the movements of the American Church." The cardinal shared this mood. Wild, misleading statements concerning his motives and his policies in Rome were appearing in American newspapers under European datelines. Greatly annoyed, the cardinal felt prompted to say: "On this side of the Atlantic intrigues and deceitful diplomacy are reduced to a science." Not often did Gibbons speak in such sharp tones even to his intimate friends. It was evident that his temper was growing short.

The gloom was justified. Although most major controversies had been settled by the summer of 1895, the most serious of all was about to erupt — the problem known as Americanism. Among the leaders of the American Church there were two fairly discernible schools of thought. One, to which men like Gibbons, Ireland, and Keane generally adhered, interpreted the Church's attitude in a tolerant manner, in the dual hope that this approach would assimilate the thousands of foreign-born Catholics to their American home, and at the same time deprive enemies of the argument that the Church was un-American. The other, numbering bishops like Corrigan, Katzer, and McQuaid, took a more strictly legalistic view, feared the germ of philosophical liberalism they detected in the opposition; they were less inclined to a spirit of accommodation to American ways. At times the ranks broke, to be sure. For example, Cahenslyism, which rallied so many of the conservative German bishops, had no more unflinching enemy than McQuaid, while the resistance to an Italian delegate, which gathered in most of the democratically minded bishops, found the progressive John Ireland in the opposite camp. In neither wing was there a bishop who was not entirely orthodox in doctrine and fundamentally loyal to the United States.

In April, 1891, Monsignor Thomas S. Preston, Vicar-General of the Archdiocese of New York, published an article, "American Catholicity," in which he deprecated the views that American Cath-

olicism was more consonant with the spirit of the age and less hostile
to those who differed from Catholics in faith and morals, that the
American form of government was the best possible and most suited
to the Catholic religion, and that all religions were good and conducive to the salvation of men, while the Catholic religion was only
better and more complete. On this issue of Church and State, Preston
said: "We yield to no one in devotion to our own country; nevertheless, we cannot hold that the best form of government is that in
which the Church is entirely separated from the State and the State
from the Church." He also believed that good Catholics were bound
to work by every legitimate means for the restoration of the temporal
power of the Pope.

These views were shared by Preston's superior, Archbishop Corrigan. A year after Preston's article, when the Superior General of
the Paulists, Augustine F. Hewit, asked the archbishop to write something for the *Catholic World,* Corrigan courteously declined and sent
a private memorandum to Hewit in which he said: "When last in
Rome, I was directed to repress certain Liberalizing tendencies
observed in 'The Catholic World.' " A far more important indication
that so-called liberal tendencies were being watched — and at times
reported to the Holy See — came the following year. The cause of
complaint was the Catholic participation in the World's Parliament
of Religions held at Chicago in the fall of 1893 in connection with
the Columbian Exposition. At the American Catholic Congress held
during the exposition, Archbishop Satolli had words of high praise for
both Church and State in the United States, and in concluding he said:

> Go forward, in one hand bearing the book of christian truth and in
> the other the constitution of the United States. Christian truth and
> American liberty will make you free, happy, and prosperous. They
> will put you on the road to progress. May your steps ever persevere
> on that road.

Then on the fourth day of the World's Parliament of Religions,
Bishop Keane read a paper written by Gibbons, "The Needs of
Humanity Supplied by the Catholic Religion." In an address carefully
worded for the mixed audience, the cardinal summarized the outstanding work done by the Church in purifying the marriage bond,
proclaiming the sanctity of human life, and providing remedies for
human misery in the persons of orphans, erring women, widows, the
sick, and the slaves. Gibbons reminded his audience that every man

had a mission from God to help his fellowman. In conclusion, the cardinal said: "Though we differ in faith, thank God there is one platform on which we stand united, and that is the platform of charity and benevolence!"

Knowing the sensitivity of Rome about mixed religious gatherings, the cardinal was at pains to explain to Cardinal Rampolla that the bishops had felt it would be well to help offset the agnosticism and atheism of the day and, moreover, to make known the truths of Catholicism to people who were entirely ignorant of or even prejudiced against them. He stated that during the days of the parliament the Catholic bureau of information had distributed around 18,000 books, brochures, and tracts. Gibbons told Rampolla that the Catholic Church's doctrines, morals, and discipline were explained in all their sincerity without the least spirit of compromise or concession. There had been no attempt made at a false union of the churches, nor had any such idea been proposed. About a month later Rampolla acknowledged Gibbons' letter. The Pope recognized the burden imposed by the parliament on Gibbons and his colleagues; the fact that the delicate and dangerous aspects of such gatherings were avoided was certainly due to the perspicacity of His Eminence of Baltimore. The Holy See seemed satisfied.

The following fall, at the seventh German-American Katholikentag assembled in Louisville, Father Henry M. Tappert, an assistant pastor from Covington, Kentucky, repeated a charge that he had made the previous month at the congress of German Catholics in Cologne, that liberalism, the great enemy of the day, had made great inroads on American Catholic leaders:

It holds sway over certain Catholics who have inscribed on their banner: "Union of the Church with the age, with modern ideas, with Americanism." Hence the extolling of modern liberties, not as a requisite for a justified tolerance, but as the ideal of political and ecclesiastical wisdom; hence the cautiousness of preaching Catholic truth, under which truth and Catholicity suffer; hence the more than sparing attitude of this third kind of liberalism towards secret societies; hence the unreasonable breaking away from sane Catholic tradition in the temperance and liquor question; hence, finally, that coquetting with a more or less general, all-embracing christianity to which a far-reaching expression was given at the Chicago religious parliament of unholy memory.

Tappert went on to say that from this same source arose the praise of the public schools and "that ridiculous boastfulness about Americanism" that reproached other Catholics for their attachment to the language and customs of their forefathers. Tappert succeeded in expressing most of the charges made by conservative American Catholics during the controversy over Americanism.

These charges — "these clouds of whispers of suspicion" about "the general tendency of so-called 'liberalism' among us," O'Connell called them — led to anxiety when word circulated that the Pope had decided to write a letter to the Church in the United States. When it appeared under the title *Longinqua oceani* on January 6, 1895, the Pope gave high praise to the American nation and expressed esteem and affection for the young and vigorous branch of the Church. The only sentence likely to give rise to unfavorable comment from non-Catholics was Leo XIII's statement that it would be erroneous to think that in the United States was to be sought "the most desirable status of the Church, or that it would be universally lawful or expedient for State and Church to be, as in America, dissevered and divorced."

The generally sympathetic reception of the encyclical was reflected by Archbishop Corrigan. Archbishop Ireland was less impressed. "I am sorry," said Ireland, "so much was expected, & so little came. . . . That unfortunate allusion to Church & State cannot be explained to Americans."

Gibbons, publicly silent, meanwhile quietly published his third book, *The Ambassador of Christ,* addressed principally to the clergy. In a text just under 400 pages running over thirty-one chapters, the cardinal covered virtually every aspect of the priesthood from its divine origin through the virtues that should especially characterize the priest in his relations to God, to himself, and to the fellowmen whom he served. Gibbons revealed the paramount importance he attached to the priest as a man of books by giving seven chapters to the need for constant study: The Sacred Scripture, the writings of the Fathers of the Church, dogmatic and moral theology, canon law, the Greek and Latin classics, and English literature. His own taste received particular emphasis in the chapter called "The Study of Men and the Times," in which he explained the importance of public issues to the Church and the necessity, therefore, for priests to inform themselves on social, political, and economic problems. In a sermon that he called "Obedience to All Lawful Authority" he deplored a lack of reverence for those in authority as one of the greatest social diseases of the age. Gibbons would not have citizens uncritical of their government, but he pleaded for calm, dispassionate judgment on the acts of those in authority, rather than reckless and partisan carping.

In his preoccupation with the things of the mind, the author of *The Ambassador of Christ* did not forget practical works, and there were chapters on the priest as a preacher, catechist, instructor of converts, as well as chapters on ministerial relations with the parochial school, the parish choir, the sick, and the dead. The volume closed with a chapter called "Consolations and Rewards of the Priest."

Gibbons' comment on politics and the state had some relevance to the forthcoming presidential campaign between William McKinley and the young Democrat, William Jennings Bryan. It was the last time that the A.P.A. was to figure seriously in national politics, but during the campaign its attacks grew so threatening that some candidates for public office, in the hope of winning votes, showed signs of equivocating on the principles of religious liberty for Catholics. Quite contrary to his customary policy in political matters, Gibbons decided to speak out. In language very strong for the mild Archbishop of Baltimore, he said:

> . . . much as I would regret the entire identification of any religious body as such with any political party, I am convinced that the members of a religious body whose rights, civil and religious, are attacked, will naturally and unanimously espouse the cause of the party which has the courage openly to avow the principles of civil and religious liberty according to the constitution. Patience is a virtue, but it is not the only virtue. When pushed too far it may degenerate into pusillanimity.

While the Democratic platform went a long way toward meeting Gibbons' demands, it failed to attract enough votes to carry the election, and McKinley emerged the victor.

In the midst of the political turmoil, the struggle between the opposing factions within the American Church cropped up again, this time at the Catholic University of America. In the last days of September, 1896, Cardinal Gibbons received a letter from Cardinal Rampolla dismissing Keane from his post as rector of the university. With a view to softening the blow, Keane was promised the rank of archbishop, with freedom to remain in the United States or to come to Rome. This altogether unexpected decision of the Holy See had behind it the full force of the opposition to Keane and his associates in the hierarchy. The conservatives like Corrigan, Mc-Quaid, and their episcopal friends, the leaders among the German Catholic nationalists, and some of the more active members of the Society of Jesus had scored a new triumph. For the moment those charged with spreading philosophical liberalism in the American Church appeared to be in complete rout. Bishop Keane, a forthright man with pronounced views on the German question, on the Knights of Labor, and on the condemnation of the writings of Henry George, felt an especially strong compulsion to urge upon American Catholics an uncompromising loyalty to their country. Occasionally the bishop indiscreetly gave his enemies an opportunity to make capital, for example, when he delivered the Dudleian lecture in Appleton Chapel at Harvard University in October, 1890, in his episcopal robes and closed the ceremony by imparting his blessing to the audience. In addition, internal disturbances that had arisen during his administration of the university had become widely known and were undoubtedly reported to the Holy See. The cumulative effect of all this evidence had damaged Keane's reputation in the Eternal City.

At the opening of the new academic year, the retiring rector announced his departure to the assembled faculty and students, and the cardinal chancellor, the most deeply affected of all those present, was reported to have said: "I am a hard man to move, but today I am moved with the most profound sorrow I have ever felt in a long life full of sorrow."

Seldom in the history of the American Church, either before or since, did the Catholic and secular press react so universally and so unfavorably to an action of the Holy See affecting this country. In fact, as the weeks wore on, the press became quite irresponsible. By November it was being reported that Cardinal Gibbons and Archbishop Ireland might be removed from their sees. Bishop McQuaid, on the other hand, was gleeful. He told Archbishop Corrigan: "What collapses on every side! Gibbons, Ireland, and Keane! ! ! They were cock of the walk for a while and dictated to the country and thought to run our diocese for us. They may change their policy and repent. They can never repair the harm done in the past." In reply to an appeal from Archbishop Sebastiano Martinelli, the second apostolic delegate, Rampolla authorized a denial of the reports about the deposition of bishops. The publication of Rampolla's telegram set at rest the more absurd published rumors, although it did not succeed in killing all the inaccuracies current at the time.

Gibbons continued his efforts to retrieve the reputations of his friends O'Connell and Keane. In early September, 1896, he had written to Serafino Cardinal Vannutelli, a friend of O'Connell's, asking if he could not do something for the monsignor, and a month after Keane had gone to Rome, the cardinal reminded Rampolla that Leo XIII's letter promising Keane an honorable post at the Vatican had been made public. Gibbons warned that further postponement would give substance to the rumors then emanating from Rome that nothing was to be done. On the very day that Gibbons wrote his letter, Keane was made titular Archbishop of Damascus and given other offices and titles in the Roman Curia that made his status honorable and dignified.

On January 19, 1897, when the cardinal chancellor installed Father Thomas J. Conaty as second rector of the university, he used the occasion for a pronouncement on the relations of Church and State in the United States that indicated that he still held fast to his brand of Americanism:

> If I had the privilege of modifying the Constitution of the United States, I would not expunge or alter a single paragraph, a single line, or a single word of that important instrument. The Constitution is admirably adapted to the growth and expansion of the Catholic religion, and the Catholic religion is admirably adapted to the genius of the Constitution.

What Keane called the "war of ideas" did not abate, either in the United States or in Europe. Especially in France, the debate over Americanism was becoming bitter and passionate. The startling growth and impressive strength of the Church in this country naturally excited the curiosity of the Catholics of the Old World. At a time when the German Church had only recently emerged from Bismarck's *Kulturkampf,* when the anticlerical government of Italy was making it increasingly difficult for the Church to carry on in that country, and when France was in the throes of one of its worst crises between Church and State, the robust Church of the United States seemed to democratically minded European Catholics to offer a useful model for their own branches of the Universal Church.

The enthusiasm for things American was particularly high among the Catholic republicans of France.

But to French Catholic royalists, the independent status of the American Church in its relations to the State yielded promise of little more than the ultimate separation of Church and State in France, a goal toward which they rightly believed the government of the hated republic was inexorably moving. To these conservative minds the republic — whether in France or in the United States — represented an offspring of the French Revolution, and in that tradition they could see nothing beneficial for Catholicism.

In their anxiety to push the policy known as the *Ralliement,* by which the Catholics would reconcile themselves to the republican form of government, a number of French Catholics were prepared to put forth extraordinary efforts. In the mind of some of these men Walter Elliott's *Life of Father Hecker* embodied the very ideas that they sought to promote among their coreligionists. Unfortunately, Elliott's expressions concerning some of Hecker's ideas on subjects like the need for a new apologetics to win converts, the relations of Church and State, the question of vows taken by members of religious orders, and the action of the Holy Spirit on individual souls could easily lead to misinterpretation. To the French edition, partly reconstructed and inaccurately translated, the Abbé Félix Klein of the Catholic Institute of Paris added a glowing preface, which the *Tablet* of London later said out-Heckered Hecker. The French life of the founder of the Paulists was an immediate success, and within a short time after its publication in Paris in 1897 it passed through seven editions. Yet the more it was read the more did the storm grow, the French Catholic republicans hailing it as a kind of charter for their program, and the conservative and royalist Catholics maintaining that it contained the seeds of heresy that they characterized under the name of Americanism.

The discussion took on such proportions that Monsignor O'Connell read a paper entitled "A New Idea in the Life of Father Hecker" at the fourth International Catholic Scientific Congress in Fribourg, August 20. O'Connell traced the basic ideas of American institutions back to the Declaration of Independence, which created a government by the people with the ultimate source of all power and political rights in God. O'Connell recalled the words of praise uttered by Leo XIII for the American Constitution in 1887, and he went on to say that never did anyone surpass in eloquence Cardinal Satolli himself when he spoke at Chicago in 1893 and recommended the Gospel and the American Constitution taken together as the complete charter of human life. In moderate language the monsignor insisted that Americanism, when fairly considered, meant nothing else than the loyal devotion that Catholics in the United States bore to the principles on which their government was founded, and the conscientious conviction that these principles afforded Catholics in this country favorable opportunities for promoting the glory of God, the growth of the Church, and the salvation of souls.

Gibbons thought that the happily chosen reference to Satolli's memorable remark about the Bible and the Constitution ought to have a telling effect in Rome. Revealing his thorough sympathy with the speech, the cardinal wrote to O'Connell:

> "If this is treason, let them make the most of it," to use the words of Patrick Henry.

La Quinzaine of Paris reprinted the Fribourg address with high approval, Vincenzo Cardinal Vannutelli pronounced it a "bravissimo discorso," and the first one to send O'Connell his thanks was Archbishop Corrigan!

With a major battle over Americanism shaping up, Elliott approached the cardinal for a letter praising Hecker and the Paulists. Gibbons' response left nothing to be desired. He stated that he regarded Hecker as a providential agent for the spread of the Catholic faith in the United States:

> His spirit was that of a faithful child of Holy Church, every way Catholic in the fullest meaning of the term, and his life adorned with the fruits of personal piety; but especially he was inspired with a zeal for souls of the true apostolic order, aggressive and yet prudent, attracting Protestants and yet entirely orthodox.

With words of the highest commendation for the Paulist Fathers, Gibbons concluded: "I am very pleased to learn that Father Hecker's apostolic career is every day more and more appreciated in Europe by the publication and circulation of his life and writings."

This powerful endorsement, promptly published in the *Univers,* headed off the *imprimatur* of François Cardinal Richard, Archbishop of Paris, for a forthcoming book against Americanism by Abbé Charles Maignen, for Richard disliked conflicts between bishops.

Balked in their efforts to enlist the Archbishop of Paris, the enemies of Americanism appealed to Alberto Lepidi, O.P., Master of the Sacred Palace in Rome. Lepidi granted the *imprimatur,* and the book appeared early in 1898 under the title *Etudes sur l'Américanisme: le Père Hecker: est-il un saint?* In the indictment drawn up against Americanism, Elliott, Ireland, Keane, and O'Connell were accused of limiting the external submission to the Church, advocating a false liberalism in their dealings with non-Catholics, supporting a complete separation of Church and State, opposing the evangelical virtues and the older religious orders, and advocating the practice of the active virtues as against the passive and the natural virtues as against the supernatural.

Gibbons was indignant at the Maignen book:

> I regard the attacks of Protestantism as mild compared with the un-principled course of these so-called Catholics. Our mission is surely a hard one here. While trying to exhibit the Church in all her beauty, we are assailed by those who would exhibit her in an odious light. But truth will prevail.

In April, 1898, the United States' declaration of war against Spain gave a new cause for complaint. In the eyes of unfriendly European critics, the bluster that accompanied American reaction to theological criticism resembled the bravado with which Americans greeted their country's triumph over Catholic Spain and its entry into the race for world empire.

During the summer of 1898 Cardinal Gibbons sought the counsel of his friends, and by late August he forwarded a protest to the Holy See. The book of Charles Maignen revealed, said Gibbons, the most violent hatred of Hecker and the Paulists. Americanism was spoken of as a quasi-heretical and schismatic doctrine, and the most ignoble insults were heaped upon American prelates whose love of the Church and of souls made them worthy of every respect and honor. He protested against

> these revolting calumnies against an episcopate and a clergy entirely devoted to the salvation of souls and filled with veneration for the Holy See and in particular for the sacred person of Leo XIII.

Gibbons stated that Maignen created the impression that Americans were hardly Catholics, that they lacked obedience to the teachings of the Holy See, and that they nurtured a strong spirit of schism among them. Yet, he went on:

> I have no hesitation in affirming, you have not in the whole world an episcopate, a clergy, and believers more fundamentally Catholic, firmer in their faith and more wholly devoted to the Holy See. In this, moreover, we are only following our traditions. The Sovereign Pontiff Pius IX was able to say in complete truthfulness that nowhere was he more completely the Pope than in the United States, and His Holiness Leo XIII could say the same.

"The imprimatur of the master of the Sacred Palace," Gibbons asserted, "granted to this libel gives it the meaning of a serious work and one worthy of confidence." For many it would no longer be Maignen who accused the Catholics of the United States but rather the Holy See.

Later in the year O'Connell reported from Rome that Gibbons' letter had made quite an impact. During the vacation period, the decree condemning Hecker had actually been placed on the Pope's desk for his signature. "Just at that time," O'Connell wrote, "a letter came from Card. Gibbons that 'shook him.' " When the Pontiff was pressed to sign, he refused and announced that he would from then on handle the case personally. Despite frantic attempts to avert a papal letter, the Pontiff affixed his signature to the famous *Testem benevolentiae* on January 22, 1899. Rampolla told Gibbons that the Pope could no longer delay in making his mind known on the subject, in view of the controversies raging among the Catholics of France which were likely to create further dissension. "When Your Eminence sees the letter," he said, "you will be immediately freed of any misgiving and will be perfectly satisfied."

Keane had a somewhat less complacent view:

> We must simply make the best of it, and carry on our game of explaining away to the American people the administrative blunders of our superiors.

Archbishop Ireland was similarly distressed: "Fanatics conjured up an 'Americanism,' & put such before the Pope. Lepidi & Mazzella wrote the body of the letter. I cannot pray that God forgive them."

In his letter, addressed to the Cardinal of Baltimore, Leo XIII denied that the Church should show indulgence to modern popular theories and, relaxing its ancient rigor, leave each individual freer to act in pursuance of his own natural bent. With this premise, the Pope listed the faulty opinions, under the name "Americanism," that deserved condemnation: first, that all external guidance should be rejected as superfluous for those who desired to devote themselves to the acquisition of Christian perfection; second, that the natural virtues should be extolled much more than formerly since they were in accordance with the ways of the present age; third, that the virtues should be divided into active and passive; fourth, that the vows taken by members of religious orders were out of keeping with the spirit of the age and narrowed the limits of human liberty. The Pontiff expressed his confidence that the bishops of the United States would be the first to repudiate the ideas that he had outlined for censure.

On the other hand, the Pope said, if the name of Americanism designated the characteristic qualities that reflected honor on the people of the United States, just as other nations had special characteristics, or if Americanism referred to the institutions, laws, and customs that prevailed in the United States, then surely there was no reason why these should be questioned.

Deeply regretting the appearance of *Testem benevolentiae,* Gibbons maintained complete silence in public. He could not, however, ignore the duty of an acknowledgment of the letter. For a month he thought and consulted with his advisers before he addressed himself to Leo XIII. On March 17, his reply was ready, and it was dispatched to the Holy See. In it, he said:

> This doctrine, which I deliberately call extravagent and absurd, this Americanism as it has been called, has nothing in common with the views, aspirations, doctrine and conduct of Americans. I do not think that there can be found in the entire country a bishop, a priest, or even a layman with a knowledge of his religion who has ever uttered such enormities. No, that is not — it never has been and never will be — our Americanism. I am deeply grateful to Your Holiness for having yourself made this distinction . . . between the doctrines which we, along with you, reject, and those feelings of love for our country and its institutions which we share with our fellow citizens and which are such a powerful aid in accomplishing our work for the glory of God and the honor of Holy Church.

The following year the atmosphere cleared somewhat. During the summer Leo XIII invited Ireland to give an address in Rome in the presence of the Pope and many cardinals. Upon his return to this country in the autumn, Ireland brightened the cardinal's view of his standing in Rome. "He will now surely go to Rome early in [the] spring to see for himself how much good his letter on 'Americanism' did," Ireland told O'Connell. "He is a new man."

Thus encouraged, the cardinal pushed the interests of his friend Keane. In March, 1900, the death of John Hennessy, Archbishop of Dubuque, created an opening, and all were agreed that Keane should now be given a chance to return to his native land. On September 12, his sixty-first birthday, John Keane received official notification that he had been appointed second Archbishop of Dubuque. Thus one of the principal figures in the controversy over Americanism and one of Gibbons' closest friends had at last been vindicated after four years of practical exile.

By the turn of the century, then, the last great internal struggle within the Catholic Church of the United States had, for the most part, run its course. In all this anguished struggle Cardinal Gibbons had never allowed himself to be frightened off from the strong Americanism that he had always professed.

Chapter 6

Citizen and Churchman

Cardinal Gibbons' significance sprang from both his position and his personality. As occupant of the premier see of the United States, as the only American cardinal for almost a quarter of a century, he won prestige because of his office. By virtue of the confidence inspired by sound judgment, wise counsel, and supreme tact, he united himself with his fellow bishops to give enlightened leadership to the American Church for many decades. His influence extended not only to ecclesiastical affairs like the Catholic University of America, but to national problems like those created by the Spanish-American War.

The sinking of the American battleship *Maine* in the harbor of Havana on February 5, 1898, with a loss of over 250 men, led the United States to the brink of war. For three years the Cuban insurrection against Spain had excited American sympathy, and now the warmongers in the United States had the incident they needed to demand a declaration of war.

Amid the tumult Cardinal Gibbons said nothing for publication until February 28 when a requiem Mass was offered in the cathedral of Baltimore for the victims of the *Maine*. On this occasion he had words of sympathy for the bereaved families, as well as praise for the president, the cabinet, and the armed forces for their dignified bearing in the emergency. The most important part of the sermon dealt with forbearance:

> This nation is too brave, too strong, too powerful, and too just to engage in an unrighteous or precipitate war. Let us remember the eyes of the world are upon us, whose judgment we cannot despise, and that we will gain more applause and credit for ourselves by calm deliberation and masterly inactivity than by recourse to arms.

The only circumstance that the cardinal believed would warrant hostilities was evidence that the Spanish government had connived at placing explosives in the harbor to destroy the vessel.

During the first week in April the prospects for peace brightened when the Spanish government, responding to the intercession of Pope Leo XIII, prepared to grant an armistice in Cuba. The name of the Pope began to appear frequently in the news dispatches concerning the crisis, and on April 4 the Washington papers gave the first information concerning the presence of Archbishop Ireland in the capital. Ireland had been at pains to keep his movements secret, but the news leaked out. Leo XIII had asked the Archbishop of St. Paul to go to Washington as his representative. The New York *Herald* of April 5 explained that Ireland and not Gibbons had been chosen because "The Cardinal, while a shrewd diplomat, does not stand in the same relationship to the present Administration as Archbishop Ireland, whose support of Mr. McKinley during the last campaign is well remembered." At first optimistic, Ireland abandoned hope of peace on April 11, the day McKinley sent his war message to Congress, and he went to Baltimore that afternoon to confer with Cardinal Gibbons. "The two prelates," said the Baltimore *Sun,* "after discussing the situation thoroughly, agreed that nothing more could be done." On April 19 Congress passed a four-point resolution that was tantamount to a declaration of war on Spain.

When the London *Daily Chronicle* circulated reports that cast aspersions on American Catholics' support of the war effort, the cardinal issued a statement: "Catholics in the United States have but one sentiment. Whatever may have been their opinions as to the expediency of the war, now that it is on they are united in upholding the government."

Cardinal Gibbons promptly turned his attention to providing chaplains for the great number of Catholic men in the army and the navy. Early in July he called on the president to put before him the difficulties attendant on the insufficient number of Catholic chaplains. After the defeat of the Spanish fleet at Santiago on July 3 Admiral Pascual Cervera and a number of his officers were brought to Annapolis where they were detained for some weeks. Late in August the cardinal called on the superintendent of the Naval Academy and paid a visit to Cervera and his men. On August 29 he visited the 100 members of the Fifth Regiment in the City Hospital in Baltimore. In the autumn, rumors reached Gibbons that priests were not being admitted to the hospital tents at Camp Wikoff at Point Montauk, Long Island; whereupon he paid a personal visit to the camp which was described by Thomas Beer:

> . . . a buzz passed under the brown canvas, through smells of typhoid, and the titular pastor of Santa Maria in Trastavere [*sic*] walked slowly down the line of cots, pausing to speak to a red-haired Unitarian youth of Celtic expression and bestowing a blessing which, he said, would do the boy no harm.

The American invasion of Cuba, Puerto Rico, and the Philippine Islands led inevitably to grave problems for the Catholic Church. In the final week of the fighting, Gibbons heard that in one area in Puerto Rico containing eighty parishes there was only one priest, and in the city of Ponce with about 50,000 inhabitants, only eight priests. With support from the government now cut off, there were grave fears that the future of the Church in Puerto Rico would be very dark indeed. In the Philippines the native forces, under the leadership of Emilio Aguinaldo, felt a deep hatred for the Spanish bishops and religious whom they associated with the former government. On August 18 the cardinal received a cablegram from Bishop Luigi Piazzoli, Vicar Apostolic of Hong Kong, which read: "Use influence in releasing one hundred priest prisoners of insurgents Cavite." Gibbons immediately communicated with Archbishop Ireland who was then in Washington and who, in turn, saw the president. An interval of two months passed, and in October the cardinal urged the secretary of war, Russell A. Alger, to take steps for the relief of the captives:

> It cannot fail to appear inconsistent to the world at large that we should be so deeply interested in the welfare of a distant and unknown people, and in freeing them from a hard rule of another nation, and, at the same time, be indifferent to the barbarities which that people uses toward its non-combatant captives.

As a result of the cardinal's intervention, Secretary Alger succeeded in getting better treatment for the captives. He promised to continue his attempt to win their release.

The peace negotiations to bring the Spanish American War to a formal close were opened in Paris on October 1, 1898. From the outset, the Catholic Church was vitally interested in the final settlement. As early as the previous May, Monsignor Denis O'Connell had cabled Archbishop Ireland from Rome: "Help hold Philippines." On August 2, ten days before the end of hostilities, Cardinal Rampolla first expressed the anxiety of the Holy See over the future of the religious orders in the Philippines. When Ireland sounded out the president, McKinley told him that in any territories annexed by the United States the Church would be separated from the State in conformity with the American Constitution and that absolute protection of ecclesiastical properties and persons would be guaranteed.

In regard to the Philippines, McKinley urged the Holy See to obtain every possible concession before the treaty was signed. These quiet arrangements would preclude the possibility of sectarian clamor. Once the treaty was signed, the United States government would grant no concessions to Catholics or to any other denomination. President McKinley summoned Gibbons to the White House to ask his views on Philippine independence. Gibbons assured McKinley that the Church was safer under the American flag than anywhere else; as a citizen, however, he opposed annexation. Annexation, he said, was "a good thing for the Catholic Church, but, I fear, a bad one for the United States." Finally, the president resolved his doubts. On December 10, the Treaty of Paris was signed; it provided that Spain should relinquish sovereignty over Cuba and cede the Philippines, Puerto Rico, and Guam outright to the United States.

The Archbishop of Baltimore immediately turned his attention to the problem of adjusting the Church to the new American regime in the island possessions. From both Cuba and Guam, he received strong pleas for upright priests to improve the standing of the Church.

Bad as conditions were in Guam and Puerto Rico, they were even more critical in the Philippines. When Aguinaldo's men broke with the Americans over the question of independence and raised the standard of revolt, the Spanish friars were relentlessly pursued by the insurgents with a consequent serious loss both in lives and in properties belonging to the religious. During the course of Spain's three centuries of occupation, the Spanish religious had become extensive landowners, and their wealth, together with the power they wielded over the lives of the masses, had made them the object of deep hatred on the part of the insurrectionists. The abuse of power by some of the friars lent plausibility to the campaign against them, and by the time the Americans took over, the widespread opinion in the Philippines, that the friars must go, gradually spread in the United States.

To make matters worse, the Catholic Church of the Philippines was soon faced with a schism. Among the close friends of Aguinaldo was Father Gregorio Aglipay, an extreme nationalist, strongly ambitious, and violently antifriar. In October, 1899, he broke entirely with the Filipino ecclesiastical authorities, and by August, 1901, Aglipay and his followers proclaimed the Filipino Independent Church. Aglipay and his party whipped the nationalist resentment to white heat. Thousands joined the rebellion against Rome and seized parish churches and Church lands.

When the second American commission in the Philippines, headed by Judge William Howard Taft, arrived in Manila in 1900, the problem of the friars was a part of the task of establishing a civil government for the islands. Taft urged a mutual friend to have Archbishop Ireland recruit American priests to replace the Spaniards. When Taft and his colleagues finished their report, they drew a clear distinction between the interests of the Catholic Church and those of the Spanish friars. Archbishop Placide L. Chapelle of New Orleans, the apostolic delegate in the Philippines, rejected this distinction. He was convinced that the attitude taken by the Philippine Commission was "unconsciously perhaps, indirectly surely," hostile to the Church. Shortly before his departure from Manila for Rome and Washington, he informed Taft of his view. The situation had reached an impasse. Clearly matters had to be referred to Rome and Washington for final settlement.

On May 11, 1901, Cardinal Gibbons sailed for Rome. The cardinal remained in the Eternal City for a month. He had three private audiences of Leo XIII, which gave him an opportunity to explain what he knew of Philippine affairs. The cardinal apparently found his role a pleasant one, for on the eve of his return he told Ireland: "This was my most enjoyable visit to Rome."

On Gibbons' return to New York, the *Times* reported that he refused to discuss the Philippines. As he turned south to Baltimore, a crowd of 30,000 to 40,000 people welcomed him in what the Baltimore *American* called a "Royal Welcome to the Cardinal." To the *American's* reporter it was one of the most remarkable demonstrations in the history of the city; never before had a Baltimorean received such an ovation on his return after an absence of a few months. The cardinal rose to the occasion, and to the delight of the crowd he declared that there was no place like home and no home like a home in Baltimore. His attachment to the city was not, he said, to buildings and brick and mortar, but to the living monuments of all that was good and upright among his fellow citizens. In the cathedral, he added that he had always enjoyed the most friendly relations with all his fellow citizens without distinction of race or creed because he firmly believed in the words, "Behold how good and joyful a thing it is for brethren to dwell together in unity."

The Archbishop of St. Paul, in welcoming Gibbons back to the United States, reported receipt of several letters from Cardinal Rampolla, all of which led up to a formal request that the American government send a representative from Washington to treat with the Holy See about the friars' lands and other questions. Elihu Root, the secretary of war, was inclined to favor the proposal, but he was waiting for word from Taft in Manila.

Two weeks later President McKinley was struck down by an assassin's bullet in Buffalo on September 6. He died eight days later. Gibbons immediately instructed his clergy to hold memorial services in all the churches of the Archdiocese of Baltimore on September 19, the day of the funeral at Canton, Ohio. He personally presided in the cathedral on that occasion and preached the sermon. He found it difficult, he said, to think of a murder more atrocious, wanton, and meaningless than the assassination of McKinley, for no court in the civilized world was more conspicuous for moral rectitude and purity, or freer from the breath of scandal, than the official home of the late president. "He would have adorned," said the cardinal, "any court in Christendom by his civic virtues." McKinley had passed away, honored and mourned by the nation, and Theodore Roosevelt had succeeded at once to the title, honors, and responsibilities of the presidential office, Gibbons went on. In other countries the assassination of the ruler meant revolution, and revolution meant death. "What a striking illustration," said Gibbons, "of the strength of our Government!" He urged the American people to rally around Roosevelt, to sustain him in bearing the formidable burdens so suddenly thrust upon him.

With the advent of Theodore Roosevelt, Cardinal Gibbons was probably on more intimate terms with the occupant of the White House than at any other time in his life. The day after McKinley's funeral he conveyed to the new president a message of condolence from Patrick Cardinal Moran of Sydney, and he used the occasion to express the earnest hope that the new administration would be creditable to Roosevelt and would redound to the material prosperity of the country. Roosevelt replied that in thanking the Australian cardinal through Gibbons he wished to add a word of "my regard for you and my appreciation of your attitude," and that he hoped to see him soon. Thus began a deepening friendship between the two men that ended seventeen years later only with the death of Mr. Roosevelt.

Sometime late in October the cardinal and the president had a long conversation on the Philippines. Roosevelt confessed that he found the problem of the friars' lands baffling. He thought that the most it seemed possible to pay for the lands, and still win the consent of Congress, was about $7,000,000. It was his idea that the lands should then be resold in small holdings so that the friars would no longer be a factor in the economic life of the islands. At the conclusion of their discussion Gibbons said: "I will undertake, Mr. President, to obtain a settlement for you on the terms which you state."

Some days after the interview the cardinal informed Rampolla of his visit to the White House. He limited himself to general statements that conveyed the impression of the goodwill on both sides. Roosevelt, said Gibbons, was very well disposed toward Catholics and toward the Church; the Holy See would have nothing but praise for the actions that the president would take. Having thus contributed to the creation of a cordial atmosphere, Gibbons let the matter rest for the time being.

Early in December, Gibbons urged the president to send a representative to Rome to settle matters in the Philippines. Roosevelt adopted the suggestion, and named Taft, now Governor of the Philippines, head of the commission. Ten days before Taft sailed in May, 1902, he paid a lengthy visit to Gibbons in Baltimore. The cardinal gained the most favorable impressions: "He is a splendid type of an American citizen, & he is disposed to be not only just but generous to the Catholic Church." Bishop Thomas O'Gorman of Nebraska, who had preceded Taft to Rome, reported from a recent audience with Leo XIII: "The Taft Commission simply delights him."

Governor Taft remained in Rome for about a month, and by the middle of June, 1902, he was able to submit to Secretary Root the terms of purchase of the friars' lands in the Philippines, as well as further details of his negotiations with the Holy See. But it was only in December, 1903, that the 410,000 acres were finally purchased by the United States for the sum of $7,239,000 in gold. With that the case was closed insofar as the Church was concerned.

From the beginning, opposition to the purchase had been expressed in both Catholic and secular journals. The president received protests from certain Catholic groups against the injustice that they said was being done to the friars by the government. One article was bluntly entitled "The Friars Must Stay." Roosevelt was puzzled by the Catholic criticism, since the government had only acted on the request of Archbishop Ireland and with the cordial approval of Cardinal Gibbons. In sending Taft to Rome, he said he had feared anti-Catholic criticism, but it had never entered his head that he would "encounter Catholic hostility."

In one Catholic editor, however, the government found a stanch defender. Herman J. Heuser of the *American Ecclesiastical Review* struck out sharply, especially at the Germans whose papers, he said, worked closely with the religious orders that were biased in the case. Moreover, some of the Catholic editors, Heuser said, were guilty of publishing stories on such flimsy evidence that it simply made them falsehoods. "It is the *odium theologicum,*" said Heuser, "carried into the domain of social and political life by half-informed champions who see in their own interests the interests of a common cause."

At one point Gibbons himself contributed to the president's discomfort. In April, 1904, Gibbons signed a petition requesting the United States to promise ultimate independence to the Philippine Islands. Roosevelt told the cardinal: "If such a promise was made by us one of the first consequences would be that the position of . . . American Bishops would grow literally intolerable." Gibbons at once sensed the mistake he had made. "I should deeply regret," said the cardinal, "to do anything that would in the smallest way embarrass you in your delicate task & formidable burden of maintaining peace & order in those Islands." From that time forward Gibbons resolutely opposed all efforts to hasten Philippine independence. After Theodore Roosevelt won the presidency in his own right in the election of 1904, Cardinal Gibbons sent him cordial congratulations, to which Roosevelt responded with similar warmth.

Just as matters in the Philippines settled down, Gibbons became involved, almost by inadvertence, in another international episode, this time in Africa. In March, 1904, the Congo Reform Association was founded in England to arouse world opinion against the regime of Leopold II and to compel reform of conditions little better than slavery for the natives. The association was intent upon winning American opinion to its side, and in the autumn of 1904 it delegated its secretary, Edmund D. Morel, to present a petition to President Roosevelt and to carry its case before the thirteenth International Peace Congress scheduled for the first week in October in Boston. At this point Cardinal Gibbons was drawn in by the Belgian government. Not invited to send a representative to present the king's side of the case at the Peace Congress, the government of Leopold II asked Gibbons to support its demand that the question be kept off the agenda. The cardinal agreed to lend his assistance by writing a letter to the Reverend Edward Everett Hale, one of the leading officials of the Congress, who read it at one of the sessions. Gibbons remarked that if he were present he would regard it as his duty to say a word in vindication of the policy of Leopold II in the Congo. He cited the recognition given to the regime at the Berlin conference twenty years before, quoted the Italian and British delegates to that conference in admiration of the king's policies, and attributed the present prosperity of the region to Belgian toil and sacrifice. With all these factors in mind, the cardinal said he would regret having a congress bearing the name of peace discuss a question calculated to arouse enmity and strife, and he added that it would likewise be unfair since no representative of the Belgian government had been invited to present the king's case. Gibbons' effort failed to prevent a discussion of the question; the day after his letter was read, Morel assailed the Congo regime.

When word of the cardinal's action reached King Leopold II, he promptly instructed his minister at Washington to thank Gibbons in his name. Pope Pius X likewise expressed his gratitude. Yet Gibbons did not escape criticism for his intervention in the case. Morel reproached him for not knowing the facts, and in December, 1906, the Reverend H. Gratton Guinness publicly attacked Gibbons in a Presbyterian church in Baltimore as "the strong hand in this country who prevented the government from noticing the atrocities in the Congo." The cardinal did not back down. He prepared a statement for the press in which he stated that he had had access to the facts from Catholic missionaries on the scene in the Congo, and from that source he had been informed that the stories of abuse were greatly exaggerated. Gibbons credited Leopold II with being a wise and humane ruler who promptly redressed cruelty when he learned of it. The king's recent decrees giving the natives additional lands and ameliorating the condition of the laborers were cited as evidences of his goodwill. "I fear," said the cardinal, "that this agitation against King Leopold's administration is animated partly by religious jealousy and partly by commercial rivalry." Gibbons disclaimed any personal interest in the affair, and in reiterating his motive as that of wishing to defend a small nation in the interest of fair play, he concluded by saying: "I would willingly make the same defence in behalf of Holland, Sweden, Denmark, or any of the weaker Powers if circumstances demanded."

As Gibbons suggested, religious jealousy and commercial rivalry had played their part in the movement for reform. But the evidence still weighed heavily against the government of the Belgian king as having been guilty of serious exploitation of the natives and, at times, of inhuman treatment of the Negro population.

Gibbons erred in becoming involved. The cardinal's apparently complete reliance on the word of the king's government and on the reports that reached him periodically from missionaries betrayed him into a position difficult to defend. When challenged, he presumably did not see a sufficiently cogent reason for reversing his position. For one of the few times in Gibbons' long life, his normally keen judgment went astray and exposed him to the charge of partisanship and of ignorance of the facts governing an issue. The cardinal should have steered clear of the case.

Closer to home, the cardinal continued his concern for the Catholic University. By 1901, very serious disorders in the finances, as well as a spirit of opposition to the rector among a group of trustees and professors, made it appear that Bishop Conaty should retire at the end of his first term. In the spring of 1902, talk naturally turned to a successor. Cardinal Satolli, now Prefect of the Congregation of Studies, intimated to Monsignor O'Connell, the former rector of the American College in Rome who was the vicar of Gibbons' church in Rome, that he might be the next rector. When this news was sent to Gibbons, it filled his heart with joy. The action of Rome was delayed, but in January, 1903, the Congregation of Studies, "thinking to please to [sic] Your Eminence," as Satolli expressed it, had named O'Connell. O'Connell himself cabled the cardinal to express his joy over the appointment. From Baltimore, Gibbons' chancellor told O'Connell that he had never seen the cardinal so elated. Archbishop Ireland could scarcely believe that the appointment had been made. "What a revolution in the temper of Rome there is implied in his nomination!" said the archbishop, recalling the stormy days of the Americanism controversy.

The university was then in its fourteenth year, but the period of strain had not yet passed. Many of the hierarchy still withheld their support, the scars of internal feuds were not fully healed, both students and financial resources were still scarce, and some of the officials of the Roman Curia had doubts about the university's future. It was no surprise, then, that apart from reasons of friendship the cardinal should welcome so wholeheartedly as rector one in whom he placed such great confidence.

On April 22, 1903, the new rector was formally inaugurated immediately after the semiannual meeting of the board of trustees. It had been evident for a long time that the university needed more ample sources of income than those yielded by occasional benefactions and by students' fees. O'Connell lost no time in getting to the heart of the matter, and at this meeting he presented to the trustees a highly detailed account of the university's finances. The report was not very encouraging: current liabilities of $201,233.33, only $56,251.11 to meet the obligations. In order to overcome this debt and to build up an endowment, O'Connell proposed that the trustees petition the Holy See to order an annual collection for ten years in all the dioceses of the United States. The trustees agreed and empowered O'Connell to present their request to Pope Leo XIII. In fulfillment of this mission, the rector sailed for Rome on July 1.

In the summer of 1903 when Pope Leo XIII had reached his ninety-third year, it became evident that the end was not far off. On July 8 Gibbons received a cablegram from Rampolla that the Pope was not expected to live, and at this news the cardinal quickly made arrangements to sail with Patrick C. Gavan, his chancellor, who would serve him as conclavist at the approaching election. They landed at Le Havre on July 16 and then proceeded to Paris. Leo XIII died on July 20, and the cardinal then set out for Rome where he was to have the distinction of being the first American to take part in the election of a pope.

The conclave opened on the evening of July 31 with all but two of the sixty-four cardinals present. On the two first scrutinies the voting ran strongly in favor of Cardinal Rampolla, and it appeared that he might be elected. In fact, as Gibbons later related, prospects appeared so favorable for the secretary of state that after the second scrutiny the Cardinal of Baltimore, who was seated at Rampolla's right, turned and congratulated him. But before the third scrutiny on August 2, John Cardinal Puzyna, Bishop of Cracow, rose in the conclave and pronounced the veto of the Emperor Francis Joseph of Austria-Hungary against Rampolla's candidacy. The imperial veto brought forth vigorous protests against this interference in the affairs of the Church by a lay State. Nonetheless, whatever chances Rampolla had had for the Papacy were now destroyed, and the balloting began to incline toward Guiseppe Cardinal Sarto, Patriarch of Venice.

At this point, however, a difficulty arose when Sarto made it known that he wished his colleagues to pass him by. His reluctance threatened a stalemate. While affairs were in this uncertain state, Cardinal Satolli paid a visit to Gibbons' room. After conferring for some time, Gibbons volunteered a suggestion, which he later said he hoped was an inspiration. He told Satolli to go to Sarto and to beg him for the love of God to bow to the selection, to yield to the action of the Holy Spirit. The Cardinal of Baltimore waited until the middle of the afternoon, but Satolli did not return. When they had again assembled in the conclave, however, Satolli came and whispered to Gibbons "*Accept.*" Thereupon the news was made known to all the cardinals that Sarto would accept the Papacy if elected. At the next scrutiny he received thirty-five votes and, as Gibbons reported, "All left the conclave like boys out of school for they felt the end was near." On the following morning, August 4, in the seventh scrutiny Sarto received fifty votes, was declared elected, and took the name of Pius X. The new Pope granted an audience to the American cardinal on the evening the conclave ended, and in another private audience gave his approval to an annual collection for the Catholic University of America.

By reason of the papal approval, a subsequent appeal of the chancellor, and the publicity given to the subject by the bishops, priests, and Catholic press, the first annual collection proved very gratifying — a total of $105,051.58. All but three of the dioceses responded to the call, the most conspicuous absentee being Bishop McQuaid's Diocese of Rochester. In an optimistic vein the cardinal chancellor remarked: "This present year is the most prosperous & auspicious that has dawned on the Catholic University since its foundation."

Actually, these bright prospects were soon overcast by an event that would mark 1904 as one of the darkest years in the university's annals. The origin of the crisis lay far back in the administration of Bishop Conaty. As early as April, 1902, a special committee of the board of trustees had reported that the management of the university funds had suffered from not only a lack of competency and of business methods, but "an almost culpable negligence. . . ." Although the business methods of the treasurer, Thomas E. Waggaman, a Washington lawyer and real-estate man, left much to be desired, the blame for the muddled state of affairs could not be laid solely at his door, since the trustees and administrative officers had for years neglected to demand an accounting of the institution's investments.

On August 22, 1904, all hopes for solvency were suddenly dashed when it became known that three Washington banks were prepared to enter involuntary bankruptcy proceedings against Waggaman. The prospect of Waggaman's bankruptcy threatened all the university's investments. It was a trying moment for Cardinal Gibbons. He hurriedly drafted a letter to the trustees, explaining that Waggaman's entire indebtedness to the university amounted to $876,168.98; as collateral, the institution held the deed of trust on some real estate in the Woodley section of Washington, a chattel mortgage on Waggaman's art gallery, which was valued by its owner at $600,000, a bond of Waggaman's father-in-law and son for $200,000, and other securities amounting to $75,000. Gibbons then said:

> The only regular source of revenue the University can depend on is the annual collection, which amounted last year to $104,023.86.

He then came to his appeal for help:

> The time has come now for the Trustees to exert themselves in an heroic manner and to preserve their honor and integrity before the world. The salvation of the University depends on the early action of the Board of Directors. What I would suggest is that each mem-

ber of the Board who feels capable of raising that amount should contribute $50,000, payable in five or ten annual installments.

Although the tone of the chancellor's letter was calm, actually he had been dreadfully shaken by the blow. Father George A. Dougherty, O'Connell's secretary, wired the rector in Seattle: "Eminenza very distressed. Situation uncertain." In a letter the following day he told the rector that the day the crisis broke he had found the cardinal in a state bordering on collapse; Gibbons had suggested that the board suppress the Schools of Law and Technology and cut the salaries of the faculty.

But regardless of pain and embarrassment, Cardinal Gibbons rallied nobly. In its most severe trial the university found no greater source of strength than the assurance of his loyalty and the prestige of his name. He turned to a number of valued friends among the hierarchy and the laity to lend him $1,000 a year for five years so that he might be enabled, in turn, to give it to the university. The depth of his feeling was revealed in the appeal he made to Bishop J. F. Regis Canevin of Pittsburgh: "It is not pleasant for flesh & blood to become a beggar in my declining years, but God wills it to Whom I bow in all humility." As the time neared for the new academic year, Gibbons requested the rector to ask the professors to come to see him as they arrived so that he might urge upon them the reasons for reducing their salaries.

Other problems relating to the university were laid before the chancellor. Archbishop Sebastian G. Messmer of Milwaukee had warned Gibbons the previous spring that O'Connell was inviting criticism by failing to respect the constitutional right of the academic senate and the faculty to voice their opinions regarding policies and decisions. Messmer suggested the names of four priests of German extraction as suitable candidates for the office of vice-rector; he gave it as his opinion that the appointment of one of these men would do much to overcome the prejudice of the German Catholics against the university.

The day before the meeting of the trustees on November 17, 1904, Gibbons was presented with a communication from Cardinal Satolli suggesting that lay students not be admitted to the university and that greater emphasis be given to the School of Theology. Coming when the trustees were eagerly seeking sources of increased revenue, Satolli's letter met with a very unfavorable reception on all sides. The trustees discussed the matter at length, and finally resolved unanimously that Gibbons should thank the prefect for his solicitude for the university but tell him courteously that his suggestion could not be complied with. With this no more was heard of the proposal, and in the autumn of 1905 the university was opened to lay undergraduates as well as to lay graduate students.

In view of the financial strain, the second annual collection scheduled to be taken up on the first Sunday in Advent, 1904, assumed a more than ordinary importance. In preparing a letter to the hierarchy, Gibbons readily followed a suggestion of Spalding's that a full account of the financial condition of the institution be included. He noted that the university had no floating debt nor any deficit at the end of the previous year and stated that the losses suffered through the bankruptcy of the treasurer were in part covered by securities; but he added that the university's income was not sufficient to cover the necessary expenses. The cardinal pleaded strongly with the hierarchy to come behind the collection.

The Archbishop of New York, John M. Farley, was delighted with the chancellor's frank appeal but annoyed at the failure of trustees like Archbishops Ireland, Keane, and Riordan to respond with $1,000 personally to the guarantee fund. A day or two later the cardinal was told of Ireland's disappointment in learning that Farley was giving only $10,000 and Ryan of Philadelphia only $5,000. "The possessors of such large sees, each one with enormous revenues," said Ireland, "should have given much larger sums." These reflections of the East and the West among the university trustees probably afforded a moment of amusement to the harassed chancellor. He was very careful, however, not to involve himself in the trustees' varying estimates of what their colleagues should contribute.

By the autumn of 1905 the chancellor was in a position to offer the university's friends a much brighter prospect. When he mailed his letter to the hierarchy for the next annual collection, he told the bishops that the entire debt of the institution was then only $50,000 and that $355,000 was invested in first-class securities. The amount of the collection on this occasion reached the satisfactory sum of $100,551.30. With the success of this endeavor, together with the gradually mounting guarantee fund, the cardinal could rightly feel that the worst of the storm had passed. The university eventually realized the sum of $361,589.08 from its claims against Waggaman, less by far than the total indebtedness of the treasurer to the university, but more than anyone had dared to hope for. Those who were close to the university in the crisis appreciated Gibbons' extraordinary effort. When the cornerstone of Gibbons Hall was laid on October 12, 1911, Archbishop Farley said:

> But while Cardinal Gibbons thus rendered invaluable service from the beginning in every juncture, never in its history was his indomitable courage, the quality most needed in every vast undertaking, so notably shown as in the dark days of its greatest trial.

Fortunately, the relations of Cardinal Gibbons with the university were not all troublesome. To offset the reverses he had the satisfaction of witnessing the extension of the university's work and the gradual addition of new affiliates. For example, on April 23, 1903, Gibbons laid the cornerstone of the Apostolic Mission House on the campus, a building intended for priests who would take special training for missionary labors in the United States, and on the same day he turned the first spade of earth for the College of the Immaculate Conception, the house of studies of the Dominican friars, a structure that he dedicated on August 20, 1905. In the spring of the year 1905 the provincial of the Oblate Fathers purchased land across the street from the campus for a house of studies. Plans for a Sulpician seminary matured more slowly, and it was not until September, 1919, that Gibbons dedicated the Sulpician Seminary at Washington, and then only as a strictly Sulpician project, not as an intergral part of the university.

During the years of Monsignor O'Connell's rectorship the university suffered the loss of one of its most loyal and helpful trustees when a stroke of paralysis incapacitated John Lancaster Spalding. No one appreciated the loss more keenly than the chancellor. In telling Spalding of the reluctance with which the board of trustees accepted his resignation at their meeting in 1907, the cardinal said:

> In doing so, however, they recognized all your great services to the University in the past, and how in a sense you could be considered its founder and its ever-constant protector.

Later that year, the theological movement known in the Church as "modernism" reached its climax with the issuance of Pius X's encyclical, *Pascendi dominici gregis,* on September 8, 1907. When the trustees of the Catholic University of America met on November 16 they unanimously assented to the condemnation of the false doctrines enumerated in the encyclical. At the same meeting Gibbons appointed a committee of five to make recommendations concerning books in the library of the university that might contain modernist teachings. In fulfillment of his duty the cardinal addressed a letter to Pius X in which he stated the adhesion of the board of trustees to the encyclical. He also reported the spontaneous adhesion of all the instructors in the university and his personal assurance that as chancellor he would rigorously use his authority if necessary.

The modernist movement was European; its application to the Church of the United States was on the whole slight. In only one instance did the issues raised by the modernist movement call forth action from the cardinal chancellor. In this case, involving the complicated story of Henry A. Poels, associate professor of Old Testament Scripture, Gibbons found himself in the uncomfortable position of appearing to force the resignation of a scholar who, in full conscience and with priestly humility, could not accept the decision of the Biblical Commission that Moses must be held to have been the main and inspired author of the Pentateuch. Poels thought that although the Holy Father did not require Poels' resignation from the university, Gibbons was attempting to effect it merely "to please the Cardinal Secretary of State, even if I have to be wronged."

The position of Cardinal Gibbons in the Poels case entailed a great deal of anxiety. As chancellor of the university he was responsible to the Holy See for the doctrinal orthodoxy of the institution, and at a time when there was such widespread uneasiness in Catholic circles over the dangers of modernism, the cardinal was more than ordinarily sensitive. Moreover, as Gibbons had good reason to remember, less than fifteen years before, the university had passed through two severe trials: the controversy over the schools, which involved Professor Bouquillon, and the Americanism trouble in which Bishop Keane was removed from the office of rector. It was not surprising, then, that the cardinal should have felt that the university could not well stand to have its orthodoxy questioned again, and that therefore Poels' contract should not be renewed.

Monsignor O'Connell had gone to Rome in the summer of 1906 where he found the officials of the Holy See in a very agreeable mood toward the university. He told Gibbons that he learned of a desire among some to accord him an official acknowledgment for what he had done, as well as to accentuate the position of the rector. Without mentioning directly advancement to the episcopacy, O'Connell quoted his Roman sources as having referred to the fact "that all his predecessors had that character." The idea, of course, was altogether pleasing to the university's chancellor, and in the early winter of that year he wrote to Cardinals Satolli and Gotti with high praise of the rector; he urged that O'Connell be made a bishop. Rome did not respond to the original prompting, and in the autumn of 1907 the cardinal wrote again, this time to the pope himself. A few weeks later Raphael Cardinal Merry del Val informed him that the appointment would come in the next consistory. At last the nomination of O'Connell to the titular See of Sebaste was announced. Gibbons was overjoyed. He told the rector:

> You may know, but hardly to its full extent, how happy I was made this morning by your elevation to the Episcopate. It is just a month today since I wrote to the Holy Father.
> Now you can say with Card. Newman: "At last I am vindicated." Thanks to God.

On May 3, 1908, Cardinal Gibbons consecrated his eighteenth bishop when he performed the ceremony for his friend, Denis O'Connell, in the cathedral of Baltimore.

As O'Connell's first term ended, he made it clear that he did not wish to be reappointed. Despite the achievements of his rectorship, he was not happy. The root causes of his discontent are not too clear, and probably only Gibbons knew the complete background. O'Connell had made enemies within the university by his methods, and this hostility persisted after the question of conflicting jurisdiction between the rector and the academic senate had been settled in 1906 in the former's favor. The atmosphere continued to be unfriendly to the rector. At the semiannual meeting of the board of trustees in November, 1907, the trustees voted for a second term for O'Connell, but then, when O'Connell made it known officially that he did not wish a second term, the balloting ended with a unanimous vote for John Carroll, Bishop of Helena. Gibbons promptly informed Carroll that in accordance with the university's constitution, only his name would be forwarded to Rome. At the same time, the cardinal, with the consent of Archbishop Riordan of San Francisco, recommended O'Connell's appointment as auxiliary bishop of that city. On Christmas Eve, 1908, the third rector of the university was named Auxiliary Bishop of San Francisco.

Meanwhile Bishop Carroll was hurrying his preparations in Helena to finish the plans for his cathedral and college so that he might be free to take up his new duties in Washington when O'Connell's term would expire on January 11, 1909. But a week after that date Rome instructed the apostolic delegate by cable to inform Gibbons that the Pope did not deem it opportune to transfer Carroll from his diocese. Until candidates could be presented, Pius X named Thomas J. Shahan as prorector.

In compliance with the wishes of the Holy See the trustees at their meeting on April 22–23, 1909, drew up a *terna* for the rectorship with Shahan in first place. Gibbons forwarded the list to Rome and accompanied it with a powerful endorsement of Shahan. The appointment came through in a month's time. In the early autumn the chancellor requested of the Holy See that Shahan be made a domestic prelate, an honor that was likewise readily granted and with which Gibbons invested the new rector on December 16, 1909, in the chapel of Caldwell Hall.

During Roosevelt's second administration, disputes raging in the Philippines finally moved toward settlement. In 1906 the Supreme Court of the Philippines confirmed the Church's title to the ecclesiastical buildings put up originally for the use of its communicants. A thornier problem was the adjustment of the claims made by the Church for damages done to its properties during the time they were occupied by the American military forces.

The Archbishop of Manila, Jeremiah J. Harty, became aroused about the matter and, early in 1906, sent Gibbons a lengthy document sharply critical of the government. He asked the cardinal to forward the document to the president. The communication from Harty met with anything but a friendly reception at the White House. Roosevelt was distinctly annoyed by the strictures against the government's conduct in the islands; while he acknowledged that anything coming from Gibbons would have his careful consideration, the opening sentence of Harty's document, he said, prejudiced him against the whole of it. The offending sentence read:

From the time of American occupation of the Philippines the Catholic Church has been harassed and confounded with an apparently studied purpose on the part of the Government of the United States to control as its own if not to confiscate outright great charities of undoubted private origin.

Roosevelt maintained that such a statement was simply untrue. Nevertheless, he would submit the matter to Taft.

Gibbons found the role of mediator unenviable. He informed Archbishop Harty that Roosevelt had been "evidently displeased with the severe tone of the paper, & the manner in which the Administration was arraigned." The following day he told the president that he regretted having been requested to send him Harty's communication on account of the brusqueness of its language and the sweeping character of its complaints.

The presidential ire at the Archbishop of Manila was heightened when Harty published his letter. Now President Roosevelt was genuinely irritated. He was sincerely in favor of an appropriation for the damage claims, and he told Taft in June, 1906, that he would have sent a message to Congress on the Church's claims some time before had it not been for the publication of Harty's letter. If he acted now it would be construed as attempting to influence the fall elections, whereas he was determined to make it clear beyond a peradventure of a doubt that in dealing with the Church he was influenced solely by a sense of equity. Not until more than two years later was the final settlement made. In March, 1908, the sum of $403,030.19 was approved for payment to the Church in the Philippines.

In Puerto Rico, serious threats to the properties of the Church in the islands arose periodically. The changes in government, along with the departure of the Spaniards and the arrival of the Americans, had entailed a good deal of confusion over land titles. When the archbishops met in April, 1907, an appeal was read from Bishop William A. Jones, O.S.A., expressing the hope that the metropolitans would intervene with the United States government to have the disputed titles clearly vested in the Church so that the matter could be settled outside the courts. Nonetheless, it did reach the courts, and in June, 1908, the Supreme Court handed down its decision upholding the previous judgment of the Puerto Rico court in favor of the property rights of the Church.

By reason of the measure of self-government allowed to Cuba there was, of course, far more leeway for the local politicians to make trouble for the Church there than in Puerto Rico. When the Liberal Party won the elections of November, 1908, and took power with President José Miguel Gómez, the situation became grave. In the spring of 1910 the Apostolic Delegate to Cuba and Puerto Rico, Archbishop Giuseppe Aversa, informed the Holy See that the government was threatening to prohibit all external manifestations of religion and to forbid foreign priests and religious from entering the country. Once more the Holy See requested Gibbons to use his influence with the American government. The cardinal conferred in Washington with President Taft and Secretary of State Philander C. Knox, who were both sympathetic. In response to an inquiry, President Gómez assured Washington that the unfavorable legislation was not likely to pass, and that if it did he would oppose it. Taft passed this information on to the cardinal with the remark: "I hope you will regard this as ending the matter." Gibbons promptly summarized developments for Archbishop Diomede Falconio so that the apostolic delegate might, in turn, let Rome know that the danger had been averted. In the course of these negotiations, Gibbons reaffirmed his familiar stand on Church and State. In an important article in the *North American Review* in March, 1909, he was at pains to explain the Church's theological doctrine on the ideal union of Church and State. He made the distinction, however, that such an arrangement was not always the happiest solution in all countries; "while the union is ideally best, history assuredly does not prove that it is always practically best." Gibbons concluded his article with a paragraph that made his position quite clear:

American Catholics rejoice in our separation of Church and State; and I can conceive no combination of circumstances likely to arise which should make a union desirable either to Church or State. We know the blessings of our present arrangement; it gives us liberty and binds together priests and people in a union better than that of Church and State. Other countries, other manners; we do not believe our system adapted to all conditions; we leave it to Church and State in other lands to solve their problems for their own best interests. For ourselves, we thank God we live in America, 'in this happy country of ours,' to quote Mr. Roosevelt, where 'religion and liberty are natural allies.'

It was ironical that Gibbons should have quoted Roosevelt in this article, for their friendship proved to be the occasion of some embarrassment to the cardinal in the spring of 1910 after Roosevelt had retired from office.

The ex-President arrived in Rome the first week in April on his return from a hunting trip in Africa, and the visit provoked a public storm when he grew angry at the Vatican's request that he cancel an engagement with Methodists and, in turn, lost his temper with the Protestant group when one of their number made an insulting reference to Pius X. In the end Roosevelt left Rome without visiting either the Vatican or the Methodists. The affair caused great commotion on both sides of the Atlantic, and political circles worried about its effect on the American electorate. Gibbons visited President Taft at the White House soon after the news broke, and as he was leaving he remarked: "The President and I both regret this incident."

Yet despite the tension, the unfortunate incident did not cause a break in the friendship of Gibbons and Roosevelt, for in the following year, the former president came to Baltimore for the civic celebration of the cardinal's jubilee, publicly lauding him in the highest terms.

The ceremonies surrounding Cardinal Gibbons' silver jubilee as a bishop in 1893, dramatic as they were, were far overshadowed by the splendor with which the nation did him honor in 1911 as he reached the fiftieth anniversary of his priesthood and the twenty-fifth of his cardinalate. By that time his position in national life had been firmly established; his name was a household word throughout the land, and the occupant of the White House, William Howard Taft, numbered him among his intimate friends. On May 19, 1911, the Baltimore *Sun* announced the resolutions passed by the Baltimore city council giving its warm approval to a civic celebration for their foremost citizen who was described as "a pattern for Americans, an illustrious example to all men, without distinction of creed or party. . . ." Among the earliest to signify that he would be there was Theodore Roosevelt, who said: "The Cardinal is a trump; and I earnestly desire to do him honor."

Two days before the demonstration the New York *Herald* published a lengthy interview with Gibbons, all of which was given over to a discussion of what he believed to be the greatest defects in

American life. The evils that the old churchman arraigned were Mormonism and divorce, the imperfect and secularized system of public education, the desecration of the Christian Sabbath, the unreasonable delays in carrying into effect decisions of the criminal courts, and the corruption and frauds that often attended elections.

On the afternoon of June 6 a crowd estimated at 20,000 persons gathered in the Fifth Regiment Armory in Baltimore for the civic celebration of the cardinal's jubilee. President Taft arrived from Washington on a special train that carried Vice-President James S. Sherman, Champ Clark, speaker of the House of Representatives, members of the cabinet and the supreme court, and large delegations from both houses of Congress. In fact, as the Washington *Post* reported the next day, "The business of the United States government, superficially at least, was at a standstill for four hours. . . . Assistant secretaries held down the lid in most of the government departments. . . ." Chief Justice Edward D. White made a special trip from New Orleans for the event. Ten speeches were made during the course of the afternoon. Governor Austin Crothers led off with a welcome from Maryland to the distinguished assemblage. He was followed in turn by the president, Sherman, Roosevelt, Senator Elihu Root, Ambassador James Bryce of Great Britain, Clark, Joseph G. Cannon, former speaker of the House of Representatives, Mayor James H. Preston of Baltimore, and finally the cardinal. All the speeches were brief, but the encomia heaped upon the guest of honor added up to the most remarkable demonstration of universal esteem for a private citizen ever witnessed in the United States. Taft said that the present assembly could find few counterparts in history. They had gathered, he said, not as members of any religious denomination nor in any official capacity, but rather to honor in Cardinal Gibbons one who in his long and useful life had "spared no effort in the cause of good citizenship and the uplifting of his fellow men." The president lauded the services that Gibbons had given to the nation by his inculcation of respect for constituted authority and for religious tolerance and by his continuous whole-hearted interest in the moral and material welfare of all elements of the population. "But what we are especially delighted to see confirmed in him and his life," said Taft, "is the entire consistency which he has demonstrated between earnest and single-minded patriotism and love of country on the one hand, and sincere devotion to his church and God upon the other."

Thus the tributes flowed on until it reached the moment when the cardinal rose to reply. He felt satisfied, he said, that the speakers had portrayed their subject, not as he was in reality, but as he ought to be. "But I have become so enamoured of your portrait," he continued, "that it shall be the endeavor of my life to imitate and resemble that portrait more and more during the few years that remain to me in this world." Gibbons claimed one merit, an earnest and ardent love of his native country and of its political institutions. He was persuaded that the government of the United States was one of the most precious heirlooms ever transmitted to posterity. He would have all Americans impress upon their minds the truths that the president and his colleagues were divinely appointed ministers of the law, that they represented Him by whom kings reigned and lawmakers decreed just things. He concluded by saying: "And, therefore, it should be the duty and the delight of every citizen to co-operate with our Chief Magistrate and his aides, and to bless them as they are steering along the destinies of our beloved and our glorious republic."

June 6, 1911, would ever remain as one of the most memorable days in a long life filled with unusual events. And yet Gibbons took the demonstration in the same unruffled manner with which he had met most of the striking circumstances of his colorful career. In fact, it was later said of him: "There was not in all the thousands a more unassuming man than he who was the central figure of the demonstration."

The golden jubilee of Gibbons' priesthood was climaxed in October of 1911 by a three-day celebration largely ecclesiastical in character. Three issues, said the cardinal in a sermon in his cathedral, were now before the American people, and he was opposed to all of them: the election of United States senators by popular vote, the making of the acts of state legislatures subject to the suffrage of the people, and the recall of unpopular judges before the expiration of their terms of office. Gibbons was unimpressed by the argument that legislatures were subject to corruption, and, therefore, should not elect the senators, for if legislatures were corrupt, so, too, would be the people from whom the legislators sprang. Subjecting acts of the state legislatures to mass vote was, to his mind, substituting mob law for established rule. And to recall a judge for decisions that were unpopular was an insult to the dignity, independence, and self-respect of the judiciary. Far less menacing to the republic was an occasional corrupt or incompetent judge than one who would be the habitual slave of a capricious multitude, constantly adjusting his decisions to the popular whims.

On Sunday, October 15, solemn pontifical Mass was celebrated in the cathedral by the cardinal in the presence of the apostolic delegate, Archbishop Falconio, nine other archbishops, and forty-six bishops. The sermon at the Mass was preached by Archbishop John J. Glennon of St. Louis, who stated that Gibbons' career had been unique in the history of the Church. Speaking of the cardinals of an earlier day, he said:

> We may not deny their greatness, their learning, their consecration; but, unlike any one member of either group, our Cardinal stands with the same devotion to his country as Richelieu had for France, cultivating a citizenship as unstained as Newman, and while reaching out to a broader democracy than even Cardinal Manning, he still remains pre-eminent in his unquestioned devotion to Holy Church.

The year of his jubilee, Gibbons gave unrestrained support to a new missionary society of American priests. The two persons chiefly responsible were Fathers Thomas F. Price of the Vicariate Apostolic of North Carolina and James A. Walsh, director of the Society for the Propagation of the Faith in the Archdiocese of Boston. Gibbons was well acquainted with Price from his days in North Carolina where years before he had given this first native priest of the state his first Communion, confirmed him, and shown him great kindness in the pursuit of his vocation. It was, therefore, no stranger who presented himself on Charles Street in the early spring of 1911 to seek the cardinal's approval of the plan for the foreign missions. Gibbons gave him a warm reception and suggested that he consult the apostolic delegate. Shortly thereafter, he likewise addressed a lengthy letter to the metropolitans in which he cited the need for a seminary in the United States to train priests for the foreign missions. He noted Cardinal Manning's observation concerning the increase of vocations in England after the Church there had bestirred itself for the missions abroad, quoted Cardinal Vaughan's warning that the prosperity of the American Church would hardly endure if it failed to assume its share of the missionary endeavor in foreign lands, and noted that the American Protestants had been in the foreign mission field for over a century. Gibbons also submitted at this time a practical plan of action. He suggested the establishment of a missionary seminary that would be independent of any diocese and would be directly under the Congregation of the Propaganda. He stated that since sufficient funds were already at hand to make a humble beginning, as well as the promise of several burses, the question of money would prove no immediate obstacle.

A month later the metropolitans gathered for their annual meeting, and at that time Gibbons won their unanimous agreement. The minutes read:

> We warmly commend to the Holy Father the two priests mentioned as organizers of this Seminary, and we instruct them to proceed to Rome without delay for the purpose of securing all necessary authorization and direction from the Propaganda for the proposed work.

Walsh and Price lost no time in carrying out this mandate. In Rome they were kindly received by Pius X and Cardinals Merry del Val and Gotti. As Price said, the doors were thrown wide open to them as the result of Gibbons' and Falconio's letters of recommendation. One thing remained to be decided at once, and that was the name the new society should take. Price told Gibbons of "our united desire that you should have the honor of naming it." He then suggested as a name the Catholic Foreign Mission Society of America so that it would emphasize that the Catholic Church of the United States was now actively in the field. The cardinal approved the name and it was, therefore, adopted. The young society prospered, and on September 8, 1918, Father Price set out for China as the superior of a group composed of himself and three other priests, the first of the many Maryknoll missionaries to devote their lives to spreading the faith in the Orient.

The year after his jubilee, Gibbons finally found a suitable opening to secure his favorite, Denis O'Connell, as one of his suffragans. After the death of Bishop Van de Vyver of Richmond on October 16, 1911, the cardinal presided at his own residence over the meeting of the Richmond consultors on November 15, and he rejoiced when O'Connell received five of the six votes for the first place. A week later the bishops of the province also chose him as first on their *terna;* Gibbons jubilantly informed his friend that he now had high hopes of success.

Early the following year the cardinal learned of O'Connell's appointment to Richmond. There were probably few ceremonies during his many years as metropolitan of the Province of Baltimore that Gibbons performed with a fuller heart than that of installing Denis O'Connell as seventh Bishop of Richmond in St. Peter's Cathedral on March 19. In his sermon on that occasion he stated that it was rare, indeed, for any bishop to be chosen for a diocese with such exceptional concurrence as O'Connell had enjoyed. Addressing the clergy directly, the cardinal said he was persuaded that if they had the selection of their ordinary, they would have named O'Connell. "Like the people assembled in the Church of Milan," he continued, "who suddenly cried out: 'Let Ambrose be our Bishop,' you would have exclaimed: 'Let Denis J. O'Connell be placed over us.'"

By the spring of 1912 Gibbons was nearing his seventy-eighth birthday, and his auxiliary bishop, Owen B. Corrigan, pastor of St. Gregory's Church in Baltimore, and nine of his consultors and irremovable rectors presented him with a formal request that he take steps to insure a successor of his own choice by asking for a coadjutor. The petitioners stated that they had so long enjoyed the happiness and peace of his fatherly administration that, in view of what had taken place in other American dioceses, they could not regard the future without serious apprehension. While they prayed and had every reason to expect that the cardinal would be with them for many years, yet the archdiocese must some day suffer its greatest loss, a loss that would be aggravated a hundredfold if they were totally unprepared for it. For that reason they humbly begged Gibbons to mitigate the sorrow of the future by preserving them from the evils of a vacant see, by taking action now while he was in perfect health and in a position to have his wishes favorably considered by Rome. The cardinal was reminded that the evils incident to a vacancy in any diocese would be greatly increased in the case of the premier see because of its proximity to the seat of government, to the Apostolic Delegation, and to the Catholic University of America. Therefore, it was proposed that Gibbons select three names to be presented to the Holy See; the consultors and irremovable rectors would pledge themselves to vote officially for these three persons. To assure the cardinal of the spirit that motivated their suggestion, the petitioners stated:

We should be pained beyond expression if our action should give rise in your mind to a doubt of our affectionate loyalty to Your Eminence. Our action is prompted by no disaffection towards your benevolent administration either in the past or in the present. We desire no change. Should you in your wisdom and generosity accede to our wishes, we beg that all jurisdiction and authority be retained absolutely by Your Eminence, and that the Coadjutor be given a vacant parish or provided with a residence at the Seminary.

This petition met with no success.

One persistent rumor did, however, move Gibbons to act. He ordinarily discounted rumors, but by the winter of 1913–1914 the reports had grown so persistent that the Holy See intended to divide the Archdiocese of Baltimore and erect a new see at Washington that the old cardinal decided upon a trip to Rome to lay his protest directly before the Holy Father against an eventuality of this kind. He informed the pope in measured words that many bishops, out of their love and veneration for the See of Baltimore, looked upon this proposal with disfavor; they had urged Gibbons to make known to the Pontiff certain grave reasons why it should not be carried out. Insofar as Washington was concerned, the Catholics there had neither the numbers nor the resources to support a bishop; heavy debts compelled some of their parishes to have recourse to Baltimore to meet their obligations. As for Baltimore, such a separation would lessen the prestige of the premier see which, in comparison to other American dioceses like New York, Chicago, Boston, and Philadelphia, was very small. Furthermore, the Archbishop of Baltimore was by appointment of the Holy See *ex officio* chancellor of the Catholic University of America; many inconveniences would arise were the university to be separated from the chancellor's ecclesiastical jurisdiction. "In the interest of truth," said Gibbons, "I must say that when the University went through its most critical period, were it not for myself and the Clergy of Baltimore, it would have ceased to exist." As for himself, Gibbons remarked that his life was now far advanced. He prayed, therefore, that his declining years might not be clouded by the humiliation of a dismemberment of his archdiocese. "The Holy See could not in a more acceptable manner crown my earthly career," he said, "than by sparing me this tribulation which would bring me with sorrow to my grave." Gibbons' protest proved effective. In fact, a quarter of a century lapsed before the names of the two cities were joined in a dual jurisdiction under a single ordinary on July 22, 1939, and not until November 15, 1947, was a complete separation effected when the two archdioceses were given their own archbishops.

With the elections of 1912 approaching, one last major concern redirected the cardinal's attention to the Philippines. Early in 1912 agitation began within the Democratic Party to have inserted in its platform a statement that would commit the party to early independence for the islands. When news of this reached Manila, Archbishop Harty became genuinely alarmed. He hastened word to Baltimore asking the cardinal to induce the American hierarchy to work against independence. He said it was the consensus of the white men in the Philippines that the natives were not yet ready to govern themselves and would not be ready for a long time. In the lengthy communication Harty detailed other reasons for his view and concluded by saying: "Sooner or later Japan would swoop down on the islands, annex them, and blot out any vestige of Christianity that might be found." Two days later Harty remarked that if it were known in the islands that the resident American bishops were working against independence they would be compelled, as he said, "to get out of the Philippines by night — thankful if our lives were spared." Therefore, the utmost discretion was necessary.

As summer approached, Gibbons informed Ireland that he was to open the Democratic national convention with prayer the following month in his see city. Ireland — a pronounced Republican — replied: "Be on your guard while invoking blessings upon the Democratic Convention. Pray hard for the country, not so much for the party. I still hope that Mr. Taft will be nominated & elected."

The Democrats wrote Philippine independence into their platform and went on to win the election with their candidate, Woodrow Wilson. Taft deplored the plank, and after the election he asked Gibbons to come to the White House to discuss the issue.

The president and the cardinal lunched together on November 23 and went over all aspects of the question. As a result of their conference Gibbons got in touch with members of the American hierarchy and urged them to work against the Jones independence bill. He stated that early independence for the islands would be a serious blow to the Catholic Church there and would place its properties in dire jeopardy. The cardinal reported that the president had suggested that the energy of the hierarchy be exerted quickly to forestall independence. Gibbons urged the bishops to bring to bear all the influence at their command upon their congressmen and other important citizens. "The President," he said, "was particularly emphatic in the expression of these views, adding that the Catholic Church is the great bulwark against Socialism, the wanton destruction of property, and the violation of property rights, and that her power is sorely needed in the islands."

Both President Taft and W. Cameron Forbes, governor general of the Philippines, were gratified at the cardinal's action. Forbes forwarded a package of documents on Philippine affairs to give Gibbons fuller information on the subject, and a few days later he told him: "I am sure your action will have immense effect, and I am also sure that if this matter is followed up, the bill can be killed in its infancy." Cardinal Merry del Val was likewise pleased; he too doubted that the Filipinos were yet ready to govern themselves. He was certain that they were not prepared for their own ecclesiastical government. To his mind a native espicopate was not within sight, not within his lifetime. If it proved impossible to stop independence in one form or another, Merry del Val hoped that at least some sort of American protectorate could be retained that would safeguard the freedom of the Church and preserve Catholic education in the islands.

Later that year, the Boston *Evening Transcript* carried a feature story entitled, "Cardinal Gibbons on 'Our Duty in the Philippines.' " In the interview itself the cardinal stated he was irrevocably opposed to a scuttle policy in the Philippines, "today, tomorrow or at any fixed time in the future. . . ." He said he had maintained that taking the Philippines in the first place was open to question; but once in, the United States had the responsibility to finish the job. It was evident that Gibbons' opposition to the Jones bill was not political but moral in character. He noted that the Filipinos had not been consulted; but that even if a majority desired independence, he believed them utterly unprepared for the responsibility. Moreover, if the United States withdrew, there was danger of a lapse into barbarism and infidelity. Withdrawal would work an injustice on a large number of Americans who had invested in the islands. And the president, who was especially well informed about the islands, was altogether opposed. In conclusion the cardinal said:

I have no patience with the argument that the Philippine Islands are the source of an annual deficit to this country. Even were that true, the fact would not warrant a cowardly abandonment of the clear and accepted duty of the American people toward the Filipinos.

The interview in the Boston *Transcript* created quite a stir. Some days after it appeared Gibbons told Cardinal Merry del Val that almost every paper of importance in the country had carried it. He enclosed a copy of the interview and said that he had purposely emphasized law and order rather than religious interests for fear of arousing sectarian bias. He thought that a congressional majority would defeat the Jones bill; if it did pass while Taft was in the White House, it would certainly be vetoed. The incoming president, it was true, was supposed to be in favor of it because of the pledge of his party platform, but, said the cardinal, "he recently told a friend of mine that soon after his inauguration, he would call me in conference on the subject."

One who expressed himself as pained by the Gibbons interview was Manuel L. Quezon, resident commissioner of the Philippine Islands in Washington. He was only reluctantly led to believe, he said, that the interview really represented the cardinal's views. He recalled how the Spanish friars had lost prestige by working against a liberalizing regime in the islands; there was a danger, said Quezon, that American churchmen would now suffer a similar loss of standing with the people. The entire letter breathed an air of hurt surprise, and Quezon concluded by drawing attention to a clipping showing a group of Filipino priests writing to President-elect Wilson asking for independence for their country.

The opposition of the Cardinal of Baltimore played a part in temporarily checking the Wilson administration from pushing the bill in Congress. Even more important, his experience in dealing with the problems created by America's empire prepared him for the larger role he was destined to fill during and after World War I.

Chapter 7

The Final Years

Though Cardinal Gibbons lived past his eighty-sixth birthday, his health had never been robust. Slight of build, a little less than average height, he quickly felt any severe strain. From the early days of his priesthood, he suffered from a sensitive stomach and consequent periods of nervous exhaustion. When as an old man he was asked the formula to attain great age, he replied: "Acquire an incurable ailment in your youth." As a result of this condition he always confined his diet to the simplest dishes. Stewed chicken, corncakes, and smearcase or cottage cheese were among his favorites; he liked a little straight whisky before his meals and often enjoyed "bonny clabber," chilled milk that had begun to ferment. Even when dining out Gibbons adhered strictly to his simple diet. On one occasion his hostess had gone to considerable trouble to secure fresh crabs for a Friday dinner only to have the cardinal request a boiled egg!

The regularity of Gibbons' life helped to preserve his health. He rose at six o'clock each morning, took about a half hour for his toilet and for setting-up exercises, and then devoted about fifteen minutes to prayers at the *prie-dieu* in his room in preparation for his daily Mass, which he always said punctually at seven o'clock. Following Mass he made a thanksgiving of fifteen or twenty minutes at his kneeler in the cathedral sanctuary and then took a light breakfast at eight, read the Baltimore *Sun* and a part of his breviary. From nine to about noon of each day he either received callers or attended to his correspondence and other business. Around noon the cardinal changed from his house cassock to civilian attire and, with cane in hand, took a brisk walk through the neighborhood. A leisurely dinner about one o'clock was his principal meal; Gibbons was always intent that the conversation at table remain free from business matters.

Following dinner, the cardinal smoked a cigar and always took a siesta of a half hour, which, he claimed, enabled him to rise refreshed for renewed work. After further reading in his breviary he was ready for more business. About four-thirty or five o'clock each afternoon, weather permitting, he stepped forth into Charles Street for a second and longer walk. Returning to his residence about five-thirty, he then recited his rosary walking up and down the corridor. A modest supper about six-thirty was followed by another cigar during recreation. After that he recited Matins and Lauds from the breviary in anticipation of the following day. By nine o'clock each evening, unless he had gone out for dinner, the cardinal usually retired to his room where he read and worked at his high rolltop desk before night prayers, which were recited in time for him to be in bed at ten o'clock.

As a Baltimorean, Gibbons loved the city of his birth devotedly. By necessity absent from home for long periods of time, he was always happiest when he returned to Baltimore. While Gibbons was always attentive to his duties in the District of Columbia, nowhere in Washington did he feel the same contentment that he experienced in the old Baltimore mansion at 408 North Charles Street. For the first twenty years of his administration, he had no auxiliary bishop, and thus through the repeated confirmation tours to all parts of his jurisdiction, he came to know the priests and people very well. He delighted in the rich historical traditions of certain rural sections where the people had preserved the faith planted by the English Catholics 250 years before.

Almost every year he spent several weeks around the beginning of Lent with his brother John and his sisters Mary and Bridget in New Orleans. Each summer Gibbons took a holiday of several weeks at the seashore, in the earlier years at Cape May, New Jersey, or Southampton, Long Island, and in his last years at Spring Lake, New Jersey. His favorite refuge was always with the Shrivers of Union Mills, Maryland, a rural settlement about seven miles from Westminster. In the simple and dignified atmosphere of this Catholic family Cardinal Gibbons felt thoroughly at home. He frequently remarked that he knew of no finer Catholic family than the Shrivers. At Union Mills, as in the city, a definite program was followed: time apportioned for Mass and prayers, for reading the papers and answering the mail, for walks through the countryside or an occasional game of horseshoes or quoits in the summer and sledding in the winter. In the evening he was exceedingly fond of euchre. He did not play auction bridge since he disliked sitting out as dummy. The euchre games, the long walks, and the sociable chats at Union Mills never displaced his customary devotions, and each evening after supper Gibbons led the Shriver family in reciting the rosary as he walked up and down the porch in the summer and strode through the long parlor in the winter. The Shriver girls served him as temporary secretaries and prepared the dishes he relished, while their brothers drove him back and forth to the city, discussed current baseball or horse-racing news, and sometimes accompanied him on his walks or afforded him opposition at horseshoes. The life at Union Mills was simple, but everything about Cardinal Gibbons was simple, and that is one reason why it appealed to him so strongly.

To one of the simple temperament of Cardinal Gibbons even the suggestion of armed conflict between nations was abhorrent, and he never lost an opportunity to speak out in behalf of peaceful measures when he felt that his words might prove helpful. In 1913 he lent his support to an arbitration treaty between the United States and Great Britain as a device that would serve not only the principals but the whole civilized world. The United States and Great Britain had been more successful in reconciling legitimate authority with personal liberty than any other countries in the world, he said; therefore,

> Let Britannia and Columbia join hands across the Atlantic and their outstretched arms will form a sacred arch of peace which will excite the admiration of the nations, and will proclaim to the world the hope that with God's help the earth shall never more be deluged with blood shed in fratricidal war.

To his regret, no satisfactory arbitration treaty with England emerged.

Far more serious problems were inherited from the Taft administration. Ever since the overthrow of President Porfirio Diaz of Mexico in May, 1911, internal revolution gravely threatened thousands of American residents and millions of dollars of property owned by American business firms. Moreover, the fall of the Diaz regime brought on a persecution of the Catholic Church that grew in intensity as one revolutionary junta succeeded another at Mexico City. As American lives and property were lost, sentiment mounted in the United States for armed intervention, and by the spring of 1914 war hysteria was sweeping the nation.

Cardinal Gibbons both deplored the prospect of war and regretted the suffering of the Church in Mexico. On the occasion of his eightieth birthday, he gave an interview in which he emphatically denounced Venustiano Carranza and his rival, Francisco Villa, for their depredations against the clergy. The interview brought a quick response from Washington. Two days after it appeared, Senator Blair Lee of Maryland called on the cardinal at the request of President Wilson and Secretary Bryan. Lee brought a copy of a dispatch that the American government had sent to Carranza and Villa regarding the persecution of the Church. "The President and the Secretary of State," said an accompanying memorandum, "desire to advise the Cardinal that they feel reasonably sure of being able to prevent any objectionable recurrence." Wilson's dispatch led Carranza to instruct his Washington agent to assure the cardinal's representative in the capital that the rights of the Church in Mexico would be protected. All this information the cardinal relayed to the papal secretary of state, Cardinal Merry del Val.

Two days after his letter to Merry del Val the cardinal received a call from Hubert L. Hall of the Department of State. Hall, who had lived for some years in Mexico, informed Gibbons that Carranza had repudiated and condemned Villa's conduct toward the Church and had promised to carry out Wilson's instructions about the protection of its interests. The cardinal was willing enough to credit Carranza with sincerity, at least from self-interest, but he was not at all sure that Carranza could keep Villa and other rebellious agencies in check. He asked Hall to tell Secretary Bryan that if the rulers in Mexico behaved toward the Church there with the justice and charity that marked the conduct of the government of the United States, they would find their best support in the Catholic religion and in the hierarchy.

Meanwhile Cardinal Gibbons cautioned the Maryland provincial of the Jesuits that *America,* the Jesuit weekly, should mute its apprehensions over Carranza's arrival in Mexico City. He felt it would please the administration in Washington if the representatives of the Church would now abstain from harsh criticism, follow what he called "a benevolent though vigilant attitude," and give Carranza an opportunity to fulfill his promises.

At this juncture Gibbons' attention was distracted from the Mexican troubles by the death on August 20, 1914, of Pope Pius X.

The cardinal had just returned from Rome five weeks before. After having taken care of the work that had accumulated in his absence, the cardinal had left Baltimore on August 19 for Spring Lake. Within a few hours his vacation was cut short. The old cardinal was reluctant to make the long journey again. But his chancellor, Father Louis R. Stickney, persuaded him that as the dean of the American hierarchy he should be present at the conclave. Stickney arranged to have the *Canopic,* which was sailing from Boston that day with Cardinal O'Connell aboard, come to New York to pick up the Cardinal of Baltimore. On August 21, therefore, the day after the Pope's death, the two American cardinals set out. Cardinal Farley, who happened to be in Switzerland at the time, was in advance of his fellow countrymen.

The outbreak of World War I less than a month before heightened the dramatic character of the trip on the *Canopic.* The law governing a papal conclave stipulated that the cardinals begin their sessions ten days after the death of the Pope. In ordinary circumstances the timing would have been very close, but with an allied ship calculating the hazards from German submarines, the chances of arriving on time were further reduced. Gibbons and his companions landed at Naples on the morning of September 3. The conclave had opened on August 31, and on the morning of September 3, the choice had fallen on Giacomo Cardinal della Chiesa, Archbishop of Bologna. When Gibbons reached the Eternal City, therefore, he found the crowds rejoicing in the election of the new Pope, Benedict XV. Gibbons rushed to the Vatican where he and O'Connell had the distinction of having the first audience granted by the new Pontiff.

Gibbons remained in Rome for nine days to participate in the ceremonies that inaugurated the new reign. He also used the occasion of a subsequent audience with Benedict XV to request a red hat for Archbishop Ireland. Gibbons recounted to the new Pope all that Ireland had done for the Church, and, as he himself said, he took the bull by the horns in expressing the wish that some great recognition be made of these eminent services. When Ireland heard of this incident, he was deeply grateful, but not surprised; he said he had known Gibbons too long and too well to be surprised at any act of affectionate kindness that Gibbons might perform in his behalf. But the red hat never came to St. Paul.

After Gibbons arrived home, he continued his policy of watchful waiting on Mexico, convinced that annoying attacks upon the president, in the guise of petitions and resolutions, "might possibly result, not in securing any assistance in our cause, but in setting the entire Administration against us." Though he denounced the lawlessness of Carranza and Villa, he refused to embarrass President Wilson even when Carranza received *de facto* recognition in 1915. By 1917, when the new Mexican constitution contained serious violations of religious liberty and of the freedom to educate in religious schools, the increasing gravity of American relations with Germany prompted the president to support Carranza. Amid the clamor of World War I the voices of protest raised by Catholics were drowned out. Thus the Mexican revolution continued to run its course.

The inevitable suffering caused by the European war soon brought appeals for relief. In the early winter of 1914 the cardinal received an urgent cablegram from the Netherlands in behalf of the starving Belgians. "A word from Your Eminence to the American people," it said, "will touch the hearts and open pockets of thousands, who if they knew the terrible devastation and desolation of innocent Belgians, would for humanity's sake give freely." Gibbons acted at once, and $2,500 from the Archdiocese of Baltimore was turned over to the Maryland Committee for Belgian Relief.

When the American Jewish Relief Committee appealed for the vast numbers of Jewish people in dire straits, Gibbons instructed his secretary to inform the committee that he was confident the Catholic people of the United States would respond generously to this latest appeal. Late in the war Benedict XV asked Gibbons to appeal to President Wilson to get American Red Cross aid in to the starving Serbians. The difficulties were many, for the promises of the enemy powers to transmit and distribute relief could not be relied upon. "But you may be sure," said Wilson, "that if any way can be found, I shall be glad to find it."

Before World War I was a year old the Germans resorted to submarine warfare with the consequence that American lives were lost in increasing numbers. Resentment naturally heightened, and when the *Lusitania* was sunk off the Irish coast on May 7, 1915, with the loss of 128 American citizens, the press rang with denunciations. Gibbons, after expressing sorrow for the families of the victims and asking for prayers for the president, urged Americans to be calm and prudent. "Popular sentiment," he said, "is not a standard to be followed too hastily."

A week later, the apostolic delegate communicated to Gibbons the opinion of the papal secretary of state that the threat of revolutionary disturbances in Italy made it advisable that the American College be placed under the official protection of the United States. The cardinal got in touch immediately with Secretary Bryan who, in turn, cabled Ambassador Thomas Nelson Page at Rome to place the college under American protection if that should prove necessary.

When a German submarine commander violated his instructions and, on August 19, 1915, sank the *Arabic,* a British ship, with the loss of two American lives, the danger of a diplomatic break between the United States and Germany was for some days frighteningly real. Pietro Cardinal Gasparri cabled a request from Rome that Gibbons inform President Wilson that the Holy See had advised Germany to settle the question over the *Arabic* in a friendly manner and to refrain from sinking similar ships in the future. The cardinal was instructed to carry out his mission in a strictly confidential way. Four days later Gibbons called at the White House and read Wilson the Pope's dispatch. The President expressed his pleasure and requested the cardinal to convey his thanks to Benedict XV. Robert Lansing, the new secretary of state, also praised the Pope's dispatch; he later told Gibbons that it probably had much influence in the amicable decision that the German government had made.

Once more the press went astray, reporting that Gibbons had carried a message from the Pope asking the president to tender his good offices to the belligerents to bring about an armistice. The cardinal refused to disclose the purposes of his visit, other than to acknowledge that he had brought a message from Benedict XV to Wilson and that it had an "indirect bearing" on peace between the warring nations. In spite of the care with which Gibbons chose his words, the Baltimore *Sun,* the New York *Times,* and other papers continued to speculate on the possibilities of an armistice through the concerted action of the Vatican and the White House. The cardinal was unable to clear up the confusion, for the Holy See notified him by cablegram that he should not make any public statement about his visit to the White House.

The growing danger of involvement in the European conflict

touched off a variety of schemes for averting the menace to American peace. In the days before Henry Ford's ill-starred peace ship sailed for Scandinavia in the hope of bringing about an armistice through the neutral nations, Gibbons was quoted as seeing no hope in Ford's scheme. When a petition against Wilson's preparedness campaign was circulated by the Reverend Frederick Lynch, secretary of the Church Peace Union, Gibbons declined to give his signature; he would take no step that might embarrass the president in "his conscientious efforts to make reasonably secure the honor of our country." But the League to Enforce Peace, which had been organized in June, 1915, with William Howard Taft as its president, was a group to which the cardinal could give wholehearted approval. The platform of the league advocated arbitration of disputes between nations, but it left room for a nation to resort to war if necessary.

At few periods in Cardinal Gibbons' long life did his extraordinary qualities of leadership show to better advantage than during the years of World War I. In the steadily deepening crisis, his voice was heard with a respect accorded to few, if any, Americans outside official circles. Americans of every creed and walk of life had come to admire his wisdom, his patriotism, and his moral leadership. The Baltimore *Sun* of June 8, 1916, was not exaggerating when it hailed Gibbons on the thirtieth anniversary of his cardinalate in an enthusiastic editorial called "A Great American":

> We doubt whether anywhere in the world-wide territory in which his Church has raised the cross there can be found any other Cardinal or any other priest who touches humanity at so many points, who exercises such an influence among persons of every class and condition, believers and unbelievers, Catholics and Protestants, Jews and Gentiles. To all he seems to speak in their own tongues by some Pentecostal power, or by some subtle affinity that makes nothing human foreign to him. . . .

By the close of that year Gibbons had become the senior bishop of the Catholic world. But the deference shown to him was not because of age, but rather because of the gentle and kindly manner, the sound judgment, and the expansive affection with which he seemed to embrace all his fellow citizens.

The cardinal was willing to risk his prestige in unpopular causes. In the summer of 1916, for example, he favored the movement for universal military service. Gibbons believed that military discipline would help to develop young men's character and to improve their physical condition, as well as to instill in them the idea of obedience to lawful authority. The cardinal said he was persuaded that the president's preparedness campaign would make for peace rather than for war. Any nation thinking of an attack would be deterred, he said, "by recognition of the fact that our country is prepared for every emergency." This stand won the prompt gratitude of ex-President Roosevelt, who stated that he wished as an American to thank Gibbons for the pronouncement. The following year Roosevelt added this striking testimonial: "Taking your life as a whole, I think you now occupy the position of being the most respected, and venerated, and useful citizen of our country."

By the beginning of 1917, hopes for peace vanished. After the German announcement of unrestricted submarine warfare, the United States severed diplomatic relations on February 3. On March 16 and 17, three American ships, homeward bound, were attacked without warning and sunk by German submarines. On April 2 the president delivered his war message, and four days later war was declared on Germany. Cardinal Gibbons rose to the occasion. In a prepared statement for the press, he said:

> In the present emergency it behooves every American citizen to do his duty, and to uphold the hands of the President and the Legislative department in the solemn obligations that confront us.
> The primary duty of a citizen is loyalty to country. This loyalty is manifested more by acts than by words; by solemn service rather than by empty declaration. It is exhibited by an absolute and unreserved obedience to his country's call.
> Both Houses of Congress with the Executive are charged and sworn to frame those laws that are demanded by the present crisis. Whatever, therefore, Congress may decide should be unequivocally complied with by every patriotic citizen. The members of both Houses of Congress are the instruments of God in guiding us in our civic duties. It behooves all of us, therefore, to pray that the Lord of Hosts may inspire our national legislature and Executive to frame such laws in the present crisis as will redound to the glory of our country, to righteousness of conduct and to the permanent peace of the nations of the world.

The cardinal's statement was widely publicized and elicited favorable comment. Theodore Roosevelt wired from Oyster Bay: "With all my heart I thank you as an American for your noble and patriotic appeal."

As the war progressed, Gibbons was as good as his word about implementing one's loyalty to country. In May, 1917, he directed a pastoral letter to the priests and people of the Archdiocese of Baltimore in which he urged that they subscribe to the liberty-loan drive. "Let it not be said that we were weighed in the balance of patriotism and found wanting," said the cardinal. Late in the same month the cardinal's strong endorsement of the Red Cross was given to the press, and when Herbert C. Hoover came to Baltimore, he won Gibbons' assistance for the food-conservation drive, though Gibbons opposed the "bone-dry" amendment in the food administration bill. A few days after Hoover's visit the cardinal addressed another pastoral letter to his people, in which he confidently called on them to cooperate fully in the government's endeavors to conserve food.

The cardinal's desire to help the government did not cause him to neglect the Church's best interests. In June, 1916, Newton D. Baker, secretary of war, had given his approval to the distribution of army chaplaincies on the basis of the strength of the various denominations. A year later, however, this decision was reversed in favor of the old basis of alloting to the Catholics 16/67 of the total. When this news reached Gibbons he informed Baker of his disappointment, stated that Catholics had not been given their just proportion, and alluded to the unfortunate timing of this decision when Catholics were manifesting so fine a spirit of loyalty. The cardinal said there would be a heartier response to every sacrifice demanded of American Catholic boys, if they felt that their government was doing its utmost to furnish them the spiritual and moral helps they needed in the camp and in the field.

Cardinal Gibbons also kept in touch with the war efforts of private Catholic groups. He took time to write his congratulations to the Knights of Columbus for their plans to aid the servicemen. Later in the summer of 1917 the cardinal fully endorsed the meeting held on August 11–12 at the Catholic University of America under the chairmanship of John J. Burke, C.S.P., of the Chaplains' Aid Association of New York, to organize Catholic war efforts on a more unified scale. In November Gibbons addressed a letter to the American hierarchy, in which he asked the bishops if they would consent to the formation of a National Catholic War Council by the metropolitans. The response to Gibbons' appeal was generally favorable, and some weeks later the cardinal invited four bishops to act as an administrative committee to direct all Catholic activities in support of the war. Those selected were Peter J. Muldoon of Rockford, Joseph Schrembs of Toledo, William T. Russell of Charleston, and Patrick J. Hayes, Auxiliary Bishop of New York. In January, 1918, the committee met at the Catholic University of America with Bishop Muldoon as chairman and John F. Fenlon, S.S., as secretary. From that time to the close of the war the difficult problems that beset the committee were canvassed at regular intervals with Cardinal Gibbons and the other archbishops of the country.

As the embattled peoples of the world neared the end of the third year of fighting, sentiment for peace ran fairly high in all countries. Shortly after the failure of the Austrian peace proposals carried on through Prince Sixtus of Bourbon, Pope Benedict XV made his famous attempt to end the war on August 1, 1917. After informal soundings in Berlin and the allied capitals, the Pontiff proposed a definite set of points on which peace might be made: disarmament, arbitration of disputes, freedom of the seas, evacuation and restoration of occupied territories, renunciation of indemnities, and conciliatory examination of conflicting claims such as those relating to Alsace-Lorraine and the Trentino. After Gibbons took some measure of public opinion, he issued a full statement on the individual points raised by Benedict XV and sought to meet the principal criticism leveled against the papal proposals, namely, that they favored Germany. "If anybody calls this a pro-German document they must use words without meaning," he said, "for they include the destruction of Germany's military power, and subjection of her in future to a board of arbitration which would be able to coerce her if she tried to evade her obligations. . . ." He granted that the Pope's effort might be called noble idealism, which might or might not be realizable in fact, but the cardinal thought the principles laid down by the Pontiff offered the only hope for permanent peace.

But the allied governments were determined to abolish the German imperial government before they would end the war, and the well-intentioned effort of Benedict XV came to naught.

The growing antiwar feeling led in October, 1917, to the organization by a group of nationally known citizens into a League of National Unity. The cardinal was made honorary chairman. The group intended to arouse Americans of all creeds, classes, and occupations to the need for prosecuting the war to a successful finish. As Gibbons told the president:

> We are working to the end that our countrymen may see the folly and grave disobedience of unjust and ill-tempered criticism of national policies. We are bending our efforts to point out to our fellowmen that they in all probability see the present situation from only one angle, whereas the Government sees it from every viewpoint, and is therefore alone in the position to judge of the expediency of national affairs.

Wilson replied that he appreciated Gibbons' consenting to preside over the influential group that had so generously undertaken to support the administration's efforts to make the character of the war clear to the American people.

The designation by President Wilson of Sunday, October 28, 1917, as a day of prayer for the success of American arms was, of course, the sort of thing that met with a warm response from Gibbons. He preached on the occasion in his cathedral, insisting upon the citizens' paramount duty of obedience to their government, and their obligation in wartime to criticize its policies cautiously. The cardinal had no doubts about the endurance of the republic. But, said Gibbons, if the United States was to endure, it must rest on a stronger foundation than the genius of statesmen, the patriotism of the people, and the wisdom of the law. It must be based on a devout recognition of the overruling Providence who directed the affairs of nations and of men. "We have no union between church and state," the cardinal stated, "but this does not imply any antagonism between the two powers. Church and state amicably move in parallel lines, helping one another in their respective field of labor."

When in November, 1917, the Bolshevik government published the secret treaties binding the Allies, Gibbons joined in the clamor against the new evidence of the active hostility of the Italian government against the Vatican. By Article XV of the Secret Treaty of London of April 26, 1915, France, Great Britain, and Russia had agreed to "support such opposition as Italy may make to any proposal in the direction of introducing a representative of the Holy See in any peace negotiations or negotiations for the settlement of questions raised by the present war." The Vatican resented this unfair discrimination. As Gibbons became aware of pressures on the allies to ignore the clause, he arranged an interview in Washington with Lord Rufus Reading, the British ambassador, in February, 1918. In this conference, Gibbons urged that the clause excluding the Pope from the peace conference be eliminated. He pointed to the favorable effect that elimination would have on Catholic opinion both in the United States and in the British Empire. Furthermore, he warned that the American archbishops at their Easter meeting in 1918 might protest against this implied insult to the Holy See; this protest might lead to counterprotests that would produce a division of opinion better avoided during the war. Gibbons pointed to his own persistent policy of fostering good feeling toward the allies among the American people. "I firmly believe," he concluded, "that I am asking for what is best for the future welfare and relations of England and the United States."

Lord Reading informed the cardinal the following month that the British government had never contemplated and would never contemplate binding itself to a foreign government to obstruct what Reading called "any activities which the Holy See may wish to initiate on any subject connected with Peace or War." Yet Reading's reply made it clear that the British government would not sponsor the admission of the Pope's representative at the peace conference.

In June Cardinal Gasparri stated that when Gibbons would next see Wilson, he should tell him that Article 15 was insulting not only to the Holy See but to the Catholic hierarchy and people as well. All difficulty would be removed if Wilson would tell the Italian foreign minister that Article 15 should be either suppressed entirely, or at least modified. "Only the President of the United States," he said, "can say a friendly and at the same time an efficacious word to the Italian government."

Although the cardinal approached Wilson several times between mid-August and the close of the war on the question of an armistice, he apparently did not raise the issue of papal representation at the peace conference. By the early autumn of 1918 it must have become evident to even the most sanguine officials at the Vatican that nothing would be done to modify Article 15. Even when Gibbons, under prodding from Cardinal Gasparri, tried to get the territorial sovereignty of the Pope onto the agenda of the Paris peace conference in January, 1919, his efforts proved ineffectual against the hostility of the Italian delegation and the opposition or indifference of the other great powers.

In spite of all that Gibbons and his fellow Catholics in the United States and the other belligerent countries did to place the position of the Church and the true neutrality of the Holy See before the public, insinuations and unfair charges continued to be made. So persistent were the criticisms of the Holy See that Cardinal Gibbons undertook to answer them in an article entitled "The War Policy of the Pope," published in *America,* February 23, 1918. He first paid tribute to the fair-mindedness of Americans in listening to both sides of a question, and then judging it on its merits. He then outlined the extremely delicate position of the Pontiff as the common spiritual father of so many children at war with one another. The cardinal met the charge of papal silence by citing the numerous occasions on which Benedict had spoken for peace, in behalf of prisoners of war, and against the cruelties perpetrated against noncombatants. He cited the expressions of sympathy for the Belgians, whose sufferings the Pope had been accused of overlooking. As evidence of the feeling about papal policy in the camp of the enemy, he quoted the statement in the Hamburg *Fremdenblatt* of January 29, 1917, that the one belligerent power against which the Vatican had spoken was Germany. Speaking of the terrible ordeal through which the Pope was passing, Gibbons remarked: "Every act of his is watched, scrutinized by jealous, critical, hostile eyes, only too ready to find fault and to register blame." In closing, the cardinal expressed confidence that the people would continue to support the President in a spirit that would be "an earnest of complete victory and of a return of the happy peace for which he and the Holy Father are earnestly laboring, each in his own sphere."

Gibbons' article was widely reprinted in American and in European newspapers. According to an Associated Press dispatch to the Philadelphia *Public Ledger* of March 21, the Holy Father ordered the article to be translated and distributed, considering it to be "the most able exposition that had been given of the circumstances of his unique and difficult position."

The closing months of the war offered no surcease to the demands made upon the energy of the Cardinal of Baltimore. As the date approached for the Philadelphia convention of the League to Enforce Peace, Gibbons stated that he would recommend active participation on the part of the Catholic clergy. "Personally I feel," said the cardinal to ex-President Taft, "that the inauguration of such a league as you plan is essential at this stage of the world's history, otherwise we are likely to see retrogression instead of further progress in human affairs."

By the fall of 1918 it was evident that the end of the war was not far off. On October 4, Germany and Austria-Hungary appealed to Wilson for an armistice on the basis of his Fourteen Points. News of the armistice negotiations was transmitted officially to the Holy See by the Austrian government, and the Pope cabled an appeal to the president begging Wilson to hasten the end of the ruthless scourge that had too long afflicted humanity. Cardinal Gibbons was requested to see the president and to urge him to consider the Austrian appeal and thus to have the glory of bringing a speedy end to the conflict. The cardinal chose to write a letter instead of calling personally at the White House since, as he said, he did not wish to trespass on Wilson's valuable time, nor did he wish to offer "any occasion for comment which would likely be caused by my calling on you personally."

The President was grateful for the consideration of his time, although, as he said, "I must say that even amidst the rush of these days it would have been a welcome relief to have the pleasure of seeing you in person once more." He had every inclination of the heart to respond to the suggestion of Benedict XV and he hoped the Pope did not doubt that. But American relations with Austria-Hungary had become greatly complicated since his address on the Fourteen Points the previous January; the recognition of Czechoslovakia on September 3 and of the national aspirations of the peoples of Yugoslavia created obligations in honor toward them. Consequently Wilson concluded with the hope that Gibbons would convey to the Pope his great appreciation for the message and for the spirit that had prompted it.

The exhausting ordeal of World War I was at last brought to a close with the armistice of November 11. The Cardinal of Baltimore ordered his priests to substitute the prayer of thanksgiving in the Mass in place of the prayer for peace. To make certain that the victory would be celebrated in a fitting manner he gave instructions that a solemn service be held in all the churches of the archdiocese on Thanksgiving Day, November 28, at which the Church's official prayer of jubilation, the *Te Deum,* should be sung.

The era of World War I brought out more strikingly than ever before the unique position that Cardinal Gibbons had come to occupy in American public affairs. His influence far transcended the boundaries of his own archdiocese or even of his own country. In 1919 the celebration of Gibbons' fifty years in the episcopacy signalized this unique position. Pope Benedict XV told him that he had won the esteem of all Americans in so illustrious a manner that it was hardly surprising that men of every order should now join in paying him honor. President Wilson headed a large group of distinguished citizens who sent their good wishes, and Bishop William T. Manning of the Protestant Episcopal Church and Rabbi William Rosenau were among those who bespoke the high regard in which Gibbons was held by American religious leaders of other faiths. Henry Noble MacCracken, president of Vassar College, stated: "Upon the roll which history will set up as those whom she delights to honor because they lived American idealism up to the measure of her opportunity, your name, Sir, will surely stand among the very first." Alphonse A. DeWachter, Auxiliary Bishop of Malines, speaking from London in the name of the Belgian hierarchy who were not yet free to communicate on account of war conditions, told Gibbons that the whole Catholic world was in admiration of his long and fruitful career. On October 16, Jules Jusserand, French ambassador to the United States, extended the congratulations of his government:

> The fame and respect which Your Eminence enjoys in your native country are not restricted to her boundaries. The same are felt for you in France, where your great influence, ever exercised in favor of noble causes, and in these latter years in favor of the noblest of all, that of the reign of justice in this world, have won for you the admiration of everyone.

The actual date of the celebation in Baltimore found the city and the nation in the grip of a devastating influenza epidemic, so the principal commemoration took place on February 20, 1919, at Washington. On that date there assembled at the Franciscan monastery for the pontifical Mass, Gibbons, two other cardinals, O'Connell and Louis Begin of Quebec; the special envoy of Benedict XV, Archbishop Bonaventura Cerretti; the apostolic delegate, ten other archbishops, fifty-eight bishops, along with a large gathering of clergy and laity. Their kindness on this occasion was accompanied by a large purse that they presented to him at the dinner that followed at the university. Taken by surprise at this generous gesture, the old cardinal forgot to thank them publicly. He endeavored to make amends, therefore, by writing to them his gratitude for the gift, but still more, for their warm sentiments of esteem and affection.

If the victory over Spain in 1898 had made the United States a world power, the defeat of Germany and Austria-Hungary twenty years later projected American leadership into responsibilities of a much graver character. The Catholic Church appreciated the enhanced position of the United States and its president, and during the next two years the Pope and his secretary of state sought American assistance in the postwar problems that faced the Church in Europe. For any approach on the part of the Holy See to the American government, the Cardinal of Baltimore continued to be, of course, the ideal medium.

Immediately after the war petitions for food to prevent starvation were received with increasing urgency by the Holy See, and Cardinal Gasparri cabled asking Gibbons to intercede with the president in behalf of the victims of the famine in Germany. The president, not unmindful of the conditions in Europe, assured Gibbons that the papal request would receive the most considerate attention possible in the circumstances.

The needs that Hoover surveyed during his visit to Europe late in 1918 proved to be far beyond the original calculations. A year later, therefore, he appealed through Gibbons for a letter from Benedict XV to relieve in particular the plight of over three million children. "Remembering the enormous stabilizing value of the letter sent you by his Holiness in 1916," said Hoover, "I feel sure you will recognize the importance of help from such an authoritative source." Gibbons acted at once. The Holy Father promptly forwarded a warm recommendation of Hoover's efforts in appealing to the generosity of all Americans irrespective of creed or party. Gibbons adopted a similar tone in the United States, supporting the Jewish War Relief Committee and the Salvation Army, along with the Catholic agencies. He often made personal contributions as well. When Archbishop Cerretti was returning to Rome in the spring of 1919, Gibbons sent the Pontiff a sum of $5,000 for his charities. Belgium and its Catholic University of Louvain seemed to have a special appeal for the charity of Cardinal Gibbons, partly because of the plucky stand that the little country had made through the war years, and partly because of the noble bearing of Désiré Joseph Cardinal Mercier, Archbishop of Malines, whose fearless resistance to the German invaders had won worldwide fame long before the war had ended. At Gibbons' invitation, Mercier came to the United States in the fall of 1919. Following his visit to Baltimore, Mercier was received by the president. Thereafter the Belgian cardinal visited a number of cities throughout the country, where enthusiastic throngs gathered to pay tribute to his peerless leadership.

Some time before the departure of the president for Europe, Gibbons, "as an American as well as a Catholic, as one who is bound to you by the bonds of patriotism as I am bound to the Holy Father in the bonds of religion," requested Wilson to visit the Pope:

> I ask you to do this not only because it will be a great consolation to the Holy Father who so admires and trusts you, not only because it will bind the hearts of Catholics to you forever, but because it will delight the hearts of all good men, who whether they agree with the Holy Father in religion or not, at least recognize him as the representative of the greatest moral authority left in the world, and because you, Mr. President, in the opinion of all men, are the one who raised the late war from the plane of national jealousies into the plane of idealism and made it a conflict and a struggle for justice, for righteousness, for liberty and for nothing else.

Wilson in fact did visit Benedict XV on January 4, at the end of his stay in Rome, and later the same day the Pontiff paid a high tribute to the American chief executive.

After the Treaty of Versailles was signed and the American president submitted the treaty embodying the covenant of the League of Nations to the United States Senate, Under-Secretary of State Frank L. Polk asked a Washington pastor to ascertain if the cardinal would issue a statement for publication in favor of the League of Nations. Gibbons was reminded that some bishops had come out against the League because Ireland had failed to win self-determination while other bishops had insinuated that religious prejudice had deprived the Irish cause of a hearing at Paris. Polk feared that religious prejudice might be introduced into the coming congressional elections. For that reason, he thought "that if your Eminence would publicly say a word in defense of the League, the testimony would be used as an offset to any anti-League agitation because of Catholicity." Gibbons' response came in the form of an interview to the press on his eighty-fifth birthday:

It is my firm conviction that after thorough and honest discussion in both houses of Congress, both parties will finally arrive at a common agreement, based upon a just and sincere league of nations that will give us a reasonable guarantee against the horrors of war in the future as well as well-grounded assurance of lasting peace without in any way impairing American sovereignty or surrendering any American right and without involving us in entangling alliances. I am sure that an early adoption of the league of nations will infuse intense joy throughout the United States without distinction of party and will be hailed with satisfaction by the allied powers of Europe.

After reading the statement of the cardinal in the Washington *Post,* the president wrote him as follows:

You have perceived, as is habitual with you, the really profound interests of humanity and of Christianity which are involved in the issue of the adoption of the League Covenant, and it is with profound pleasure that I find myself aligned alongside of you in this great cause, to which the anxious and prayerful thought of every Christian man, it seems to me, must turn with hope that will permit no denial.

Cardinal Gibbons continued to the close of his life to try to convince his fellow countrymen of the wisdom of entering the League of Nations. In the winter of 1919 he joined a group of distinguished Americans in petitioning the president to accept the amendments offered by Senator Henry Cabot Lodge to the Treaty of Versailles, in order that the League of Nations might not be entirely lost. But neither Wilson nor Lodge would yield, the treaty failed to pass, and the United States remained outside the League.

Gibbons' ideas met defeat on domestic legislation as well. Since the Cleveland administration, presidents had resisted legislation to apply a literacy test to immigrants. The cardinal, as the ranking dignitary of a Church that was made up so largely of immigrants and as the son of immigrant parents, naturally commended their stand. The reappearance of the proposed legislation in the Wilson administration found Gibbons again in the camp of the opposition. What would the United States have amounted to as a nation, he asked, if after the Revolution its founders had closed its portals to honest but illiterate immigrants? Gibbons cherished the hope that his country might remain the refuge of virtuous men who conscientiously believed their native lands did not afford them the advantages that good men craved. Although Wilson vetoed the bill embodying a literacy test, it was enacted into law over the president's head in 1917.

Another defeat for Gibbons' position on a public question involved the ratification in January, 1919, of the eighteenth amendment to the Constitution. The cardinal was aware of the abuses of intemperance; his remedy was not national prohibition, but a strict licensing system. To cure the evil of excessive drinking he approved local option, giving voters in a community the right to forbid the sale of intoxicating liquor. At the time the United States entered World War I the prohibitionists redoubled their efforts and put the campaign on the basis of a war measure. The New York *Times* of April 29, 1917, carried a feature article on the question, in which it quoted Gibbons as saying: "I would regard the passage of a Federal prohibition law as a national catastrophe, little short of a crime against the spiritual and physical well-being of the American people." As the prospect of a constitutional amendment drew closer he stepped up his opposition. On February 6, 1918, the New York *Times* published the cardinal's statement that the state legislatures should not bow to fanaticism. He predicted that if prohibition became a law, illicit stills, making low-grade whisky, would spring up all over the land. Once more he characterized the enactment of such a law as a calamity. "Those favoring it," he said, "won't be satisfied and will try to impose other obnoxious laws until our liberty will be worth little."

Gibbons also opposed the constitutional amendment that guaranteed women's suffrage. The insistence on woman's participation in politics, the cardinal said, was calculated to rob her of all that was amiable and gentle and to give her nothing in return but masculine boldness and effrontery. Moreover, this insistence habitually emphasized woman's rights without a word about her responsibilities. The result was that women were distracted from their true vocation, the home and the cultivation of the domestic virtues of love for their husbands and children. Because women did not vote, it did not follow that they were deprived of the right of suffrage by proxy. So powerful was the influence of a sensible matron over her husband and sons, he maintained, that they would often follow her counsel. Woman was queen indeed, said the cardinal, but her empire was the domestic kingdom. Though she was debarred from voting, it was she who brought into the world the nation's future citizens; it was she who molded the characters of its future statesmen.

But the views of Gibbons and the opposition failed to gain the ascendancy, and on August 26, 1920, the nineteenth amendment to the Constitution granting the vote to women was declared ratified. On September 20 he gave out an extended statement which was published in most of the Catholic papers of the country. At the outset he remarked:

> While I have always been opposed to Woman's Suffrage because I felt that political activities would tend to withdraw women from the more delicate and sacred pursuits of home life, now however, that the vote is theirs, I strongly urge upon all of them the exercise of suffrage, not only as a right but as a strict social duty.

He added that it behooved Catholic women to take their new social duty seriously in the hope that they could minimize the evil forces that might menace the family and the home, the most essential factors in Christian civilization.

One of the most important problems facing the American Church upon the return of peace was the future status of the National Catholic War Council. Some opposition to the N.C.W.C. had arisen within the ranks of the hierarchy, and when Gibbons asked Muldoon to cooperate with the League to Enforce Peace, the bishop replied that he feared the program was too expensive and would involve too many hands. Then he added: "Some of the Bishops, as you know, do not look any too kindly on the National Catholic War Council and might be very willing to take our approval of the League as indicating that we were over-stepping our charter." Nevertheless, at the formal celebration of Gibbons' golden jubilee in 1919, Archbishop Cerretti expressed the Pontiff's wish that the American bishops join him in his efforts for a just and lasting peace and for the adjustment along the lines of Christian ethics of the many difficulties in the world of education and of labor. Later the same day a committee was appointed by the cardinal to investigate the best means of carrying out the Pope's desires. On the following day this committee recommended that in the future the entire hierarchy assemble in an annual meeting and that a standing committee of five bishops be appointed by Gibbons to supervise Catholic activities. The report was unanimously adopted. Two months later Benedict XV gave the new project his full approval.

After the appointment of the provisional committee, Gibbons communicated with his fellow metropolitans. Hitherto, he said, because of the courtesy of his colleagues in the hierarchy and because of the presence of the national capital within the limits of the Archdiocese of Baltimore, the burden of the Church's general interests had in great measure rested on him. "My experience has made me feel keenly," said Gibbons, "the necessity of such a committee which with adequate authority and the aid of subcommittees could accomplish more than any individual, however able or willing he might be." All recognized that the Catholic Church in the United States, partly through defective organization, was not exerting an influence proportionate to its numbers and to the individual prominence of many American Catholics. Diocesan units were well organized, but the American Church as a whole was suffering from "the lack of a unified force that might be directed to the furthering of those general policies which are vital to all." Gibbons then sketched his ideas of how a permanent committee, chosen by secret ballot at the meeting of the entire hierarchy, might represent the interests of the Church at large as well as the various sections of the country. To the bishops of the executive committee, Gibbons said he regarded the suggestion for their committee as a divine call. He believed that the formation of the committee would launch a new epoch in the Church of the United States.

On September 24, 1919, 92 of the 101 ordinaries of the United States gathered at the Catholic University of America. At the opening session Cardinal Gibbons once more stated his conviction that their present assembly held an extraordinary significance for the future of American Catholicism. The meeting then heard the report of Bishop Muldoon on the proposed departments — missions, education, press and literature, social service, Catholic societies and lay activities — and proceeded to discuss the question. Only one serious objection arose. Bishop Charles E. McDonnell of Brooklyn believed that such an organization would conflict with the constitution of the Church, according to which no bishop could exercise jurisdiction in another diocese without delegation from the Holy See.

The discussion of the first morning session produced a discouraging effect upon Gibbons; he feared nothing worthwhile would be accomplished. But Muldoon told him not to worry, that affairs would take a turn for the better, and that with the possible exception of the budget, the entire program would be finally accepted. As the bishop said later: "This seemed to cheer his good old heart."

After further talk. Bishop J. F. Regis Canevin of Pittsburgh moved that Muldoon's report be accepted, Archbishop Keane of Dubuque seconded the motion, and it carried. On the following day the hierarchy elected the administrative committee of the N.C.W.C. by secret ballot. Soon thereafter Father Burke, chairman of the Committee on Special War Activities of the old National Catholic War Council, was unanimously elected executive secretary to preside over the headquarters of the National Catholic Welfare Council in Washington. Cardinal Gibbons was able to win from the Paulist superior-general permission for Father Burke to devote his full time to the N.C.W.C.

By the time the country prepared for the presidential election campaign of 1920, the Cardinal of Baltimore was nearing his eighty-sixth birthday. By coincidence he was scheduled to be in Chicago the second week of June, 1920, the same week in which the Republicans gathered for their nominating convention. Gibbons was invited by the convention committee to offer the opening prayer on June 10, and he accepted the invitation. The nomination of Warren G. Harding that followed soon thereafter drew the cardinal's congratulations to the candidate. In the autumn of that year the cardinal told his brother privately that he favored Harding. But when he preached in the cathedral two days before the election, his preference of candidates was carefully concealed. Gibbons had prayed over the Democrats in Baltimore in 1912 and over the Republicans in Chicago in 1920, but to neither party did he make any public commitment, and those who might have been curious about his political faith could only indulge their imaginations.

After Harding's election, the president-elect expressed the hope that among the first whom it would be his privilege to receive in the White House would be the cardinal. But by the day of Harding's inauguration on March 4, 1921, the cardinal was less than three weeks removed from death, and he was thus denied the pleasure of seeing his candidate as the occupant of the executive mansion.

As the years went on, Gibbons never lost his zeal for the university, and in the last summer of his life he was still rallying the American hierarchy to the university's support. In the final letter that he wrote in preparation for the annual collection he remarked:

> The years of my earthly life are drawing to a close, and in the way of nature I must ere long appear before my judge. I could have no greater happiness in these remaining years than to know that the Catholic University of America was placed on a solid basis for the present, in keeping with its admitted needs, with its encouraging growth and progress, and with the educational interest of our Catholic people.

Six months before he died Cardinal Gibbons presided for the last time as president of the university's board of trustees. He was encouraged by the rector's report that the annual collection of the year before had amounted to $150,000, that generous donations had been received for the National Shrine of the Immaculate Conception on the university campus, that the faculty now numbered eighty-seven, and that, because of the end of the war, there was an increase of 336 students over the previous year. Two days later Gibbons laid the cornerstone for the great church recently begun on the campus. It was the last important function over which the aged chancellor presided at the university.

At the annual meeting of the hierarchy in 1920, Gibbons had to deal one more time with the thorny problem of national loyalties within the Church. As time had passed, the acute character of the German problem had passed with it; but the new century, with its greatly accelerated immigration from eastern Europe, created new difficulties for Gibbons. Archbishop Giovanni Bonzano, the new apostolic delegate, had sent him a group of documents that revealed that the Polish minister to the Holy See had intervened at the Vatican in behalf of the appointment of bishops of Polish descent to the American hierarchy. In replying, the cardinal told Bonzano he would bring the matter to the attention of the bishops' meeting about to convene, but, as for himself, he had always followed the practice of recommending to vacant sees the most suitable candidates without consideration of nationality. At the meeting of the hierarchy Gibbons delivered a strong speech against recognition of any national groups within the American Church. "Ours is the American Church," said the cardinal, "and not Irish, German, Italian or Polish — and we will keep it American." One bishop who was present later wrote of Gibbons' remarks: "He was at his best, and seemed only about fifty years [of age]."

Two months later the Archbishop of Baltimore forwarded to Cardinal Gasparri a very strongly worded protest against the action of the Polish legation at the Holy See. Gibbons quoted the two pertinent resolutions, passed unanimously at the meeting of the American hierarchy in September, that condemned the interference of any foreign government in the affairs of the Church of the United States and the conduct of any body of clergy who would appeal to laymen or to a foreign government to coerce the episcopate in the selection of candidates for vacant sees. He stigmatized the move for Polish bishops as a step toward isolating the Polish Catholics from the rest of their coreligionists, and he branded the attempt to preserve a distinct Polish nationality in the United States as "absolutely injurious both to the Church and to the Country." Thus did the aged cardinal deal in his last days with what John Gilmary Shea had called "a canker eating away the life of the Church in the United States."

Late in the year 1920 symptoms of a break in the cardinal's normal health appeared. On November 7 he had an engagement to administer confirmation at St. Patrick's Church in Havre de Grace, Maryland. In the course of a sermon Gibbons suddenly faltered and almost fell down. Yet after a few moments he steadied himself and finished the sermon from a chair with his accustomed earnestness. He later confirmed a class of over 100 children and adults, and before the day was out held two receptions. Upon his return to Baltimore, the old churchman continued to suffer periodic recurrences of labored breathing, difficulty in ascending the stairs, and momentary losses of consciousness. But his general appearance offered reassurance to his close associates.

The following month his physician, Dr. Charles O'Donovan, attributed the condition of the cardinal to nothing except the increasing physical weakness of one of advanced age. This general debilitation continued at Union Mills, and on December 9 Gibbons said Mass for the last time in the Shriver oratory. Soon he was unable to leave his bed unaided, and on December 17 the cardinal was anointed. Once more he rallied, and he was able to assist at Christmas Midnight Mass in his bedroom. It was the first Christmas in fifty-two years that James Gibbons had not celebrated a pontifical Mass.

In the closing days of 1920 Cardinal Gibbons gave the final interview of his life to Bruce Barton, then a reporter for the *American Magazine*. He told Barton that he liked young men, and when the reporter commented on the youthful appearance of the priests of his household, Gibbons replied: "Until you are forty, seek the companionship of men who are older. After that, keep a vital contact with those who are younger." He said that until his recent illness he used to walk every afternoon from five to six o'clock with one or more of the students from St. Mary's Seminary. "And do you want to know what I say to them?" he asked. "I say, 'Young man, *expect* great things! Of God, your fellow men, yourself, and America.'"

The reporter then inquired what program of life the cardinal would recommend for success. Gibbons replied: work, patience, and thrift. Theodore Roosevelt was, to his mind, a man who owed much of his success to his tireless labor, and in Abraham Lincoln, Gibbons found a prototype for patience. As for thrift, he confessed that to urge it might sound trite. It was trite, but he had no apology to make in offering it as a necessary quality for success in life. "The law of God is the law of thrift," he remarked, "and no man transgresses that law, either in his personal or business affairs, without incurring a penalty."

The cardinal knew the conditions in the business world that made it so difficult for young men at that time to find employment and to get established. He then quoted the Biblical verse, "Whom the Lord loveth He chasteneth." He admitted that it was a very hard verse, indeed, for American youth to learn. But those who were old like himself knew its meaning, for the chastening of adversity was an act of God's love, not of His punishment, since human nature was not fitted to stand the strain of unremitting prosperity. What the world needed most, according to Gibbons, were men of character and ideals, like the hero of *Tom Brown's School Days* who knelt down and offered up his prayers in the dormitory at Rugby in spite of all taunts; it needed men who had the courage to stick to virtue, truth, and high thinking through adversity and prosperity alike. Such men were not made by easy times alone; they came only through the molding and hardening of trial, disappointment, and difficulty.

Barton had told Gibbons that the interview would appear around the time of Easter. That led the cardinal to a brief review of our Lord's exaltation on Palm Sunday and the dreadful fate that He suffered on Good Friday. The thought prompted the old man to say:

> This is the message of Easter — the message of eternal Faith. At the darkest hour the stone of discouragement is rolled away; despair is lost in glory. And only those whose hope has died, a martyr to their doubts, fail to share in the splendor of the resurrection.

The Barton interview was an unusually buoyant message from an enfeebled old man in his eighty-sixth year who was then only about three months removed from death.

Early the next year, the last article that the cardinal wrote was published in the *Catholic Review* of Baltimore. "As the years go by," he said, "I am more than ever convinced that the Constitution of the United States is the greatest instrument of government that ever issued from the hand of man." He emphasized the personal liberties that had found protection in the document, and he instanced especially that of religious freedom. Other features of the Constitution that earned his praise were the autonomy enjoyed by the several states and the sacred privilege of the ballot.

It was appropriate that the last article from Gibbons' pen should have been devoted to this subject. He had spoken many times of the sacred character of the Constitution, but probably none was more eloquent than this final summary.

Gibbons understood the gravity of his illness, and as the year 1920 drew to a close, he begged to return to Baltimore so that he could die in his own home. After the doctors had given their consent, arrangements were made to convey the invalid to the city. On January 3 he left Union Mills. Back again in the beloved environment of the old mansion where he had lived for over forty-three years, Gibbons' strength picked up somewhat, and although he was no longer equal to his customary walks, he was well enough through the next two and a half months to take frequent automobile rides through the city.

After his customary ride on Sunday, March 20, the Bon Secours Sister who was nursing the cardinal noticed a sudden change and summoned the priests. The following morning he received Holy Communion for the last time, having previously been anointed and made the profession of faith prescribed for a dying bishop. The cardinal became unconscious on Tuesday evening and remained in that condition through most of the next day. Near midnight of Wednesday he woke and told Father Stickney, rector of the cathedral, that he would die on the morrow. In the absence of his regular confessor he requested Stickney to hear his confession, and soon thereafter he lapsed again into unconsciousness until death took him on the morning of Holy Thursday, March 24, at 11:30 o'clock.

Hardly had the news of the cardinal's death been flashed to the country and the world when a stream of cables, telegrams, and letters from men and women in every walk of life began flowing into the episcopal residence. Cardinal Gasparri cabled, in the name of Pope Benedict XV: "The august Pontiff has learned with profound sorrow of the death of His Eminence Cardinal Gibbons. He offered up prayers for the soul of the worthy prelate and sends heartfelt condolences to Your Lordship, to the clergy and to the faithful of the Archdiocese." Within a few hours after the cardinal's death President Warren G. Harding sent the following telegram:

> In common with all our people I mourn the death of Cardinal Gibbons. His long and most notable service to country and to church makes us all his debtors. He was ever ready to lend his encouragement to any movement for the betterment of his fellowmen. He was the very finest type of citizen and churchman. It was my good fortune to know him personally and I held him in the highest esteem and veneration. His death is a distinct loss to the country, but it brings to fuller appreciation a great and admirable life.

Practically all the leading secular papers from the Atlantic to the Pacific gave generous space to Gibbons' history and expressed their glowing appreciation of the significance of his life to the Church and to the nation. The New York *Times* on March 25 said that for many years his name had been one that "had the majesty of ecclesiastical, moral, and intellectual authority, the dignity, influence and power of a great nature and mind." To the *Times*, "He was one of the wisest men in the world." The New York *Herald* of the same day declared;

In the sense that Francis of Assisi is everybody's saint, James Gibbons was everybody's Cardinal. No matter what their religious beliefs, Americans who knew him held him in the highest respect and esteem.

Because the cardinal's death had occurred in Holy Week, his remains were not brought to the cathedral until Monday, March 28. There the body lay in state before the high altar, his red hat resting against the foot of the casket and his numerous decorations from foreign governments and from civic organizations displayed nearby. It was estimated that over 200,000 people were admitted to the cathedral during those three days and nights. Long lines that formed a block away on Mulberry Street slowly moved forward to view for the last time the face of one whom they had learned to love in life.

By the morning of March 31 there had arrived in Baltimore two of Gibbons' fellow members of the College of Cardinals, O'Connell of Boston and Begin of Quebec, along with Archbishop Bonzano, who as apostolic delegate to the United States was to celebrate the pontifical requiem, nine other archbishops, and forty-three bishops. The President of the United States was represented at the funeral by Postmaster General Will H. Hays. Among the mourners were Chief Justice White, the governors of Maryland and Ohio, members from the two houses of Congress, the envoys of a dozen foreign nations, and a score of Protestant and Jewish clergymen, together with a vast throng of minor prelates and priests from Baltimore and other cities. The cathedral was filled to capacity. The funeral sermon was preached by Archbishop Glennon of St. Louis. At the end of the funeral Mass the customary absolutions were performed by four of the late cardinal's suffragans. With that the long ceremony came to a close and the distinguished assemblage dispersed. Later in the day the body of the cardinal was carried from the cathedral to the crypt amid the tolling of the bells of the city's Catholic churches. There, beneath the cathedral he had loved so dearly, the mortal remains of James Gibbons were laid away beside the tombs of six of his predecessors in the See of Baltimore as Bishop Corrigan gave the final absolution and the assembled clergy chanted the solemn tones of the *De profundis.*

The secret wellsprings of Cardinal Gibbons' greatness, which the leading figures of the Church and State proclaimed in so unprecedented a way, lay hidden deep in those subtle and intangible qualities that men call character. The character of Gibbons was not a complex one; in fact, his dominant characteristic was simplicity. All the living witnesses of his career agree that the simplicity of his manner, tastes, habits, entertainments, and style of writing and preaching was his distinguishing attractive feature. Extolled as perhaps no churchman in modern times has ever been, he never lost his graceful simplicity; the gentle dignity and quiet self-respect with which he bore his exalted rank as a prince of the Church rested serenely upon the conscious certainty that his high office neither needed nor suffered any self-assertion.

The simplicity of the man was conveyed in a hundred different ways. He never owned a horse and carriage, nor later an automobile. He always walked whenever that was possible, even in Rome where tradition dictated that cardinals should move about the city in carriages. The same held true for the entertainments that amused the cardinal during his hours of relaxation. Any man who could pass an entire evening playing euchre with his friends, while away an hour at horseshoes or quoits, or show a fondness for old and familiar music like "Lead, Kindly Light," had, indeed, a great deal of the common touch about him. Men especially felt at ease with the great churchman when he would light up a cigar after dinner and sit down among them for a friendly chat. Gibbons liked baseball, and he followed the game closely enough to discuss it intelligently. Horse racing was also a sport in which he showed a keen interest. Now and then he would place a modest bet on a horse through one of the Shriver boys, and on one occasion in New Orleans the cardinal attended the races. Gibbons took delight in dining out with friends. "I dine out," he once said, "because Christ dined out."

This simplicity of manner and taste sprang in part from the cardinal's intense interest in people, not in their stations in life nor in the wealth or prestige that attached to their names. He had a truly remarkable memory for names and faces which, of course, proved exceedingly flattering to those whom he met. Everyone seemed to hold some kind of interest for Gibbons, and he once remarked that he had never met anyone from whom he had not learned something. On his visits to Rome, he never failed to see his students from the Archdiocese of Baltimore. His priests were at liberty to call to see him without appointment at any time, and even children felt free to ring the doorbell at 408 N. Charles Street and to ask for His Eminence.

His reputation for approachability occasionally involved Gibbons in situations that afforded opportunity for the exercise of his well-known tact. The cardinal once met a woman at a social gathering whose curiosity exceeded her discretion; she made bold to ask him how far he thought the infallibility of the Pope extended. With the faintest smile he replied, "Madame, that is not an easy question. All I can say is that a few months ago in Rome His Holiness called me, 'Jibbons.' " As one who overheard the exchange later wrote, "The subtlety of this reply was probably lost on the inquirer." The delicacy with which Gibbons invariably governed his personal relations was partly motivated by the dread he always entertained of hurting the feelings of another person. One afternoon some children called on Gibbons to present the cardinal with a few trifling mementos of their handiwork. Their chaperon deprecated the value of the gifts but emphasized the children's motive. Immediately the children's faces revealed their hurt. Gibbons sensed their feelings at once, rose from his chair, went to the table, and picked up the trinkets, and as he looked them over carefully he exclaimed several times, as if to himself, "Aren't they wonderful!" He then turned and passed them around to the priests and others in the parlor, and by that time the faces of the children were again wreathed in smiles.

Another outstanding characteristic of the man was his sympathy and generosity to those in distress. Hardly a month passed without some new manifestations of the cardinal's fulfilling the priestly role of healing and consoling, of comforting and providing for the unfortunate. When Bishop Messmer of Green Bay asked if Gibbons would take a priest who had compromised his usefulness in Green Bay by intemperance, the cardinal replied that, although he had no vacant chaplaincies, he had given instructions to the Sisters at St. Agnes Hospital to provide a room for the priest for a year at Gibbons' expense.

Gibbons' consideration for all persons and his generosity toward those in trouble were more than matched by his fidelity to close friends. Archbishop Ireland acknowledged more than once what it had meant to have the cardinal defend him against unjust attack; Denis O'Connell was a notable example of Gibbons' fidelity when a friend had fallen into disfavor; John Keane's perplexities in moments of trial were calmed in no small measure by Gibbons' sympathetic counsel. Bishop Shahan, a special favorite in the last years of Gibbons' life, was not only supported in his administration of the university but sustained as well in his more ambitious projects like the National Shrine of the Immaculate Conception.

But whatever may be said of the winning characteristics of the Cardinal of Baltimore, it was the priestly quality of his daily life that most attracted those who came into frequent contact with him and who found spiritual encouragement by the otherworldly temper of his mind. That quality gave meaning to his kindness toward others. Priestly he was in every word and action of his life; yet there was nothing particularly striking about the cardinal's piety. Unlike Newman and Manning, Gibbons left no intimate journals of his inner spiritual life. He was not given to speculation; there was little of the ascetic or mystic about him. The cardinal was rather a man of action with an intensely practical turn of mind. Yet the fidelity with which he observed all the religious devotions of his priestly office gave a tone to his daily living and established him in the minds of others as a true man of God. Without much apparent soul-searching, James Gibbons went serenely on his way. This priestly bearing was always with him at the altar, in the pulpit, and in his confessional near the sanctuary railing where in his more vigorous years he heard confessions on Saturday afternoons and after his morning Mass whenever a request was made of him. He had a keen sense of the ecclesiastical proprieties. It was no mere accident that St. Francis de Sales was Gibbons' favorite saint, for there was a sweetness and kindliness of manner about the Cardinal of Baltimore that suggested the great Bishop of Geneva. His was a spiritual greatness resting upon a foundation of natural benignity that precluded harsh treatment or mean expression about anyone. Monsignor Stickney, the cardinal's house companion for thirteen years, and Bishop Shahan, who had known him well from 1891 to his death, both stated that they had never heard him utter an uncharitable word about any man.

The motto on the coat of arms of Cardinal Gibbons was *"Emitte Spiritum Tuum."* Rarely did a churchman carry out with more consistency his role as an agent for sending forth the divine spirit among men. Not alone by his books, sermons, and help to organized movements did Gibbons exercise his zeal for the spread of God's word, but by his daily contact with men, by his bearing, by the cast of his thoughts, and even by his choice of words in ordinary conversation. One friend noted his alterness to inject a spiritual note into mundane matters; but "it is exercised in such a benign, dispassionate, evangelical manner that it never shocks the different religious sentiment or the agnostic indifference of his interlocutor. He is always a missionary who speaks to convince educated people and not to intimidate uncultivated people."

Yet Cardinal Gibbons was no exception to the universal law of human frailty. A certain observable vanity, although it escaped the more unpleasant features of strong pride, manifested itself in inoffensive ways, such as his desire to win at cards, his love for the splendor of ecclesiastical processions wherein he was arrayed in his scarlet robes, and his skill in drawing to himself a table conversation that showed signs of straying into other channels. Yet his vain little foibles, guileless and transparent as they were, were never allowed to develop into an exhibition of pride that gave serious offense to his equals and repelled those of lower rank.

More serious, perhaps, was the cardinal's tendency at times to shift his ground in unpleasant situations. On occasion, his failure to face up strongly to a problem caused embarrassment to his associates: in 1886, for example, when he wavered in his support of a national university and called forth a rebuke from Bishop Keane. A number of instances made apparent his deep aversion to giving offense; but, as Keane reminded him, at times his effort to please everyone jeopardized the prospect of his pleasing anyone.

But to magnify these few cases of temporizing to the point of implying cowardice would be to miss the true measure of his moral courage. No man who staked his reputation before the highest tribunals in the Church as Gibbons did in the case of the Knights of Labor, or in his masterful speech at Rome in March, 1887, on the relations of Church and State in the United States, could be said to lack courage. Neither was it the conduct of a weak man to defend with all the power he could summon the policies of Archbishop Ireland in regard to the schools, and the American Church itself against the charges of a heretical Americanism. Nor was it weakness that prompted Gibbons to persist to the end against placing Henry George's *Progress and Poverty* on the *Index of Forbidden Books,* when in doing so he experienced the pain of alienation from Archbishop Corrigan who for years had been a close friend and counselor. Nor was it weakness at Milwaukee in August, 1891, when he gave his bold sermon against the evils of excessive nationalism within the Church. In the process of arriving at a final decision, it is true, he resorted on occasions to stratagems that bolder spirits like Ireland and McQuaid would have scorned. Yet who will say that his conciliatory way of meeting trouble was not at times the better way? If there were times when Gibbons' mildness restrained him when he might better have gone forward, there were also times when that peaceable spirit guided his steps into the path of true wisdom and redounded to the advantage of the Church.

Allied to this tendency to avoid unpleasant issues was his desire to put the best construction on disagreeable events. The effusive letter that he wrote to Pope Leo XIII in January, 1893, after the latter had established the Apostolic Delegation in Washington, was one example of this trait. His generous heart likewise betrayed him into unwise judgments in regard to his close friends; the heart almost certainly overruled the head in his support of some men for the episcopacy.

Apart entirely from these minor moral faults, Gibbons revealed deficiencies of another nature. He was quite unoriginal. No great project came from his personal initiative. The Third Plenary Council of 1884 arose at the suggestion of the bishops of the Middle West, and the defense of the Knights of Labor probably owed as much in origin to Keane and Ireland as it did to Gibbons. The same lack of originality appeared in his sermons and writings, none of which showed evidence of the gifted researcher, orator, or prose writer. In the field of administration, Gibbons' long tenure of the See of Baltimore yielded few striking accomplishments. As he grew older, he was lax in initiating new parishes and in advancing parochial schools. A young vigorous coadjutor might have remedied these deficiencies; but Gibbons' attachment to old ways and reluctance to have close at hand an archbishop with whom he would have to share his authority made the plan unattractive.

Yet the failure to find brilliance of mind, depth of learning, mastery of administrative detail, resourceful and fighting qualities of leadership, powerful oratory, and majestic diction did not mean that Cardinal Gibbons was not a singularly gifted man. His prudence, discretion, and delicacy of perception — gifts of an altogether uncommon order — were employed to the utmost advantage in his dealings with others. Men are not easily led unless leadership is strengthened by love and high respect. The profound love that the cardinal engendered for his person enabled him to accomplish wonders where more gifted men would have failed. As one who knew him well said after he was gone: "Cardinal Gibbons was powerful because he was simple, and his simplicity invited love. It never demanded service."

Beyond simplicity the cardinal possessed to a marked degree what St. Thomas Aquinas considered the chief virtue of those who govern, the sense of reasonable proportion in all his judgments. That quality raised the execution of policies by the simple and unpretentious cardinal to the lofty level of statesmanship.

Eleven years after the death of Cardinal Gibbons the Knights of Columbus erected a handsome bronze statue of the great prelate in a prominent spot facing down 16th Street in Washington. On Sunday, August 14, 1932, President Herbert Hoover accepted the statue in the name of the United States as a gift from the Knights. Hoover spoke of his acquaintance with the cardinal during the days of World War I and of the high regard that he had shared with all Americans for the radiant sweetness of Gibbons' spirit and the kindliness of his wisdom. The cardinal's life, Hoover said, had been a remarkable demonstration of the power of a quietly noble personality to spread its influence to those who lived far beyond the range of his physical presence. And in seeking to express the spirit and the depth of the love and influence that the cardinal had exterted on his fellowmen, the president came close to the secret of Gibbons' greatness when he said:

> He loved God, and to a degree that is seldom equaled he succeeded in carrying into the minds of other people the feeling that the truths of religion are really their primary aids in solving the perplexities of every day living.

Index